Praise For Karl Drinkwater

"Drinkwater creates fantastically believable characters."

On The Shelf Reviews

"Each book remains in my mind for a long time after. Anything he writes is a must-read."

Pink Quill Books

"Karl Drinkwater has the skill of making it near impossible to stop reading. Expect late nights. Simply outstanding."

Jera's Jamboree

"An intelligent and empathetic writer who has a clear understanding of the world around him and the truly horrific experiences life can bring. A literary gem."

Cooking The Books

"Drinkwater is a dab hand at creating an air of dread."

Altered Instinct

FROM IDEA TO ITEM

"A gifted writer. Each book brings its own uniqueness to the table, and a table Drinkwater sets is one I will visit every time."

Scintilla.info

From Idea To Item

Karl Drinkwater

Organic Apocalypse

FROM IDEA TO ITEM

Copyright © Karl Drinkwater 2025
All rights reserved.

Any use of this publication to train generative artificial intelligence (AI) technologies is expressly prohibited. Creativity should be applauded and protected, not stolen.

Cover design by Karl Drinkwater

Published by Organic Apocalypse
ISBN 978-1-911278-40-5 (Ebook)
ISBN 978-1-911278-41-2 (Paperback)

Organic Apocalypse Copyright Manifesto

Organic Apocalypse believes culture should be shared. We support far more reuse than copyright law and licensing organisations currently allow. We respect our buyers, reviewers, libraries and educators.

You can copy or quote up to 50% of our publications, for any non-commercial purpose, as long as the awesome source is acknowledged.

You may sell our print books when you've finished with them. Or pass them on to other people and share the love. You buy a copy, you own it.

We don't add DRM to our e-books. Feel free to convert between formats (including scanning, e-formats, braille, audio) and store a backup for your own use.

Contents

Introduction		VII
1.	Stages In Book Production	1
2.	Two Types Of Publishing	30
3.	Money Money Money	85
4.	Polishing The Draft	127
5.	Formatting	151
6.	Cover Design	257
7.	Metadata	292
8.	Distribution	329
9.	Marketing	411
10.	The Secret Sauce	531
About The Author		539
Other Titles By Karl Drinkwater		541

Author's Notes	543
Endnotes	546

Introduction

As well as being an author, I spend a lot of time teaching, mentoring, and advising new writers.

In 2023 I taught a session on the different routes to publication, as part of the *Market of Possibility*[1] in Dumfries, Scotland. The focus was on publishing options for new authors, whilst explaining some of the mysteries of traditional publishing and working with agents. Along the way I talked about the stages of quality book production.

The attendees told me they'd learnt a lot and wished the information was available in a book. So here it is, an overview for prospective authors to peruse at their leisure, covering modern publishing options for authors and the things they need to know. Contracts, publishers, editing, distribution, cover design, marketing, metadata, and figures on author earnings from international surveys.

Although in the preparation of this material I was mostly thinking in terms of fiction, much of the information applies to other types of creative work, such as poetry or non-fiction.

The key for all creatives is to take an initial *idea*, to shape and translate it into a form, to refine it (which requires mastery of technique), and hopefully the end result is an amazing *item* that people will buy and appreciate. Hence the title of this book, and the journey from inspiration to publication.

No book fits everyone, and has every answer we seek, because we come from different starting points. We have varying abilities, goals, and needs. If we try to satisfy everyone, we may satisfy no one (which is true of our fiction, too). But I do hope you'll come away having learnt one or two new things.

When I began planning this book I gave it the subtitle "A brief overview of publishing options for authors". I soon realised that my goal for a concise pamphlet had been naively optimistic. There was so much I wanted to say, new questions to answer, or topics to address. And so it grew to this weighty 120,000+ words. And it may surprise you that this book you hold was once bigger, since the first draft was almost 200,000 words. I cut 80,000 out in the process of tightening language, removing some of the extended digressions, and making the text flow better.

Welcome to my ultimate brain splurge, that could also have been called "Pretty much everything Karl knows about publishing."

STAGES IN BOOK PRODUCTION

CHAPTER 1

It is worth being clear about the steps a book goes through on the road to publication. It provides a mental framework of progress, a way to identify where you are in the process of transforming an idea into an item.

I'll list the stages, then dive into more detail on each one. I tend to divide them between those that lead to a finished draft, and those that take the draft and turn it into a published book. It's the latter sections that From Idea To Item is most focussed on, but there's no harm in covering the basics of writing a draft as well.

The Stages

Initial creation of the work

1. The idea

2. Research

3. Outlining

4. First draft

5. Pause

6. Rewriting

Publication stages

7. Developmental editing

8. Copy editing

9. Proofreading

10. Formatting

11. Cover design

12. Metadata

13. Distribution

14. Marketing

Initial Creation Of The Work

It all begins somewhere.

1. The Idea

This is where it all begins. The seed of an idea that takes root and grows into what will follow.

Inspiration comes from somewhere. A dream, or something you have read, or that happened to you. Sometimes it begins with a title. Or the first line of the book. Or even the last line. Ideas are shy, and don't always approach you from the obvious direction.

And so you muse over the idea, and the possibilities it represents. From there you come up with details, scenes, plot points, and ideas about the characters.

Drinky's Digressions: What Makes A Good Book Title?

Welcome to Drinky's Digressions. I'll use these throughout the book to expand on topics that capture my imagination and seem somehow relevant. It's like a deep dive into the always-overclocked Brain Of Drinkwater: except, unlike me, you can leave at any time. Let's proceed with my first musing!

During the process of writing a draft we often have a working title, just for ourselves. When I was writing my first space opera book I didn't have its final title in mind yet. I referred to it as *Girl On A Motherfucking Spaceship*, and only after finishing the first draft did I come up with *Lost Solace*. So the title may come at the start of the project, or it may come much later. And if you are trade published, you may not get any say in that decision at all.

But titles are important. They are one of the first promises as to what a reader will find between the covers. Titles can indicate genre and tone. We know what kind of book we have with *Quantum Warships Of Mars*, and it would be different from *Tender Touch Of An Angel*, or *SAS Maximum Impact*. So the title is a marketing tool. The way it appears emblazoned on the cover may tempt people to pick up the book.

A good book title is memorable and distinct. The last thing you want is people to get lost in vagueness and not remember the name of the book they once desired. It also needs to be original and not misleading. It would be a bad idea for me to call my new book *A Hunger Game*, or *Drifts Of Dune*.

If you're totally stuck for ideas, look at books on your shelf. Which titles work, and why? How can you categorise them? One of the following systems could work for you.

- The name of a character in the book. *Rose Madder* (Stephen King). *Tess of the d'Urbervilles* (Thomas Hardy). *Justine* (Marquis de Sade).

- Some trait of an important character: nickname, role, or physical appearance. *The Girl Who Played With Fire* (Stieg Larsson). *The Constant Gardener* (John le Carré). *White Teeth* (Zadie Smith). *Charlotte's Web* (E. B. White).

- The location where the book is set, or something to do with the main places. *The Road* (Cormac McCarthy). *Wuthering Heights* (Emily Brontë). *Anne of*

Green Gables (L.M. Montgomery).

- A time period or date related to the book. *Tenth of December* (George Saunders). *1984* (George Orwell). *The Winter's Tale* (William Shakespeare).

- A literary or thematic reference or allusion. *The Children of Men* (P. D. James). *A Scanner Darkly* (Philip K. Dick). *The Curious Incident of the Dog in the Night-Time* (Mark Haddon).

Note that there are many other categories of title, which you'll find when you browse your shelves. You can also combine any of the above.

Top Tip: Find An Interesting Premise For The Story

The trick with telling stories is to try and avoid the obvious, well-trodden path, and to find more original and interesting routes. That can apply to the plot as much as it can to writing style. Freshness is a massive selling point. It's not enough to just write a basic zombie survival novel, or a "boy meets girl, has a few tribulations, then they get together romantically" novel. They've been done millions of times. We need to combine ideas in new and exciting ways, such as "*boy zombie* meets *human girl*, has a few tribulations, then they get together romantically" (*Warm Bodies*, by Isaac Marion).

The concept itself can also be used to hook the reader. Something about it that makes them wonder what would happen next, what they would do in those circumstances.

We want people to think "I have to read this!"

While I'm talking about trying to make things fresher: remember settings, too. Don't generally set all your scenes in the same place. For example, suppose you're writing a dating novel. If every scene is set in a coffee shop, it will already feel like a rehash of other works. You've just made your job harder. Would a bucket list be so boring? No. So think of interesting locations, and variety, and places we don't often see. Love blossoming in a nuclear reactor. Deep feelings during a subaquatic archaeological dig. A series of dates where the only interactions take place during sky diving. Go wild. No doubt you will love writing the story because it will interest you, too; and that will come through for the reader.

2. Research

It is good to have a solid idea of important things before you begin writing. That's where initial research comes in.

Your research will vary by genre and story. If I'm writing a historical romance, I need to research the time period when my book is set: the language used, clothing, technology, and social structures. If I'm writing sci-fi then engineering and advanced astronomy might be beneficial to study. If my book is strongly set in a particular place, visiting or researching that place would be in order. So, when I was working on *2000 Tunes* and *Cold Fusion 2000*, both set in Manchester in the year 2000, I spent a lot of time in Manchester city centre, at the bars and galleries that the characters visit. I also reread my diaries from back when I lived and worked in Manchester, and studied maps of the city as it was in the year 2000.

Some research might be tied to your plot: investigating the feasibility of anything that your story will hinge on, before you waste time on ideas that turn out to be mistaken.

I keep folders for current and future novels, and save snippets whenever I come across a phrase, description, photo, bit of information, or scene idea that is relevant. By the time I start outlining that project I will already have a lot of material to work from. The folders can be physical, containing cut-outs from newspapers and magazines, photographs, and things printed from the web; or they could be a digital folder on your computer that you save and drag material into.

Immersing yourself in research before you begin writing helps give authentic vitality to the world you'll set your story in. Some authors plaster their walls and desk with photos and diagrams that help their mind shift into the fictional context when they write.

While you are writing a draft it's best not to stop to check facts, as it interrupts the flow. Instead, research is something you do before writing, and also again at later stages (especially fact-checking).

3. Outlining

Outlining is deciding on the main points of the story: what significant event occurs in the world or the characters' lives; what actions the characters take as a result; and what happens next. Repeat and repeat. This outline is a summary of key elements of the plot. Ideally the plot points should tell a satisfying story, and lead to some change in the world or characters, backed up by themes which make the tale more universal.

Drinky's Digressions: Plotters Versus Pantsers

Enter a room of writers and raise the issue of plotters versus pantsers, and you may also raise people's temperatures.

Some authors plot every point in minute detail, so that when they come to write the story they have a good idea of what will happen in each scene. This prevents dead ends, and helps authors to get words written, because they always know what they are going to write. This is **plotting**, or **outlining**.

Other authors prefer to let a story flow and make it up as they go along, asking "What if ... ?" and creating new scenes out of how the characters react to events. This is known as **pantsing** – "flying by the seat of their pants" (an idiom meaning "playing it by ear" rather than following a set of predetermined instructions). The characters drive the story. It can lead to exciting and unexpected twists for the author and reader; or it can lead to wasted time, dead ends, and more need for rewriting. Note that for pantsing to work, you have to already visualise strong and believable characters and interesting situations for them to exist in. Some authors refer to this as **discovery writing**.

Here are some reasons why new authors should consider plotting.

- Usually only experienced authors can use full-blown pantsing and still achieve good novels. So, if you are new to writing, then definitely err on the side of plotting, with breakdowns of your scenes and chapters. This lets you spot problems, or areas to cut, before you waste time writing them. Ask the question about every sub-plot, twist and event: "Does this contribute to the overall story, or is it just words?"

- If you use a developmental editor, it is far cheaper to ask them to look at your outline and a writing sample, than to send them the whole book. It also means things can be improved before you start writing, saving costly mistakes and wasted time later.

- If you have a good outline that covers every chapter, *you don't have to write the scenes in that order*. Some authors like to write the ending, then the beginning, tying them together with language and motifs, then fill in the middle bits later. You can even write the book in reverse if you prefer.

So, are you a plotter or a pantser?

The reality is that many authors mix the two systems, and they are not mutually incompatible. For example, I plan out the major scenes of my novels, and have notes on the key events that will happen in each chapter. But I don't do it in massive detail, and nor do I make decisions on the outcome of every conflict. The characters retain some freedom to surprise me. And while a structure prevents me from going astray, I still feel excitement as I write.

4. First Draft

This is one of the fun bits! Your enthusiasm is high. The concept is exciting. You have an idea of where you're going. Now you just have to see through the page to the world beyond, and inhabit the heads and perspectives of your characters, and get as much of that richness onto the page as possible. It doesn't matter if that "page" is a real piece of paper, or a word processor on a PC, or even recording it as audio while you pace in circles around the living room, driving those nearby batty. "Just get the words out," as I shout in creative writing classes. Welcome to the **first draft**.

You may not have the luxury of long periods of time to devote to this. You may have a family, or work, and need to steal moments wherever possible, such as on the train, waiting for a bus, sat on the toilet, or even in a hospital emergency room.

I was working full-time as a university librarian when I began my first novel. In evenings and weekends I taught aikido or spent time with family. But I found ways to do the writing. In work I always got hungry early, so would eat my food during the morning break. When dinner time came I would write for an hour. Once the hour hand reached the top of the clock I returned to work, often with another few thousand words written. That is the *little-and-often* approach. (Note: I am northern, so to me dinner time is what posh people call "lunch"; the meal is obviously really dinner because at school we had *dinner ladies* to serve it, not lunch ladies.)

For another book – *Turner* – I went on holiday. The book was set on a remote Welsh island, so I stayed on a remote Welsh island for a week. Well, actually it was longer than that, as the weather turned bad and the boat was unable to reach the island to pick us up, but that's another story that might also involve sharks and a giant sea kraken. The house I rented had no electricity (or indoor toilet, or shower), so I took all my notes and hand-wrote the novel. During my time on the island I finished a full first draft. See, that's where a good outline comes in; it makes you much more productive within whatever limited time you have available. This approach is the *all-at-once* system of doing a draft.

Whether little-and-often or all-at-once, or a mixture of both, the secret to a first draft is simply to get the words down. Don't worry about facts. If you don't know something, make it up. If you're stuck, skip ahead. Don't over-analyse what you write. Don't keep tweaking it. All that comes in the rewrite. If you try to edit as you write, you'll ruin your flow. Just keep envisioning the golden glory of a completed draft, and that will light the way.

Note that this book is mostly focussed on the stages of production, that take a work from completed draft to publication. The actual process of creating that first draft is a massive topic, bigger than my desire for chocolate. And so I'd like to do a separate book one day purely about the craft of writing, which can act as a companion to this tome you hold in your hands or are reading on a screen.

5. Pause

The draft is finished. And it may be a mess. Crossings out and arrows and areas where you changed your mind and went in a new direction.

Your brain is buzzing. Your nerves are frazzled. You feel like you've run a marathon or been on an epic bender. This is not the correct frame of mind to see the work with fresh eyes.

So congratulate yourself. Maybe even treat yourself. Put the manuscript in a drawer (or the digital equivalent). Make sure you have a backup. (You do make backups as you go, don't you? If not ... oh boy, you have pain to come, pilgrim.)

Now is the time to take a break from the book and let it sit.

That's not to say you need a break from *writing*. It's good to always write. Just do something different. That short story you wanted to submit to a magazine? Polish it up and send it. That spoken word evening in your local cafe? Write the poem that's been niggling at you, and rehearse it (a lot), then perform it at the event. Work on notes for another book. Do free writing. It doesn't matter. We're just making sure your mental machinery doesn't freeze up from disuse before you get around to one of the stages some authors hate: rewriting.

Oh, hello stage 6.

6. Rewriting

When working on a book, we have most enthusiasm at the beginning ("This is going to be *amaaaazing!*"), and when we write THE END on the final page ("I did it!"). The time between can involve a struggle to keep motivated. But surely it is all smooth sailing after the draft is finished?

Sorry. It's called a draft – rather than a **completed manuscript** – for a reason. We now need to make it fit our initial vision of excellence. To wrap up loose ends, excise the unnecessary, and retie the arteries where we removed rotting chunks of exposition.

Rewriting doesn't mean setting the whole novel aside and literally starting again (except in the worst cases). Rewriting is more about analysing and improving. It may involve literal rewriting, but of scenes, paragraphs and sentences, rather than the whole thing.

Rewriting involves hard thinking: that time when non-writers accuse you of doing nothing but chewing your pen, since they don't realise that whole worlds are being shuffled around in your god-like cranium.

This is the stage when we reread the book many times. We study it. We rewrite sections and scenes. We edit. We make changes to structure and content. We build in new ideas or remove old ones. We check facts via research. We do all this as many times as needed. The amount of work depends on the writer, and their experience. Nowadays I've learnt enough to shortcut the problems, so the first draft comes out pretty clean and close to what I envisioned. That's just practice.

But this stage of reworking our words to make them both tighter and more impactful is an incredibly valuable learning experience. It's also an important part of taking the work to the next level. If you try to jump from stage 4 (First Draft) straight to publication, then – unless you are amazingly, wonderfully, *unfairly* talented (or so rich you can spend a fortune on trying to get other people to do this stage for you) – your book will fall short of its potential.

I think of the novel as a building. It may be dilapidated and need work on the foundations, before you can get to all the dainty stuff like wall coverings and fluffy cushions. Or it could be in almost perfect condition and just need a bit of touching up.

Chances are it is somewhere in the middle of that range. So you may have to work on the structure, and move scenes around. Knock out the ones that don't work. Fill in with new ones that do, and which further the story. Some scenes might need a tweak. Others might need a literal rewrite.

New writers have problems with this stage, because they don't have the trained eye to spot where the work is needed and what interventions would best fix the problems. That's where the next sections come in. But we all get better at it over time. Experience guides us.

Rewriting is the **self-edit**, done by *you*.

Publication Stages

You've written. You've polished. A good quality third/fifth/tenth draft has been completed. Long live the draft! But you have got as far as you can on your own. It probably isn't yet publishable, because only one person has worked on it. We all have a mote in our eye when it comes to our own work. And so we move on to the editing processes provided by other people.

Now we can look at what happens to a book from the point where a decision to publish has been made. This applies both to traditionally published books, and to professional self-published books. They are alternative routes to market, but the steps to a successful launch of a good-quality book are remarkably similar.

So, steps 7-9 are different types of (professional) edit, each building on the previous ones, acting as levels of polish on the road to glittering perfection. You need more of this early in your career.

In an ideal world a book spends time at each level, but the reality is messier. Sometimes the types of edit are conflated, with a mixture of more than one taking place at the same time. There are cases where a stage can be skipped, especially if it is an established author writing something they are an expert in: I doubt if

Stephen King needs a developmental editor to point out where to strengthen a subplot.

There are even opposite scenarios, where an editing stage may occur multiple times. One of my early books was so problematic that I went through many stages of rewriting it, then worked with an external editor for a developmental edit. I considered what they said and undertook further rewrites. The book I ended up with was better, but still not right, so a different developmental editor reviewed it and made suggestions. It took three developmental editors to help restructure it enough to finally work as intended. The experience taught me a lot, but also meant in future I was much more organised with my initial outline, to avoid this situation from happening again.

7. Developmental Editing

This step has a few names. I usually refer to it as the **developmental edit**. You might also hear people call it **substantive editing**, **structural editing**, or **literary editing**. They're the same thing.

I think of this as "big picture" editing, looking at the whole book. It's not about the nitty gritty of punctuation and spelling, but the overall narrative and structure. The character arcs, tone, the plot and subplots, prose style, structure, repetition, story pacing and reversals, the way theme ties events and imagery together, the individual scene connections and overall ending, and many other elements that affect the shape of the complete story. It's often the kind of things that the author has trouble seeing for themselves, as they have been too close to the project for too long and can't see it with fresh eyes, nor emotional distance.

As well as identifying problems or areas for improvement, the editor will provide suggestions for how to fix them, to unite the whole with your creative vision. The editor can't rewrite your book and make the decisions for you, only give pointers on how to do it – whether it is throwing out unneeded characters, adding in a subplot, working on style, or coming up with a different opening or ending. You read the suggestions, decide which way to go, and rewrite as necessary. Work from a developmental edit often leads to moving content around in the manuscript, as well as deleting sections (and writing new ones in other places). The changes can seem radical at first, but the result may well be a smoother and more satisfying read. Keep polishing the stone.

Full developmental editing is the most expensive form of edit, since it can be such deep surgery on a book, involving cuts, transplants, replacements and augmentations. There is a cheaper form called a **manuscript critique**, which is more of a broad strokes summary, only highlighting the major strengths and weaknesses.

8. Copy Editing

Copy editing is sometimes called **line editing**. The copy editor isn't concerned with the overall story arc, the characterisation, the themes. A copy editor checks for errors, and ways to improve the writing. They are focussed on sentences and paragraphs. Spelling, grammar and punctuation. Style. Repetition. Cliches.

Confusing elements. Rhythm. They will check facts and tell you that the date is wrong, or the minor character of Fred Dibble was called Frank Dabble in a previous chapter.

Copy editing makes the book more readable, with no basic errors that will distract a reader and pull them out of immersion.

9. Proofreading

A book designed to professional standards will be free of errors (spelling or typographical) and also grammatically correct. A **proofreader** helps with this. They check the final version of a book for typos, grammar errors or spelling mistakes that may have slipped through. Bear in mind that after each of the previous editing stages, changes were made to the manuscript. It is quite common for those to introduce new errors, hence the continual checks.

Often *track changes* is used to highlight errors, sometimes with accompanying notes. The author can work through them and correct things as necessary.

Proofreading is the final stage of Polishing The Draft (which I'll talk about in more detail in Chapter 4). It is the last time the *text* changes. After that, it can be formatted.

Celebrate reaching this stage with some cake and a nice glass of ginger wine.

Drinky's Digressions: Which Comes First?

I have laid these processes out so we end up with perfect electronic text which can be formatted. That places proofreading before formatting.

However, some people in the publishing industry put the processes into a different order, and place proofreading *after* formatting. They argue that proofreading is the act of someone checking the physical or digital proof for formatting errors; therefore you can't have someone proofread something until *after* it has been formatted.

To my mind, this difference relates to how the processes have changed over time, and where emphasis lies.

Wikipedia[2] says: "the proofreader focuses only on reading the text to ensure the document is error-free and ready for publication. Proofreading generally focuses on correcting any final typos, spelling errors, stylistic inconsistencies (e.g., whether words or numerals are used for numbers), and punctuation errors."

But of course, that description could apply to either the digital master pre-formatting (my interpretation), or the printed copy post-formatting (the opposing interpretation), and doesn't specify which. The flexibility of interpretation means both arguments are correct. It's just different ways of defining it.

Wikipedia also hints that the stages (and what things are called) are changing over time:

> "In the past, proofreaders would place corrections or proofreading marks along the margins. In modern publishing, material is generally provided in electronic form, traditional typesetting is no longer used and thus (in general) this kind of transcription no longer occurs. Consequently the part played by pure proofreaders in the process has almost vanished: the role has been absorbed into copy editing to such an extent that their names have become interchangeable."

What seems clear to me is that the way things are done nowadays doesn't have to match how trade publishers originally did things.

But just because I put proofreading before formatting, that doesn't mean there are no printing error checks (for things like white space, widows and orphans, layout). I just consider the checks of the ebooks and printed copies as part of *formatting*, rather than a separate stage.

10. Formatting

The **designer** or **formatter** works on the way the words appear on the page (printed copies) or screen (ebooks). They make sure the book has a consistent, professional, and pleasantly readable style. They deal with things like images, running heads, digital conversion, and hyphenation, then put all the parts of a book in their correct place. Chapter 5 will be a deep dive into formatting and explain all these terms, and more.

The end files for printing and for ebooks will be quite different, as both formats have their advantages and disadvantages. For example, the ebook can have hyperlinks, but the printed book may need to have a web address written out as a footnote; ebooks don't have page numbers, but print books do.

This stage is all about the presentation *inside* a book.

11. Cover Design

The cover designer is focussed on what goes *outside* the book: images, colours, fonts and layout. They will make sure things are in the correct place, such as placing the ISBN barcode on the back of the book, and the imprint logo on the spine.

The cover is more than just wrapping paper for words. It is a key marketing element. We tempt readers to pick up a book by the cover. Only after that do they read the text on the back, and glance inside the hallowed tome at the quality content within. (For an ebook the cover will be a thumbnail in lists and a larger image on the book page, but will fulfil the same purpose: tempting people to read the book description, click to look inside the book, and read the first pages.)

The ebook's cover can be finished at any point as it has a fixed size, but the final print cover files can only be done once formatting is complete. That's because the designer needs to know the exact number of pages in the book. The page count, multiplied by paper thickness, determines how wide the cover's central spine element must be. Chapter 6 will take us through the cover design process.

12. Metadata

Meta is Greek for "about". **Metadata** is "data about data". I'm familiar with it from my career as a librarian, but in essence it is anything that describes something in structured ways, without being a part of the main content. When viewed in the abstract like that it all seems confusing, but examples will help.

- Films have age ratings. In the UK we're used to seeing PG, 15, 18. That's an element of metadata about the film.

- Computer games will tell you what systems you can play them on. Linux, Playstation, Wii, Atari 2600. That's metadata about the game.

- A tin of beans will tell you exactly what the ingredients are. That's metadata about the contents.

In all those cases the information will appear on the packaging in some way, and also in online descriptions of the product.

Books have many categories of metadata. The title, author, publisher, and year of publication, for example. Non-fiction may have a library classification number, which tells a librarian where it goes on the shelves (e.g. 920 for biographies in the Dewey Decimal Classification system).

In a paperback this information, and more, goes on the back of the title page. Online, there may be headings with that information. Either way, Chapter 7 will take us through the options.

The **blurb** (or **book description** – what you see on the back of a printed book) could be considered another form of metadata. It concisely describes the book's contents in a compelling way that tempts you to buy a copy. The book cover grabs attention, but the blurb makes the sale.

Drinky's Digressions: When Two Blurbs Go To War

It's worth being aware of the two different things that the word "blurb" might refer to.

For most authors, "blurb" refers to the short description of the story, providing a clear overview of your main characters and conflicts. It appears on the back of a paperback or hardback, or as the book's description online. It's the tease that entices the reader into the book's world and makes them want to know more. I'll give some tips on writing a good one in Chapter 7: Metadata.

To confuse matters, some authors use the word "blurb" to mean something else: the patronising endorsements that may appear on the cover of a book. For example:

> "Amazing and gripping, you will wet yourself with excitement" – Jonathan Random-Celebrity-Who-Probably-Hasn't-Read-The-Book

Authors who use "blurb" to mean "back cover summary" will instead refer to these testimonials as "puff quotes" – perhaps because they are as insubstantial as a puff of air, with the implication of being insincere.

Why is it that the term *blurb* can mean *back cover description* to one author, but *puff quotes* to another? It's because many dictionaries define "blurb" as *a short promotional description of a creative work intended to tempt people into buying it*. As such, both a summary of the book's premise, or an excerpt from a review, can fulfil that purpose. Hence different authors using the same term for different things.

For the purposes of this book, a blurb refers to the back cover summary.

Note that a blurb is not the same as a **synopsis**. A blurb is a concise temptation to the reader, whereas a synopsis is a document of a few pages, listing everything that happens and what the outcome is, aimed at enticing a publisher or agent into reading the manuscript. Although you wouldn't tell a reader the story's ending on the back of a book (they wouldn't want to buy it if they know what happens!), publishers and agents are different: they want to know that there is a story that's worth reading and that it has a satisfying conclusion.

Top Tip: An End As A Beginning

A concept related to the idea of a blurb is that of the **elevator pitch** (even though the UK term for an elevator is a lift). It's based on the fantasy that you're in an elevator with some media bigwig who has the resources to finance your dream project, which is often thought of as a film, but in this case perhaps they could publish your book and give you a juicy advance. They are a captive audience until the lift reaches their floor. You have that time – twenty seconds – to describe the work in a way that is so exciting they can't ignore it.

Sometimes that conciseness can slip into lazy comparison territory: "Harry Potter in the dystopia of 1984!"; "Before Sunrise crossed with John Wick!". But it's better if there's a way to isolate the key element that really makes your vision stand out, the compelling concept or situation that is intrinsically interesting. That's the thing that originally made you want to write the book, after all.

Two examples of possible elevator pitches for stories I admired:

- "Secret government agency tasked with protecting humanity from an intelligence so deadly and incomprehensible that you cannot see it, think about it, or even write about it, because as soon as you do so *it will kill you*." (*There Is No Antimemetics Division*, by qntm.)

- "A single mother takes her two young sons to the seaside, knowing it will be their last day out." (*Beside the*

Sea, by Véronique Olmi.)

Yes, they leave a lot unsaid, and raise questions, but that's part of their power.

It is useful to write an elevator pitch for your book early on, before you have even written a word of the story. Capture the exciting element that makes this a story you just have to tell.

Keep it as your mission statement. Put it on a sticky note on your monitor. Maybe even work it up into a blurb. Sure, it probably won't be the final version that goes on the book, but it is still a distillation of what got you interested in telling this story. It may help you keep your focus and excitement as you write the first draft.

13. Distribution

Printed books need producing and shipping, while ebooks need to enter the online distribution chain so that they appear on vendor sites. This is a complicated but vital part of the process.

At the end of this stage the book is finished, and the idea has finally become an item you can hold in your sweaty hand, whether it's a paperback, or an ebook on a portable device. Chapter 8 will cover distribution.

14. Marketing

Marketing, promotion, advertising, public relations: this is all the stuff about informing the world that the book is *coming*, and then that it is *here*. Tasks such as creating images and posts for social media, sending out review copies, informing fans, writing press releases, and making use of your author platform. Maybe it will include paid advertising, and interviews, and extravagant book launch parties. Marketing advice isn't the goal of this book, but be aware that it is a key part of a successful book launch. Chapter 9 will cover some key marketing topics.

Drinky's Digressions: What Is The Difference Between Marketing And Promotion?

Some people will argue that they are different processes. That **marketing** is about creating the conditions to draw readers to you, and is long-term (e.g. having a website). Whereas **promotion** is instead pushing information out to readers, and is short-term (e.g. an advertising campaign). Even so, most people agree that marketing and promotion aren't mutually exclusive, and there is some overlap.

I find the distinction to be blurry so just use them as synonyms for anything in my business aiming to connect the right reader to one of my books. Most activities to that end will mix long-term and platform elements with shorter-term and communication elements.

So, if you find the distinction useful, treat marketing and promotion as separate. If you don't find the distinction useful, treat them as synonyms. Potayto, potarto.

Top Tip: Divide Your Time

It's worth stating this, regardless of where you are in the process: be organised and divide up your time.

If you only have a few hours a week to devote to writing, you need to use them wisely. Even with more time, you still need to be efficient to make sure you are achieving your goals, and doing all the tasks required; not just focussing on the fun ones. This is one of the structures I use when writing full-time.

- 9-9.30am Communications
- 9.30-11am Creative Writing
- 11am-12pm Writing CPD
- 12pm-1pm Food. Fuss the cat. Shoot a zombie. Practise pole dancing. Walk in the garden.
- 1-2.30pm Creative Writing
- 2.30-3.30pm Business Stuff
- 3.30-5pm Creative Writing
- 5-5.30pm Communications

I find it helps prevent the opposing demons of distraction or paralysis. I know what to do, and at the end of the day I've got something to show for it. What do the headings mean?

Communications: a good way to start and end each day, without comms *dominating* your day. You know urgent emails will get dealt with. This can include interactions on social media, or writing blog posts.

Creative Writing: writing words, working on your new book. This time can also be spent plotting (mwuhahah), editing, rewriting, or researching something you're going to write about later.

Writing CPD: we're always learning. A bit of time each day for reading books about writing, grammar, the dictionary, articles of writing tips, notes from courses and so on. The book you hold in your hand counts. Find a single tip or fact each day to dwell on. Hopefully you can apply it to that day's creative writing.

Business Stuff: anything to do with being a self-employed author. Tax and finances; guides on running a business; website work; marketing and publicity.

So there you go. Does it sound like heaven?

The rest of this book will go into more detail about the business of writing, and the key stages of taking a fevered idea and turning it into a sacred item.

Two Types Of Publishing

Chapter 2

There are two main ways for a book to reach bookshops and online stores, and many options along both paths. The system chosen should be the best fit for the author and their work.

The central decision is whether to license rights to an intermediary or not. We'll begin with traditional publishing; called "traditional" because for a long time this was the main route from author to reader. But first, let's understand what rights we are talking about.

Copyright

When you write a book you own all the rights to it, without doing anything extra. That is due to **copyright**. Though it is recommended practice to include a copyright notice in your work.

No one else is allowed to take your work and sell it unless you give them explicit permission. That's because intellectual property law states that the copyright owner (you) has exclusive rights to publish, profit from, or perform the work, though you can license those rights to others if you so wish.

As long as you don't fully sign the copyright away, copyright stays with you and your heirs. This is why we talk about *licensing* rights, limited by term, format and territory (I'll expand on that later in this chapter). Licensing means the rights come back to you. Selling them means they are gone for good. *Only ever license rights.*

Copyright on books lasts for seventy years from the death of the author. That's in the UK, but applies in many other countries too, such as the US. So you will want to think about passing on the rights (e.g. to your family) at some point. It's your legacy to bequeath. See the section on wills in the next chapter.

The US is a bit weird, because while they give you automatic copyright on works you create, your ability to sue people for infringing your copyright is vastly reduced if you don't also register it (which costs money). So that is an extra pain. Hey, USA: if people have automatic copyright without doing anything, then take that to its logical conclusion, and don't add unnecessary hurdles in the way of enforcing our rights.

Like all laws, copyright law is relative, and the actual laws vary by country, and over time.

Copyright protects the *expression* of an idea, not the idea itself. So I can have copyright on my novel *Turner* (an expression of my ideas), but I can't copyright the idea of people trying to survive a murderous outbreak on a Welsh island.

Traditional Publishing

A **traditional publisher** (often called a **trade publisher**) does not write the books they publish. Instead, they are a service provider who acts as an intermediary between the author – you – and some of the tasks described in Chapter 1.

You, as an author, can sign a contract giving a publisher permission to print and distribute your book. In exchange, the publisher agrees to give you a certain percentage of the money they make back as **royalties** (*after* they take their own cut). Publishers are often secretive about the figures for royalties, but 10-25% of net revenues is usual in traditional publishing, depending on format. 10% is often the figure for print sales, or even less. For ebooks it might be 25%. Total royalties are generally dropping.

In some cases the publisher may also give an **advance**, which is a lump sum of cash based on how popular they think the book will be. Note that an advance isn't bonus money, it is just an advance payment of royalties. So if the publisher gives you two thousand pounds as an advance, you won't receive any more royalties until the figure for the advance is reached ("earned out"); then they will pay you royalties on every copy sold after that. Note that many books never earn out the advance.

This is what people usually mean when they say, "I'm getting published!" It is uttered in reverent tones as if it's a mystical rite of passage, but in reality it is just the author licensing exclusive publishing rights to a service provider (publisher) and hoping that the publisher will continue to promote the work for the duration of the contract.

That contract will determine how much the royalties will be, how frequently they will be paid, what the advance is (if any), what other rights the publisher has (such as negotiating TV, film, game or translation rights), and the conditions upon which the contract ends and all rights revert back to the author. There may also be unwelcome elements, such as non-compete clauses or non-disclosure agreements.

The publisher will undertake many of the tasks to get the book to market, such as editing, cover design and distribution. They pay upfront for that, and in return they keep a share of the profit on every copy of the book sold.

The point is, they are not giving you anything for free. They get paid for the work they do in publishing the book, but their payment comes from their cut of every copy sold. If they spend two thousand pounds publishing the book, and it is a hit that sells enough copies to make two *hundred* thousand pounds in profit, you can see how the economics of it works from their point of view. A publisher is therefore most interested in books that they think will sell a lot of copies, which in turn often translates into mass-market appeal.

There used to be a lot of big publishers. Due to corporate consolidation that number has dropped over the years, so that now we talk about *the Big Five*.

The Big Five

The Big Five are the largest publishing companies in the world. They are corporate media giants, owned by even bigger companies. None of them are British-owned any more.

The Big Five consist of:

- **Penguin Random House.** They are owned by the German multinational conglomerate corporation Bertelsmann. (The Big Five used to be the Big Six, but Penguin merged with Random House in 2013: I think a more charming name after the merger would have been Random Penguin House, but hey ho.)

- **HarperCollins.** They are owned by News Corp, an American mass media and publishing company. News Corp grew from the earlier News Corporation that was controlled by Rupert Murdoch; News Corporation was split following scandals and violations of ethical standards by one of their subsidiaries (News of the World). HarperCollins are also known for their support of DRM in ebooks distributed to libraries, which would remove the book from the library's collection after being lent a number of times (even though a digital file doesn't wear out like paper).

- **Simon & Schuster.** They were owned by Paramount Global, an American mass media and entertainment multinational conglomerate, until August 2023, when it was sold to hedge fund KKR for $1.62bn.

- **Hachette.** They are owned by the French media giant Hachette Livre, which is in turn a subsidiary of the Lagardère Group. Hachette used to have an imprint called Weinstein Books, shut down in 2017 after Harvey Weinstein was found guilty of sexual assault.

- **Macmillan.** Originally a British publishing company, but now owned by the German Holtzbrinck Publishing Group. Various library organisations have run campaigns against Macmillan in the past for the publisher's attempts to implement controversial restrictions on ebook lending.

Each of the Big Five have numerous **imprints** they created or acquired, and every imprint appears like a separate publisher to the public, associated with a certain kind of book. The imprint is a form of branding and differentiation, as much as anything else.

These publishing companies have the power to give books their best chance of success in the marketplace, though there are some downsides, which I'll get to.

Drinky's Digressions: What's In A Number?

In 2022 the Big Five almost became the Big Four as Penguin Random House tried to buy Simon & Schuster for 2.2 billion US dollars, but eventually the US Department of Justice blocked the acquisition due to concerns about such large consolidations being bad for authors. During the hearings in August 2022 (as reported by the New York Post)[3] the US government "argued that the largest five publishers control 90% of the market, and a combined Penguin and Simon & Schuster would control nearly half of the market for publishing rights to blockbuster books, while its nearest competitors would be less than half its size." That gives you an idea of the scale of these big publishers. Also the fact that "With the deal's dissolution, Penguin will pay a $200 million termination fee to Paramount Global". These companies are focussed on big numbers.

Limitations Of Big Publishers

Traditional publishers can only publish a limited number of books, partly due to the need to schedule everything up to two years in advance. They can't publish all the good books that get submitted, even if they wanted to. In particular, they are unlikely to publish a book which may be excellent, but which only has a small audience. In the past this often meant good books were never published.

Publishers (especially the biggest ones) want guaranteed successes, which pushes things towards mainstream commercial fiction.

As such, resources are not allocated equally. Publishers reserve the big advertising budgets and advances for the authors who are already massively successful, and are guaranteed to bring them big profits. Sometimes a more popular book will be used to subsidise a less popular one that they don't think will sell so well, but which may be the kind to win literary awards and boost their reputation. That's an exception though, not the rule.

Another issue is that publishers can't tell what the next big thing will be, only what sold well *in the past*, so they tend to try to do more of that. "What made money last year? Can we replicate it? Yes, more thrillers with the word 'Girl' in the title, and more books about wizard schools. That's the next three years planned out!" Their focus on extrapolation in order to predict future sales can make them complacent, risk averse, and more interested in mass-market appeal than in more niche works. This can lead to creative stagnation, conformity, and a lack of real choice.

The sad outcome is that many big publishers will put more marketing money into a ghost-written celebrity memoir of debatable literary merit, because they know it will sell, rather than an amazingly original book which won't have broad appeal. And this can make it hard for new authors to break into the industry, especially authors with fresh or diverse voices. Even if they are taken on by big publishers, they're likely to be required to fit into the mould.

Lastly, note that things are not always rosy for trade-published authors. In truth, they tend to keep quiet when things go wrong: whether due to legal worries about contracts, embarrassment that it wasn't the dream they expected, or just misguided loyalty and gratitude to a business partner that isn't delivering. It's only behind closed doors in the author community that many authors open up about finding the experience of trade publishing to be demoralising and unrewarding, leaving them with a book that isn't promoted, doesn't sell, and with them dropped or demoted by the publisher to the point where some authors consider giving up writing.

How To Get A Big Five Publishing Contract

The first thing to realise is that, in general, acquisitions editors at the imprints of Big Five publishers do not accept unsolicited manuscripts from authors. If you hear otherwise, or have personal contacts, then by all means go ahead. Otherwise, you are likely wasting your time contacting them.

In most cases you must have a **literary agent** who submits material they think is sellable (generally mainstream and commercial literary works) to the publisher on your behalf. If the publisher is interested, the agent will negotiate a contract. The agent can also often manage foreign rights, film adaptations, and give general advice. They get a cut of the deals they negotiate, called a **commission**, which is usually 15%-20%.

So, before even attempting to climb the mountain of a Big Five publisher, you must first climb another mountain in order to get a literary agent.

Being taken on by a literary agency does not guarantee your book will be published. I know authors who have had agents who were unable to sell the manuscript to a publisher. That isn't necessarily the agent's fault: it could be related to the manuscript, or the current market situation, or changes at publishers and their requirements. This is why agents are picky about who they take on. They want books they can sell, and authors they get on with. And even though a literary agency may have a number of agents, each one only has so many hours in a day, so there will be a limit to how many clients each agent has. And if their list is full, they will be closed to submissions until that situation changes.

(Please don't get annoyed at me for putting all these hurdles in your way. I didn't make them, and I didn't put them on the pavement. I'm just warning you so you have realistic expectations of what will happen. But I'm a nice guy, and if I had a magic wand that would let me publish your book without all this foo-faa, and make us both rich in the process, then believe me I'd wave it until my arms fell off.)

How To Find Agents

The Writers' & Artists' Yearbook[4] is an annual directory which includes a chapter on literary agents. It also covers publishers, and has useful articles on many publishing topics. You can buy a copy, but it is available in many libraries; and if not, you could ask them to order a copy, since it is useful to so many creatives. There are regional equivalents to this kind of directory in other countries.

Online and global directories such as the one hosted by Reedsy[5] let you narrow down results by country and genre. There are also regional ones, such as the Scottish Book Trust's list of literary agents in Scotland.[6]

Another approach is to identify authors you admire, in the genre you want to write in. The contact section of the author's website may well have the name of their agent for rights enquiries. Of course, that doesn't mean the agent is taking on new clients, but you'd at least have a lead for checking the website of their agency to see what their submission status is.

Some big book and genre conventions or exhibitions can be good ways of making contact with agents and publishers. Obviously the main reason to go is because you love the conference theme, but if you're friendly with everyone you meet, it could well leave a good impression, and make future communications easier.

How To Query Agents

Assuming you have identified some agents who work in your genre, and checked that they are accepting submissions, the next step is to put together a **query letter** (sometimes called a **book proposal**).

This is a formal letter which introduces the author and the book being offered for publication. It should summarise the engaging qualities of the book, and make the author sound marketable, interesting, and professional. Ideally it points to where the author and work would fit in the market (because that's how agents and big publishers think).

The query letter is important. It is the agent's first view of the way you use words, and contributes to their impression of you. A badly written query might lead to the agent not even bothering to look at your work. I'll give some tips on writing one later.

If your book isn't of interest to the agent then feel free to try again with another agency. I have author friends who received more than forty rejections before they were finally accepted. Remind yourself that rejection is often more about commercial needs than the quality of the manuscript or your creative skills.

Small And Independent Publishers

Okay, we've seen that it can be difficult to get published by an imprint of one of the Big Five publishers. Don't be too disheartened, since they obviously do take on new writers via agents. It's just worth being pragmatic about the chances of signing a contract with them. Also note that for the subset of authors who want to be published by the Big Five or nothing … well, if that is their only acceptable option, then most of their books will never be published.

Anyway, there is another, more achievable, option than the Big Five: **independent publishers**, also known as **small presses**.

By "independent publishers" I mean traditional publishers who aren't part of the Big Five. These are smaller, and often regional (as in, not based only in London, or whatever your country's capital is). Publishers like Salt[7] (Norfolk), Honno[8] and Seren[9] (Wales), or Luna Press[10] (Edinburgh). They range in size from tiny, boutique publishers aimed at a niche, to mid-size trade publishers (perhaps equivalent to one of the Big Five's imprints).

Although some independent publishers prefer submissions via an agent, many are happy to receive them direct from authors. Make sure you check their guidelines carefully to confirm that they are open to submissions, find out what they are looking for, and how to submit. Much of the information about finding and approaching agents will apply equally to approaching a smaller publisher.

Due to their different scale they are often more personal and hands-on, with a supportive family feel, unlike the hollow corporate swishness of the Big Five. This is why it is frustrating for small publishers to nurture a new author, help to get them well known ... at which point the author is poached by a Big Five publisher offering a tempting contract. The Big Five publisher gets an author with proven potential, without having to support them in the early stages. The small publisher never gets to benefit from that investment. But some authors retain loyalty to the publisher that they started with, and the close connections they have made. One writer told me that he'd been offered contracts by one of the Big Five, and also by a quirky small (but well-respected) publisher. In the end he chose the small press, and told me one of the reasons was because the independent publisher found out he loved cheese, and sent him an artisan block of fromage every week for a year.

Small and independent publishers are more likely to take a chance on books that would do well within a niche area that the Big Five shy away from. It's worth noting that some regional publishers (such as those in Wales) may be able to get grants to publish books that they think have literary merit but which won't sell many copies, for instance many poetry books. This is known as **sponsored publishing**, and some specialise in it, including Arkbound.[11]

As to finding independent publishers: the printed and online sources listed above in the agents' section apply here, too.

Bonus Tips For Query Letters

Here are some extra tips for your first interactions with an agent or publisher.

- Find out about who else they represent, what the company is like, and what their approach is. It will make it easier to pitch how your work will fit into their portfolio. Yes, there is research involved here.

- Follow their guidance on submissions. If they don't provide them, follow industry standards instead. You want to appear (and be) professional, and for everything to be presented clearly and concisely.

- It's fine to be passionate about your work. List any relevant successes, awards, reviews, sales figures, or whatever else might point towards you being a worthwhile investment.

- As long as you don't break the bounds of being professional, remember to be yourself. Let some of your voice come through, especially if it is also how you write. We don't interact with names, we interact with people. Be friendly and polite, the kind of person you'd be happy to meet and consider working with. *Interesting* can be a bonus, something marketable.

- If going via agents, you will need patience. Since an agent is only the first step, and it can be seen as rude to approach more than one at a time, there may be a lot of contacting and waiting (and some following up). And if it doesn't work out, it begins again. And if you do eventually get an agent and negotiate a contract with them, then *they* begin the process of offering your work to publishers. More waiting. If a publisher shows interest, there will be lots of contractual things to sort out. Negotiations can fail right up to the point where you sign the publishing contract. And even then, it could be up to two years before your book reaches the shelves of your local bookshop. Patience is a virtue to nurture, Grasshopper.

- While submitting and going through this process, don't sit at home twiddling your thumbs. Your book may be on their slush pile of unsolicited manuscripts for some time. Be working on your next – even better! – book. We have three score years and ten on this earth, and if you wait to write your next book after the current one sells, you may only ever write a few books. Don't pin all of your hopes on one story.

- I highly recommend visiting Query Shark.[12] It was a blog by literary agent Janet Reid where she received real pitches from authors. In return she gave honest, biting feedback, where she pointed out where they did or didn't work, and how they could be improved. Janet's snark was legendary, so it was funny as well as educational. Although Janet is no longer with us, you can benefit from just reading her feedback on the 347 that had been nibbled or ripped apart on the site. In many cases the query sender submitted revisions, and it was interesting to see the improvements with each attempt. Therefore, if you are approaching the point when you might submit a novel to agents, working your way through at least some of this blog could be invaluable.

- The first sale is the hardest. As such, agents prefer an author that they know will write a number of good books, each better than the last. The hope is that, over time, the author brings in more money (since the agent is only paid a percentage of how much you earn). They are unlikely to take on an author that states they are only ever writing one book, their magnum opus. They are also perhaps less likely to take on a client who is extremely old or with a terminal illness. As with anything, there are exceptions, but most agents look beyond the current contract to future – bigger – publishing contracts for their author. The ultimate goal is an author so popular that publishing houses will undertake a bidding war for the rights to publish the next book, or even a multi-book contract.

- Publishers and agents want to know you are sellable. Clues that could act as an indicator of future sales might include a large following on social media or email lists. By which I mean, due to the scale publishers work at, perhaps ten to fifteen thousand followers or fans. (Which is different from just having a lot of friends on Facebook.) Some kind of celebrity status can be a big help.

- Agents and publishers often talk about identifying the "ideal reader" of a work, visualising and profiling their age, sex, lifestyle and interests. Some authors take this further, and then write books *for* their ideal reader. The reduction of a market segment to a fictional individual can make it much easier to create a satisfying story for them, and help with **writing to market**: providing the stories that a particular set of fans will find satisfying. This profiling lets agents and publishers consider how big that market segment is, and calculate potential revenue, turning art into rankings based on sales (therefore popularity). If you tell them "My ideal reader is *everyone!*" they will shake their heads and wait for a better answer. So make an effort to think like this and be specific if submitting query letters.

- Likewise, what other (recent, popular) authors does your writing resemble? What are the comparable works in your genre? Yes, it is pigeon-holing. Don't blame me, I'm just the messenger (pigeon), and I acknowledge that clear divisions don't really exist, as real life has many grey shades. Although categories can be useful for knowing where to put a book in a library or bookshop, the world is gloriously messy and many books fall within multiple categories and genres. But never say that to an agent or publisher, as it isn't the answer they want to hear.

Now we'll move on to options for those who don't want to stick with the slow lottery of the traditional agent-to-publisher model.

Self-publishing

A self-published book is any book where oversight of the publishing process is managed by the author, with or without help. The world has changed and tools and services that used to be unavailable to the public are now open to everyone. As with every other type of creation, from digital art and film making, to music production and 3D printing, the process has become democratic.

This is not a bad thing. It is fantastic that your gran can write a memoir or family history and make it available in print for friends and family. Yes, it may have a basic cover, and contain some mistakes, but she is not aiming at bestseller lists. More power to her, and everyone that creates. There is an important role for writing in terms of self-development, expression and creativity, which needn't have anything to do with commercial success and markets.

As is the case whenever a medium becomes available to the masses, there will be a range of quality to the outputs. In book terms we see the scale between the unedited amateur teenage fanfic, to the professionally edited and designed book that sells a million copies. So in itself the term self-published is nothing to do with *end quality*, it is just about *production process*. Nonetheless, a terminology distinction can be useful.

So from now on, when I say **self-publishing** I am being literal and thinking of an author who really does everything (or almost everything) *themself*. I think of this as the amateur or hobbyist realm. That's not a criticism. Maybe your uncle wants to do a recipe book for his fellow ballet dancers; your son his book of existential poetry; and your best friend wants to get the novel that's been in their head for years down on paper. Self-publishing makes all that possible. The goal isn't professional quality, millions of sales or making money, it is just bringing the work to life. And they may only ever want to publish a single book.

I will differentiate that from the **independent author** (also **indie author, author-publisher** or **independent author-pub-**

lisher). To me, this is where the author is a professional running a creative business, where they have the final say in all creative choices, and release books to the highest standards that match or surpass traditionally published works. They wrote the book, and they also supervised every aspect of its publication. They may be part-time or full-time; might make all their income from writing, or just a significant part of it. But the goal is making money with high quality works. It's not a hobby, but a livelihood. It is about ultimate creative control remaining with the creator, not the middlemen. Independent authors are owners and founders of a small business, and have committed to it because of their passion.

The key thing is that professionals *don't do it alone*, which is why it is a misnomer to call their work "self-published". Professional independent authors are part of a team, just like with a traditional publisher. The books go through all the same processes that they would at any publishing house. The difference is that the *author* chooses who to hire for each task, selecting the formatters, audiobook narrators, cover designers, editors and so on, and paying them up front as a form of investment in the work. The author plans, organises, delegates, and has the final say on everything. The author retains all ownership and copyright and can publish in any formats, languages and territories they wish. Many authors prefer the creative control, the faster publishing pace, and potentially higher profits of self-publishing.

As we saw in Chapter 1, publishing a professional work involves a lot of people, and a lot of skills. Quality publishing is not free.

Or cheap, even: it isn't uncommon for an independent author to spend over £1,000 per title for all of the services.

But going with a traditional publisher does not mean you get all that for free: all the stages cost money, and one way or the other, the author pays for it. Building on what I've already said, there are two main ways to pay.

- A traditional publisher acts as a third party intermediary, and subcontracts all these services, or does them in-house. In exchange they get a slice of the profit from every copy sold (which is what they're gambling on – they invest in a title in the hopes of it being a success). So the author pays the publisher via a cut from the royalties from each copy sold.

- The author finds professionals to subcontract and pays upfront for all those services. The author is investing in themselves and their work. In exchange for spending time and money on these processes, the author keeps all rights and royalties.

As you can see, *the author always pays*, with the only difference being whether they pay upfront with an initial outlay (independent author), or later, via reduced profits per copy sold (traditional publishing).

There are companies set up to help with the processes involved in independent publishing: for a fee. Some people see this as a separate category of publishing, called *assisted* or *supported publishing*. Personally, I just see that as a standard part of being an independent author. The author can hire people to take care of different aspects of the publishing process, or they can use a single company.

At risk of sounding evangelical, I'd like to include a quote by author Barry Hutchison[13] (reprinted with permission, from his 2019 Facebook post). I think it speaks for itself when it comes to the advantages of independent author-publishing.

> "In late 2016, after struggling to get by for 10 years as a full-time traditionally published author, I published my first indie novel.
>
> Within six months, I was earning more from indie than I was earning from trad. Within a year, I knew I was never going to go back.
>
> Yesterday, I hit a major milestone for me. It was launch day for the third book in my pen name crime series and for the first time ever I broke 5 figures (USD) in a single day.
>
> I cannot even begin to get my head around it, really, after all those years of worrying if I could pay bills, and feeling guilty for pursuing a writing career when I could've been making more money in a job.

A year ago, I was convinced that indie publishing was the future of the industry. It isn't. It's the present. It's happening now. Everyone here who self-publishes has a head start on everyone still trying to land that elusive trad deal.

For contrast, I remember when HarperCollins phoned me up and told me to 'crack open the champagne' because they'd managed to get my first book into Asda (a supermarket in the UK). They ordered 10,000 copies, and sold the whole lot. I was ecstatic.

Six to eight months later, I got my royalty statement. My cut for those 10,000 copies?

Two hundred pounds.

Minus 12.5% for my agent's commission."

Drinky's Digressions: Predators

Independent publishing is not vanity publishing. **Vanity publishing** is paying a third party an inflated sum for a poor service, all smoke and mirrors trading off the lure of being able to say "Wow! I'm published!" before realising that it isn't being published at all. It is basically paying for a printer. Maybe with unethical rights grabs in the process.

I mentioned supported publishing companies above. Note that some are reputable and useful, but others (such as the Author Solutions imprints)[14] can be predatory. The bad ones are little more than vanity publishers using deceptive practices and charging huge fees. And there are many companies claiming to be publishers that fall into the same categories.

I've known authors have near-misses from some of the predatory "publishers". So as well as looking into their reputation (for example, via reviews, their social media accounts, services like the ALLi Watchdog mentioned in the next section) here are other things to be aware of:

- With traditional publishing money flows *to* the author (or, in many cases, trickles in a disappointingly slow fashion), never the other way around. If they are claiming to be a publisher but asking you for money, alarm bells should start ringing. Because maybe they make their riches from fleecing desperate authors, rather than from selling books and taking a cut.

- What are their quality controls? I recently heard of one "publisher" that told an author they'd accept her work and definitely publish it – without having read anything. A true publisher would only invest money in a book (and author) that offers a return on their investment, via sales. If they aren't being picky, they aren't proper publishers. Don't be flattered into signing up.

- Contracts are binding. I've heard all sorts of horror

stories. Make sure you understand what the contract says. Read the small print but also think about what is missing or obfuscated. See my section on contracts (Drinky's Digressions: Licensing Rights), later in this chapter.

- Beware of hard sell. If they are being pushy and putting pressure on you, especially if it follows you being rightly cautious, then that isn't a good sign.

- Look for the title and author of some of the titles they have published, on the websites of Amazon, Waterstones, Kobo, Barnes & Noble etc. If the books aren't there, then why? To sell books they have to be available everywhere. If they are only on the publisher's website for direct order, then you will only ever be found by the tiniest fraction of the potential market. That means they are a printer, not a publisher. Also look at the book covers, and the sample previews of the interiors, to see how professional they look.

- Identify what they say are their most popular books. Do some research. What are the ranks of those books in their main categories on Amazon? (The higher the position in a category, the more the book is selling.) Look at how many reviews and ratings the book has on Amazon and Goodreads, and what the reviewers say. If the publisher's top books have barely a handful of ratings and reviews, that means they probably aren't selling or being promoted. Also look at the author platforms of their top authors: their websites, social media accounts and so on. Do they have a lot of interactions and fans? Or are they unknown?

- Clarify how the books are going to be printed and distributed. Are they printing ten thousand copies, warehousing and distributing them to bookshops? Or are they using print-on-demand, which costs them nothing, but still taking the lion's share of every sale?

- Part of the contract should specify that you get some author copies free, and can buy more at a heavily discounted price. Beware of "publishers" that actually make their money by selling books back to authors, especially if they try and encourage you to order in bulk. No. You are an author, not a bookshop. It's handy to have a few books as examples, for fans and reference. But you don't need more than that. Don't turn your spare room into a book warehouse.

- Who is their editor, and how long will you work with them for? What are their credentials? I heard of one case where the author was told to pay £100 for a "programme" where it turned out they were to join a group of other authors who also had been conned into paying £100 with the idea that they critique each other's work; then pay another £400 to do it four more times. That is the opposite of the publisher editing your work!

- Trust your gut – if it feels a bit off, then it probably is.

Top Tip: Seek Support

If you are interested in the independent author route then I highly recommend joining the Alliance of Independent Authors (ALLi).[15] They provide loads of best-practice advice in their member guidebooks, magazine, website, forum and blog. They can also mediate and provide some legal and contractual advice. ALLi's goal is empowering and supporting excellence in publishing, so if you are an author you can join regardless of your route to publication.

Speaking of ALLi, they have an additional professional category of authorpreneur for independent authors who have sold more than 50,000 books. An example would be LJ Ross, who appeared on the cover of The Bookseller (30th June 2023) to celebrate the fact that she had sold eight million books, all through her own imprint. In fact, her DCI Ryan series is the UK's second best-selling book series *of all time* (outranking Harry Potter) according to The Big Indie Author Data Drop 2023.[16]

ALLi have an excellent rating system for publishing service companies,[17] which will warn you about some of the bad ones. For members they also offer an Approved Services Search of reputable companies,[18] and a collection of Discounts & Deals.[19]

Drinky's Digressions: A Question Of Quality

In every area of creative endeavour – books, music, films, games – there is a range of quality. Sometimes the lower quality entries are because the creators couldn't do any better with the skills and resources they had available. We all grow by practice.

In other cases, people work out how to trick you into buying things that have no love or craft. I'm aware of writers who use many methods to churn out low-quality books. For example, there's the semi-plagiarism of reworking existing books via purchasing Private Label Rights (PLR), meaning they buy existing content (which is often low quality but cheap), make minor changes, and release it as if they wrote the whole thing. Others increasingly use AI to churn out books to a prompt, sometimes a hundred books per day. In many ways these are professionals, with multi-million-pound businesses, extensive advertising, and huge platforms. But there's no love or art in what they do: they are *marketers*, not authors. Nonetheless, their bad reputation and bland output harms us all.

All I can say is: buyer beware. Always do due diligence before buying anything. Just as I check Ethical Consumer[20] when choosing a product (so that I don't contribute to companies that invest in war, environmental destruction, and other evils), I also look at reviews and ratings of creative works before buying them. In book terms, what other titles has the author written? Do they have seven hundred books to their name, all with one rating that shows they are churning stuff out and relying on enough people falling for it? If they don't care about repeat customers, they don't care about quality.

But the real sign is the book itself. Ebook free sample previews are your friend. Just as you would open a printed novel to check writing quality, style, and how engrossing a story is, you can do the same with ebooks.

Lastly: identify authors you trust and respect, and support them. Then you know you'll keep reading books that are labours of love, and I'll be forever grateful. Ooops, I meant *they* will be forever grateful.

Drinky's Digressions: Self-publishing Is Not New

Although modern technology has made it easier than ever, so that we no longer have to hand-crank pages in our dining room as Virginia Woolf did, self-publishing is not a new phenomenon. It was used by many famous authors, sometimes for their classic works – which would never have been seen by the world and become classics in the first place if they hadn't been self-published.

Jane Austen paid for the first print run of *Sense & Sensibility*, which is why the copies said "PRINTED FOR THE AUTHOR" on the title page. She was investing in her own writing, and took the financial risk if it failed. (Luckily it made her a substantial profit.)

The first copies of *Songs of Innocence and of Experience* were printed and illuminated by William Blake himself in 1789.

Beatrix Potter self-published *The Tale of Peter Rabbit* when traditional publishers refused to do so. They came crawling back to her eventually and published future editions, selling over twenty thousand copies in the first year (and over forty million copies since then).

Mark Twain started his own imprint due to frustrations with traditional publishers, and published *The Adventures of Huckleberry Finn* in 1885. He had over forty thousand pre-orders of what went on to become one of his most popular books.

Margaret Atwood won awards for her self-published poetry book, *Double Persephone*.

As mentioned above, Virginia Woolf and her husband Leonard had their own imprint, Hogarth Press, which published many of her books, and those of other authors. Possibly her most famous book is *Mrs. Dalloway* (1925), which she self-published.

So self-publishing isn't a new phenomenon. It's part of the literary tradition.

Comparison Of Publishing Options

There's been a lot to take in, so I'll summarise many of the elements. First I will list a facet of publishing, then the approach of Traditional Publishing (TP) and Independent Authors (IA).

Who decides on a book's quality?
(TP) The publishers act as gatekeepers (and possibly the agent before them).
(IA) The market: readers and fans.

Rights
(TP) The publisher has the publishing rights (and may acquire other rights too). Conditions depend on the contract.
(IA) You keep all the rights but can selectively license them and take up opportunities.

Who pays for editing, book design, proofreading etc?
(TP) The publisher pays upfront, but they hope to get the money back (and more) in their cut from every book sale.
(IA) The author pays the upfront costs; in return they get greater royalties.

Who takes the financial risk for publishing the book?
(TP) The publisher. They are investing in the author. (Note that the author took the financial risk in writing the book.)
(IA) The author. They are investing in themself.

Royalties
(TP) The author may get up to 25%.
(IA) The author may get up to 70% (see next chapter).

Advances
(TP) You may get an advance on royalties.
(IA) No advance: you only get paid for sales.

How is the quality of a book determined?
(TP) Initially by looking inside it; then more fully by reading it.
(IA) Initially by looking inside it; then more fully by reading it. (Yep, it's the same. Judge a book by its quality and how well it fits your interests, not its route to publication.)

Creative decisions
(TP) The publisher makes most of the decisions. Cover, title, final edit, marketing, metadata: they have the final say. The author is seen as a content provider, not a creative director.
(IA) The author keeps creative control and makes all the final decisions, including how the book is presented.

Who hires editors, cover designers etc?
(TP) The publisher.
(IA) The author, via outsourcing.

Who pays the author?
(TP) The publishers.
(IA) The distributors.

Timing
(TP) Can take up to two years for the book to reach the shelf.
(IA) Your book can be available within a week of it being fully finished.

Amount of author responsibility
(TP) Less, as the publisher is doing some of the work, especially formatting, production and distribution.
(IA) More responsibility as you are running a creative publishing business. There are a number of skills to master.

Marketing
(TP) You are expected to do a lot of it, and have an author platform. Publishers may promote the work within a short window of time before moving on.

(IA) You do it (or hire people), and have an author platform. Marketing is within a larger potential canvas of time (forever).

Bookshops
(TP) Easier to get into bookshops (but distribution has a cost). Also note that not all contracts include publishing printed books: nowadays, some are digital-only contracts.
(IA) More difficult to get into bookshops.

Awards
(TP) Easier to win awards (since conditions and large hidden costs – e.g. £10,000 "contributions" – often favour traditional publishers).
(IA) Impossible for some awards due to the way they are manipulated, but the situation is improving all the time. I'll discuss awards soon.

Film and TV deals
(TP) Possible for hit books (though still a rarity for it to go beyond being optioned).
(IA) Far less likely to be offered.

Can a formatting error or typo in a book be fixed after publication?
(TP) Due to the costs, many authors find the publisher won't make changes, so there's nothing the author can do.
(IA) It can be corrected and a new version uploaded the same day.

Sales focus and definitions of success
(TP) The initial launch period, akin to a film's make-or-break

opening weekend.

(IA) Long-term; known as the "long tail" (which I'll discuss in the next chapter).

Who decides pricing?

(TP) The publisher.

(IA) The author, who can experiment with promotions so sales don't stagnate, and can reinvigorate backlist titles or drive read-through in a series.

Barriers to entry?

(TP) Publishers (and agents) are flooded with submissions. It may be difficult or impossible to access this route, especially for niche, experimental, or controversial works.

(IA) The time and motivation to learn the processes involved and the cost of outsourcing services.

Distribution

(TP) Wide (all shops and vendors).

(IA) Can be wide, or exclusive to Amazon (in exchange for benefits).

Sales data

(TP) Delayed reporting on sales (sometimes massively).

(IA) Real-time sales figures from distributors, or only a 24 hour delay.

As you can see, one route to market is not automatically better than another. Some authors might want full creative control; others might be happy to hand that over to someone else. They are both viable options.

Drinky's Digressions: Awards And Prejudice

No, it isn't a recently discovered Jane Austen novel.

If a competition is to be legitimate it should find *the best*. The more open a competition is, and the bigger the field of books, the more likely that the winners really are the best books. Restricted awards have little connection to quality due to excellent books being excluded.

Even though the BBC National Short Story Award is publicly funded, it has always been run on the old-fashioned prejudice that you have to have been "traditionally published". It was the case in 2013, and it is still the case over a decade later in 2025. So it isn't a competition to find the best new short stories in the UK, it is a competition to find the best short stories by established writers. It is a shame that many excellent authors are prevented from entering a competition that their taxes go towards funding. But hey, the BBC is a conservative, establishment institution, so I am not surprised.

The best book awards should identify and promote excellence; introduce books to new readers; and help authors build their careers. Excluding whole categories of authors means a slapdash and prejudiced approach to achieving these things.

Awards which reject books by independent authors (The Booker Prize also has a clause to that effect), regardless of the book's quality, are failing the reading community. They are also punishing authors who retain creative control and greater rights.

TWO TYPES OF PUBLISHING

Anyone who loves books, and those who write them, should support authors that are in control of their own creations.

The key factor isn't how a book is published: it is how *good* the book is. That is the only thing that should concern readers. That is the only thing that should concern writers. That is the only thing that should concern award organisers.

Big awards can be controversial in other ways. Shortlists of unreadably dour books; nepotism; culturally biased judges; opaque judging processes; claiming that subjective responses from a limited group equate to objective criteria; and goals of enriching the organisers.

Regarding the latter, hidden costs can automatically exclude many excellent books and authors from being considered. What a prize should *not* do (if it wants to be open) is charge massive fees to enter. Costs that can be swallowed with no problem by a large publishing house such as the Big Five would be impossible for an independent author or small publishing house. This is why independent authors could not win the Costa Book Awards (that prize requires a £5,000 fee from publishers if a book is to be shortlisted), or be part of the Richard & Judy Bookclub. Even the BBC National Short Story Award charged £600 to submit a single short story in 2024. No wonder many consider these competitions to be just an extended sales promotion for the biggest publishers.

It's also worth dispelling a myth. "But surely if book prizes were open to all books, they would be inundated?" I was quoted in

Book Prizes & Awards For Indie Authors by Orna Ross (2021), talking about this topic, and I answered:

"Can the level of entries be managed? Of course. An insider told me it's really not hard to do; the Folio prize starts with a form submission about the book and goes from there. Also, if an organisation is worried about the number of entries, it can implement quality controls. This is far better than arbitrary exclusions. Apply the same criteria to all books, trade published or independent."

I say that from experience. One year I chaired a judging panel for the international Bram Stoker Awards. These awards are truly inclusive because they are open to everyone, regardless of how a book is published. All that matters is looking for the best book in each category. Many on my shortlist were amazing books, and would have been excluded entirely by some other awards due to being published by independent authors. The focus in my panel's critical discussions was on championing works, explaining why they stood out, what they did well, what made them so fresh and exciting.

In addition to the Bram Stoker Awards, be aware that The Pulitzer Prize, the Arthur C Clarke Award, the Nebula Award, the Romantic Novelists' Association Awards, the Commonwealth Book Prize, and many other major literary awards, are all open to independent authors.

Bearing all that in mind, awards fall into the category of "nice to have" rather than necessary. The time and cost in being considered can be substantial in some cases, and a drain of resources from more important endeavours. That said, if you do win any notable awards which might impress readers (and I don't mean your local writing group's monthly prize for best short story), then it is something you'll use in your marketing, such as adverts or a badge on the book cover. You might mention it in the book's blurb, your author bio, or in press releases. The importance of a major award isn't in boosting the author's ego, but in the possibility of increasing sales of the book; and, in turn, a chance of selling subsidiary TV, film or translation rights.

If you are interested in this area, it is often best to start with local or smaller-scale competitions. This can boost your confidence and profile, paving the way for bigger wins later. ALLi has a list of literary awards and contests.[21]

And don't let the idea of accolades swallow up too much time and energy from writing your next amazing book, which will be so good it can't be ignored. Nothing sells books like a new book does. (Try saying that quickly, while drunk on celebratory champagne at an awards ceremony.)

Drinky's Digressions: A Note About Industry Prejudices

I've already touched on the misunderstandings that are sometimes applied to independent authors and their work. I remember how someone once described Gladstone's Library to me as "stuck in the 1950s" because its small print included the same prejudice against independent writers ("Self-published authors are not eligible for Writer-in-Residence").[22]

How are prejudices created? The competitions discussed earlier can be one example. They reinforce the mistaken idea that the only good books are those that are traditionally published "because self-published books never win that big award". Independent authors are erased from the history and even if the organisations become more inclusive, those past award lists will always make it look like independent authors never existed. A self-fulfilling prophecy is established via discrimination.

Enlightened creatives know that the means of production doesn't relate to the quality of the output: only the author and the reading experience matter. Thankfully that bias is rapidly fading away as facts show how unsubstantiated those opinions are, and how the views reveal (as always) more about the prejudices of the speaker than the reality.

We've seen this in other creative spheres. Think about indie music, indie movies, indie games. Their independent nature becomes a mark of vitality and interest, taking risks that traditional releases won't, to create something fresh. It's about artists retaining control over their creative vision. Saying independent works are worse than corporate-created works is like saying home-made cake is worse than store-bought cake. In all publishing there is good and bad, books that suit your preferences and books that don't.

And what do readers think? In 2022 K-lytics looked at the ratings of 43,000 titles in the top 100 categories bestseller lists on Amazon for the previous few years. (The Big Indie Author Data Drop 2023.)[23] They found that readers rated books by independent authors as highly as those by traditional publishers. Both types of book had an average of 4.5 out of 5 stars. Note that most of those readers won't even have been aware of whether the book had been traditionally or independently published, as the quality was the same.

Hybrid Authors

This isn't a term for some kind of genetically-modified writer from one of my space opera novels. It is simply an author who uses both traditional publishing and independent author-publishing as appropriate. Authors shouldn't miss out on the benefits of working with a publisher; nor should they be unaware of the benefits of retaining full creative control. A hybrid approach that crosses over both systems is increasingly common amongst professional authors.

This kind of flexibility is a good thing for all involved in publishing: it's an opportunity, not something to fight over. Traditional publishing can be a good partner to work with because of the expertise, passion and connections of many small presses. Likewise we all benefit from a growth in quality literature, that creates new markets and enhances readership. We should all be working together to build that united creative industry.

Some books go from one system to another. The best-selling hits *The Martian* (Andy Weir), and *Wool* (Hugh Howey), began life as stories published by the authors. The books were such huge successes that traditional publishers came begging for the rights to distribute them. Andy Weir's *The Martian* went on to be adapted for the 2015 film directed by Ridley Scott and starring Matt Damon. And Hugh Howey's Silo series (where *Wool* was the first book) led to Howey signing a print-only deal for around $500,000 with Simon & Schuster, while Howey retained full rights to continue distributing the ebooks himself. They are both great examples of the benefits of the author being in control of how they license their work.

It can go the other way: one of my friends is a well-respected traditionally published author of many great books. Some of them are now out of print and the rights have reverted to her. The titles were doing nothing, unavailable to readers and providing no income. She decided to create digital files of the texts, get them edited, design new covers, and publish them again herself. I gave her advice on all those steps. Her other books remained distributed by traditional publishers. The end result is a win-win situation for everyone. She was especially pleased at regaining control over the works, since she really hated some of the covers her publisher had chosen, but she had been forced to accept them due to her contract stating the publisher had the final say.

The key point of the hybrid approach is that you adopt the route to market that is best for the project and your own skill set.

Brandon Sanderson has a number of useful FAQs on his website, including one on hybrid approaches, where he answers the question "Should I self-publish ebooks or try for a New York publisher?":[24]

> "I would not abandon either model. Self-publishing has proved itself so viable recently that if I were a new writer, I would be looking at doing both at the same time. Maybe taking the longer, more epic-style books to New York and doing the faster-paced, more thriller-style books online and seeing what works for you best. So the expansion of the ebook market gives you more places to go."

Although he is well known as a traditionally published author, he has also released some books himself via Kickstarters (a form of crowdfunding which I will discuss in Chapter 8). His most recent Kickstarter raised a truly record-breaking $41 million, from over 185,000 backers. All to self-publish four new books.

Brandon talked about using different types of publishing for different genres. Sometimes it is simpler than that, and relates to *formats*. An independent author can publish an ebook with ease, and receive far greater royalties than a trade-published author. But other formats may have cost implications, or perhaps the connections with bookshops and distribution channels a trade publisher commands could be advantageous. That's why some independent authors choose to release ebooks and special editions themselves, but would consider using a trade publisher for printed editions, audiobooks, and translations, only licensing the rights for those. The trade publisher becomes just another business partner when it is mutually beneficial.

Licensing Rights

As I mentioned previously, if you sign a contract with a traditional publisher (Big Five or not) you will assign some of your rights to them in exchange for payment. A hybrid author will be doing this for *some* of their works. It's worth delving into rights.

In general, an author starts out owning all the rights to their book. Some publishers and rights buyers treat the rights as a single thing, and try to claim all of them (with "all rights, all territories, all formats" contracts): even those rights they don't plan to use. Even worse, I've heard horror stories of contracts that gave the trade publisher all the rights; the publisher then sold subsidiary filming rights for a book that became a popular TV series, making the publisher a lot of money. Sounds good? Not for the author, since the contract didn't stipulate separate *payments* for sales of subsidiary rights, so the author didn't get a penny from the TV show. The publisher was bullish, and stuck to the contract, which was carefully worded in their favour. So do be aware of these traps, where the initial excitement in being offered a contract can lead to accepting grossly unfair terms and conditions that are detrimental to your future. Contracts should be equitable for both parties, not just for the publisher.

If a contract includes any of the following red flags, it should make you cautious:

- Indemnities for the more powerful party.

- A request to "assign rights". Never assign them, only license them. "Assign" means give away forever. "License" means you still own them.

- Non-disclosure agreements (NDAs, or gagging clauses) which stop you from being able to discuss some topics. Also "non-disparagement" clauses, meaning you can't criticise the company publicly, no matter what they do.

- "Do not compete" clauses. They can severely hamper authors and are vague enough to act as a continuous legal threat to your creative business.

- Clauses allowing the publisher first option on new work with no time limit, or with a requirement for you to accept their offer. It means the publisher can sit on your next book forever and you can't sell it elsewhere until they make a decision. A right of first refusal should always have a defined limit in time (such as thirty days), and also be clear about what first refusal applies to: ideally only books related to the one they have published.

- Requirements to agree to other policies outside of the contract: policies which may change over time.

- Limits to your ability to use the law, especially if the

publisher makes you agree to binding arbitration and can choose the arbiter.

- A claim of "derivative rights" which could prevent you from writing sequels or spin-offs set in the same story world you created.

- A requirement to waive your "moral rights". These are the right to be identified as the author (right of attribution), and the right not to have your work changed without your permission. If you agree to waive these rights then the publisher can make any alterations they want and even publish it under another author's name.

- Clauses allowing them to transfer contracts to another company without your consent. It might mean the new company keeps publishing the work but refuses to pay royalties, as happened with Disney: "Disney had argued that it had purchased the rights, but not the obligations of the contract."[25]

- Clauses trying for a full "grant of rights" – taking rights that they may not ever even utilise, just to stop you from selling (sublicensing) them to someone who would. At worst, they might create poor quality adaptations or sequels, damaging your reputation; they may also pay you little or nothing, to add insult to injury.

- A lack of clear and fair clauses governing reversion of rights and termination. What if you want to publish the book somewhere else because the publisher was useless? What if the publisher goes bankrupt? If there are penalties on you for ending the contract, are they reasonable? Or are the termination terms grossly unfair to the author, in order to prevent them ever cancelling the contract?

- The publisher stating they can allow companies to train AIs on your work, which could lead to AIs being able to produce competing books in your style: many authors are against this, as shown by Draft2Digital's survey.[26]

- A lack of performance standards, with no defined penalties even if they fail to deliver what was agreed.

Which leads me on to this: *rights are divisible.*

A book can be published in many formats, and the rights for the formats licensed separately. A book can be released in many territories around the world, and in many languages: again, those can all be licensed separately. Then there are rights to do adaptations: TV, games, film. And merchandising rights, to create products based around the story, setting and characters (such as the Star Wars action figures and vehicles I grew up playing with).

The concept of "selling" a book to a publisher is therefore misleading, as we're actually licensing publication rights in exchange for payment (whether royalties, or royalties plus an advance), and also for publishing services such as design and editing. As such, authors should always be wary of signing away all their rights in a work.

A canny author will view the rights not as a blob taken all at once, but as separate sub-rights, and will always seek to license rights selectively, and – where possible – *non-exclusively*. We saw this above, where Hugh Howey licensed the rights to publish print books of his titles, but he kept the rights to release the ebooks (a different format).

So always limit what you license:

- by term (time, usually in years; you can easily renew the contract at the end if the arrangement worked well for all parties);
- territory (regions or countries, but sometimes even retailers);
- language (translations);
- and format (e.g. print, audiobook, film, ebook, merchandise).

This is known as **selective rights licensing**.

Only grant the rights a publisher needs, and those they will use – and for which you'll be paid. This is the "use it or lose it" approach. There's no point licensing translation rights if the publisher has no intention of doing translations. 10% royalties of nothing is still nothing.

However, many trade publishers or rights buyers will push for the opposite: to grab as many rights as possible, for as long a time and over as wide a territory as they can. They'll say it is their standard contract, "non-negotiable". It's why I want to raise this topic, so at least you can be aware of what you might be agreeing to. The ideal may not always be possible, but if you don't understand the situation, you have no chance of negotiating a fair rights deal. Never be afraid to require the removal of awful contract terms and clauses you do not agree with. You can be sure that if you added anything the publisher was unhappy with, they would refuse to sign it until the clause was removed.

One final consideration that may help you in negotiations. Traditional publishing contracts assume they are licensing a work from a new author with no publishing skills and no audience, requiring the publisher to do everything. But if you are an experienced independent author, that doesn't apply. You may have a substantial existing readership, a polished manuscript, and an understanding of how rights licensing works. You will hopefully have more power in the negotiation to split the rights and only license the formats, languages and territories you want. Namely, those that the publisher is best situated to exploit for the benefit of them and you, whilst keeping back any rights that are more profitable for you to utilise directly, such as ebook sales where your royalties will be three times higher than the publisher will offer. You can also limit the term of the agreement, so the publisher doesn't force a "lifetime of copyright" deal. The publisher may also be more amenable to giving you a say in publishing and marketing decisions, based on your knowledge of your audience.

Remember, they are licensing rights that they think will be profitable, they aren't giving you a handout. Negotiating is standard. You want to keep as many rights as possible, and make a good profit from those you license; they want to gain as many as possible (and as cheaply as possible) "just in case". Be assertive (not aggressive or passive) and businesslike, and you'll likely be respected for it.

Drinky's Digressions: Can IP Law Go Too Far?

Intellectual Property (IP) laws are those concerning topics like copyright, trademarks, and patents. They are relevant to authors, and anyone who creates original things.

I am in a number of networks, groups and organisations with fellow authors. A vast number of queries are to do with IP-related creative restrictions: worries about titles, using trademarked terms, referring to real places and businesses, or quoting copyrighted content such as lyrics and text (or even identifying if it is copyrighted, and who owns that copyright).

And yet those same restrictions on intellectual property rarely benefit or protect the authors in turn, because IP law is a minefield that requires (expensive) legal experts to understand and navigate. It's made even more complicated by the international nature of information, so that you might live in the UK but be affected by laws from another country such as the USA's awful DMCA Act (1998).[27]

Only big companies, the rich and the powerful, have the resources to be able to use IP laws to their benefit, which is why big media conglomerates push for more restrictive (and therefore, profitable to them) IP laws. Normal people like you and me? We're more likely to fall foul of these laws than be able to use them in any meaningful way.

A few issues with copyright law off the top of my head.

- Copyright trolls, e.g. those who add copyright photos to photo sites (even licensed ones) under a false account, then when the photo is used they threaten legal action unless you pay them an exorbitant fee. Yes, this happens.

- Research that is publicly funded but hidden behind paywalls, just to boost publishers' profits.

- In the past writers freely quoted each other's works, widening knowledge and appreciation of the thing quoted. Nowadays you could be prosecuted for doing so even if you fully cite the source. Instead, you would have to track down rights holders for every single quotation, get permission, pay, and probably renegotiate and do it all again if you print more copies, do a new edition, or change format (e.g. audiobook). So nowadays it is easier to just avoid that negotiation, administration and paywall nightmare. The common attitude of publishers to their writers when, for example, a quote from a song is used is to just strip it out. "It isn't worth it." Even in 2010 it could cost £735 to quote one line of "When I'm

Sixty-four".[28] These restrictions impact on creative arts.

- Likewise in contemporary novels, authors avoid mentioning real world names, events, and products since they can't risk offending powerful companies. So we self-censor, and chunks of everyday reality can't be referred to in fiction, even though we are continually bombarded with adverts for those things from which we cannot escape.

- Things which should have passed into public domain get their copyright extended because rich corporations can pressure law makers for exceptions. For example, Disney was powerful enough to get laws changed in its favour with the Mickey Mouse Protection Act.[29] Likewise if you use stories and characters in the public domain (fairy tales and so on) which should be available to all, you have to be careful because companies like Disney may have used those names and stories in works they have then copyrighted and trademarked to the hilt. They can then clamp down on anyone telling the story of Sleeping Beauty or Aladdin in any way that resembles the Disney interpretations (which most retellings would, because they are based on the same source material) – so most creatives self-censor, and back away as part of their risk management. We end up with corporations owning stories and names that used to be part of the public domain.

- Copyright on classic works of visual art expires – but

you end up not being able to re-use that work because a gallery or museum restricts it.

- Trademarks can be used to restrict common words (and in some cases images, fonts, colours). Our communal word hoard becomes commercially owned property.

- Even taking photos in cities can break the law, as the architecture of a building in the background might be protected or restricted. Likewise you might record a video and it shows logos and images in the background – brand signs on shops, posters, whatever, perhaps exacerbated by copyrighted music playing from a nearby TV or radio. Recording or sharing the video may be illegal.

- In my career as a librarian I often had to deal with commercial licensing and collecting societies, and their heavy-handed letters and emails which threatened crippling legal implications if you didn't pay them for licences (whether you needed one or not). Educational institutions across the UK had to spend chunks of their budget on licences from these societies, rather than on staffing and learning resources. We now have a profusion of licensing and collecting societies. I remember that just for one type of organisation (independent schools) in one country (England) the librarian told me they had to budget for more than ten licences from different licensing societies, including: The Copyright Licensing Agency (CLA); The Educational Recording

Agency (ERA); Christian Copyright Licensing International (CCLI); Phonographic Performance Limited (PPL); The Performing Right Society (PRS); Mechanical-Copyright Protection Society (MCPS); Motion Picture Licensing Company (MPLC); Filmbankmedia (Public Video Screening Licence – PVS); Newspaper Licensing Agency (NLA Media Access); PMLL (Schools Printed Music Licence – SPML). No, that list is not comprehensive, there are over a hundred globally. And everything they licence should be allowed by law anyway.

Many authors believe current copyright restrictions are far too restrictive and complex to the point where it interferes with creativity and our right to share information. These areas cross over with the wonderful work done by the Electronic Frontier Foundation.[30] Caitlin Johnstone even allows her words to be reused for commercial profit without attribution, in one of the most open copyright statements I've ever seen.[31]

We need to campaign to increase what can be done with IP under fair dealing and fair use laws, whilst also simplifying the law so it is much more open. It should be simple to know what is unequivocally okay to do, and you shouldn't have to track down rights holders or get permission to do any of these things. All this benefits the whole creative community. Some examples:

- You should be allowed to quote from books, music, magazines, poems, letters, emails, journals, newspapers and websites, as long as you cite the source. It's only snippets, not the whole work, and yet it keeps the quoted work in the public consciousness.

- You should be allowed to convert between formats (including scanning, electronic formats, Braille, audio), and store a backup for your own use.

- DRM (Digital Restrictions Management) which interferes with these activities should be illegal.

- Once something has been bought, the item ceases to be controllable by the vendor. They mustn't try to prevent second-hand sales or sharing. They mustn't ever destroy, reduce, or cripple it in any way, for example using DRM or online measures.

It would be much simpler to know what we can do if we had less restrictive IP laws. It would strike a balance between re-use and rewards for creativity. We have bigger issues with works being wholesale scrunched into AI minds to regurgitate without any compensation, or even citation – nowadays it seems churlish to care about someone quoting and citing your work. That isn't a lost sale, it's free publicity.

Conclusion: The Key Publishing Paths

The tasks required to publish a book can be complex and time consuming. Many authors do not want to engage with them, and are only too happy to go with the convenience of traditional publishing, and let the publisher deal with it all. They don't mind not having the final say in the cover or book title or edits: they just want to get on with writing. It's a perfectly valid attitude, and is why traditional publishing is the best fit for some authors.

On the other hand, some authors want to be hands-on. They want to control the creative vision from start to end. For them, professional self-publishing is the best way. They don't do all the tasks themselves but they choose who to hire, and what brief to give them; they *manage the process*.

As such, one route to market is not better than another. One does not guarantee quality; one does not automatically offer the best option for an author. They are both viable options, depending on the project, the market, the skills and motivation of the author and their team. The end goal is to be read, and for our readers to gain something positive from the experience.

I've tried to keep this chapter relatively simple, but if you'd like to dive in deeper then Jane Friedman has been updating her (free!) *Key Book Publishing Paths* guide every year for a decade. Her 2025–2026 version can be read as a text version or downloaded as a pdf.[32]

Money Money Money

Chapter 3

The alternative name for this chapter, which has less resemblance to a Billy Idol song, is: "Can I make a living as a writer?"

As you can imagine, this is impossible to answer simply, because it depends on factors such as who *you* are, what you write, how well you write (both craft and art), how quickly you write, how lucky you are, and how closely your output fits current trends.

But the related question, "Can *a person* make a living as a writer?" is answerable: yes! Of course. Though it will take time and work to reach that point. I won't sugar-coat it: writing is no fast track to easy money, so if you hoped it was, let me divest you of that assumption right this minute. Many authors will spend years learning this wonderful craft and writing good books, but still never earn as much as they'd have made working behind a bar. I'll back that up with figures later on, in case you think this is an attempt to dissuade the competition. I just want to encourage a realistic idea of what you are up against, and the quality you will need to strive for, in order to stand out. Brandon Sanderson has a short FAQ called *Can I Make A Living As A Writer?* which answers the same question.[33]

In creative professions, there is a highly unequal distribution of income: in 2022, the top 1% of authors earned a third of all sales. That applies whether the author is traditionally published, or an independent author. As with all popularity contests, being well known leads to being talked about and taken seriously, which leads to free promotion, which helps to maintain your position. Whereas if you are unknown, you don't have any critical mass, don't get the sales, and don't get the reviews or commentary.

There is another problem.

Imagine a world called Booktopia where only a hundred new books (by a hundred authors) are released every year to a voracious readership. Those hundred new books would get masses of attention and sales, assuming the same human population as in our world.

Then imagine a world called Gluttonia where, instead of a hundred books, there are a million new books, from a million authors, who are all attracted to a job that seemed glorious: "Tell exciting stories, get rich!" The possibility of sharing your ideas and being loved for it, with adoring fans and lots of money, whilst working from home (or a coffee shop, or the beach, or anywhere else you like) in your pyjamas/trunks/Renaissance costume appeals to many people. Who wouldn't want to live that dream, rather than grinding away for a corporate overlord, or having to defend awful company policies to users?

For each new title released in Booktopia, there are ten thousand new releases in Gluttonia ... but only the same number of readers. It's impossible for any reader to stay on top of all the books, so many of them (even wonderful ones) sink without trace under the avalanche. And as well as new releases (**frontlist**), the **backlist** of books from previous years is also monumentally huge and still available.

That is the scenario nowadays. Everyone has an imagination and thinks they can write a book. Hence too many authors and too many books. Each year, nearly all the previously published books are still available, plus a massive influx of new ones. It makes it harder to stand out and get noticed. So much money is spent on advertising by the big players that it pushes advertising costs up for everyone. The big names get promoted at the front of (virtual and physical) bookshops and purchased by readers and librarians. The result is a massive second-hand market where they sometimes can't even give books away.

Even back in 2009 publishers knew that the number of books published tripled every few years, while sales were going down. In this 2014 Guardian article[34] a literary agent said the number of new publications is "either a sign of cultural vitality or publishing suicide ... Of course, it is utter madness to publish so many books when the average person reads between one and five books a year."

But authors know this. When a market is as saturated with products as the book market, average incomes will inevitably decline. Would subsidies help? No, it would only make things worse, by encouraging more people to write, so incomes drop even more. So when you see reports that author incomes are low it isn't really a problem in need of a fix, it is an inevitable consequence of there being so many authors and books.

The end result is that some authors will drop out, and some new authors will be put off writing for profit, and it will begin to balance out again. Authors are no different from other industries that deal with supply and demand in that respect. There's no point complaining about not making much income if we open a clothes shop next to fifty other clothes shops.

Here are some figures to paint a fuller picture.

Estimates of books released vary. Traditionally published books worldwide account for up to a million books per year, with perhaps 160,000 new titles a year in the UK alone. When you include independent authors and self-publishers that may be quadrupled, since independent authors may be publishing more than one and a half million titles a year. I've seen estimates of over 600,000 titles published by independent authors every year *just in the US*. Worldometer[35] estimates 2,200,000 new book titles will be published this year, based on UNESCO figures.

Bearing all that in mind, I work on the assumption that the total is about *two million new titles a year globally*, which is as good a figure to adopt as any, since there is no truly accurate way to measure this. For example, many books are released without an **ISBN (International Standard Book Number)** through vendors such as Amazon, and ISBNs aren't an accurate way of measuring book releases anyway.

And so, many books never find the audience they deserve, while mediocre and formulaic books may sell well due to existing fame and significant advertising budgets. It's no different from the interesting and varied independent local cafes closing every day while the likes of the big chains make billions in profit and spread their corporate banality onto every high street.

But do some authors succeed? I repeat, louder, YES! So could you succeed? YES! It's just important to have realistic expectations, to make sure you don't think you can spend a weekend bashing away at a keyboard and have an immediate bestseller that will earn you riches and fame. The truth is that most successful authors worked *hard* and wrote *a lot* and faced *many* rejections before they began to make even a partial living from writing.

Also bear in mind that, even though more than a million new books are released every year, only a small portion of those will be released in the genre or subject area you write in. And people buy a *lot* of books. Again, estimates vary, but I work on the assumption that global sales of print books are about 700 million a year, and a lot more for ebook sales.

The core message is: there is always room for an excellent book. They may be one in a hundred, but it is that one in a hundred which discerning people seek. And that's what you should aim at writing, so we end up with *the right book* reaching *the right reader*.

Drinky's Digressions: Ranganathan

When I was doing my MSc in librarianship I learnt about the five laws of library science[36] proposed by Ranganathan.[37] The second and third laws stuck in my head. "Every reader their book, and every book its reader." I will refer back to this later.

A good library will help the reader find the exact book they need. You can replace "library" with "bookshop". The problem for librarians and booksellers is that it's impossible to know about every book, and therefore the perfect book for me (as a reader) may be one they don't know about. But that won't stop my quest to find it. And the next. And the one after that.

Royalties And Economics

Royalties govern how much you get paid from the sale of every copy of a book. For traditionally published works, when you license the rights to a publisher, the contract will stipulate things such as royalty rates. They will vary by the format the book is published in (paperback, hardback, ebook, audiobook), but I'll list some commonly used figures.

Note that all my calculations are generalisations, since every contract, vendor, publisher and book are different. Also you would probably need to deduct a further 10-15% from any income figures to represent the agent's cut.

Lastly, I am working on the basis that the publisher is paying royalties on the listed retail price of the book ("retail royalties" or "list royalties"). But do check your contract, as some publishers pay "net royalties" or "royalties on net profits". That means you only get the royalties *after* all the deductions for distributors and discounts. They can fudge the figures and deduct all sorts of expenses (things they should be paying for themselves), taking them from your royalties. In that case your percentage royalties are taken from a far lower starting figure than the book's retail price, and is a much worse deal for the author. Sometimes even one changed word in a contract can massively alter how much the author will be paid.

Paperback

Around 7% retail royalties. The percentage may change, the more copies you sell, via break points. For example, it may begin at 6%, and only after a number of books are sold (e.g. 70,000) does the rate move up to 7% for that next batch. After another 70,000 sales, it might go up to 8% for the third batch. But, of course, even reaching that first increase point won't happen for most titles, and the initial print run will be far below it.

So, if a paperback sells for £10, the author might receive (at 7% retail royalties) £0.70 per copy sold.

If a paperback sells a lot of copies in the first few years – let's assume ten thousand – the traditionally published author would earn £7,000 over that three year period for that book. That's around £2,333 a year if averaged equally: though in reality the bulk of sales would be in the first year, and the third year's payment would be significantly less.

If half the number of copies sold, the royalties would be half as well, coming to £3,500 for the author, split over three years to about £1,160 a year.

If the book is reduced in price (e.g. for a supermarket promotion) then the royalties paid per copy will also be a lot less; the assumption is that volume of sales makes up for the smaller cut.

Hardback

Usually 10-15% royalties. These also sell for a higher price, so you can see why publishers often release hardbacks first. Anyone desperate to read the book is more likely to buy the version that creates more profit.

If a hardback sells for £20, the author might receive (at 15% royalties) £3 per copy sold. Normally there are far fewer total sales of hardbacks than paperbacks.

Ebook

Usually 20-25% list royalties.

Technically, ebooks should be cheaper because there are no printing, distribution or warehousing costs. But many traditional publishers now want to charge the same for an ebook as a print book, which seems like price-gouging the customer to me. Still, if people will pay £12 for an ebook, that's their choice.

So, if an ebook sells for £6, the author might receive (at 25% list royalties), £1.50 per copy sold.

Where Does The Rest Of The Money Go?

If an author receives 7% of the paperback sale price on a £10 book, who makes the rest of the money? Well, the distributors and bookshops get the book at a reduced price so that they can make a profit from selling it (otherwise, why would they?). The figures (and distributor/bookseller divisions) vary since supply chains are complex, so for now I'll simplify it by pretending the bookshop gets the whole discount. Let's say 45%, which is fairly standard. So the bookshop gets the book for £5.50 and sells it for £10, meaning they make £4.50 profit. The publisher has made £5.50. They give the author their £0.70, leaving £4.80.

However, it costs money to print a book. The cost varies depending on the initial print run if offset printing is used (which I will explain in Chapter 8: Distribution); and it costs more per copy for print-on-demand, though that saves a lot of money on warehousing. Let's assume the publisher has used offset printing, and work on the figure of £3 to print and ship each copy. That leaves £1.80 per copy for the publisher, which pays editors, typesetters, cover designers and so on. In effect, the publisher is making 18% of the sale price of a paperback.

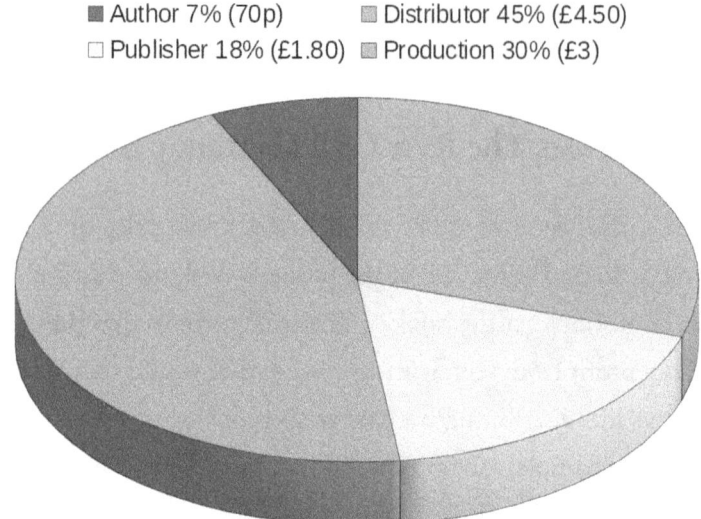

3.1 Money division for a £10 paperback, traditionally published author

Note that in all examples for traditionally published authors (here and below), if they have an agent then you need to remove 15-20% from the author's cut to represent the agent's commission.

Ebook Royalties: Traditional Publishing Versus Independent Authors

Ebooks are a useful focus for sums, since – once the work is written and formatted – making extra digital copies costs the publisher nothing. No printing, no warehouses, no paper and glue and ink, no transportation in big trucks and boats. "You want a copy?" (Author clicks fingers, accompanied by magical tintinnabulation, and a new ebook poofs into existence with a whiff of vanilla.) "There you go."

Let's compare ebook royalties for an author who is traditionally published, and an independent author.

We'll assume an ebook is being sold for £6, and the traditionally published author's contract allows them list royalties at the higher end, 25% (rather than 7% for the paperback). The author will receive **£1.50** per sale, the distributor would perhaps take 30% – £1.80 – and the publisher would pocket the remaining £2.70. In effect, the publisher gets 45% of the sale price on an ebook.

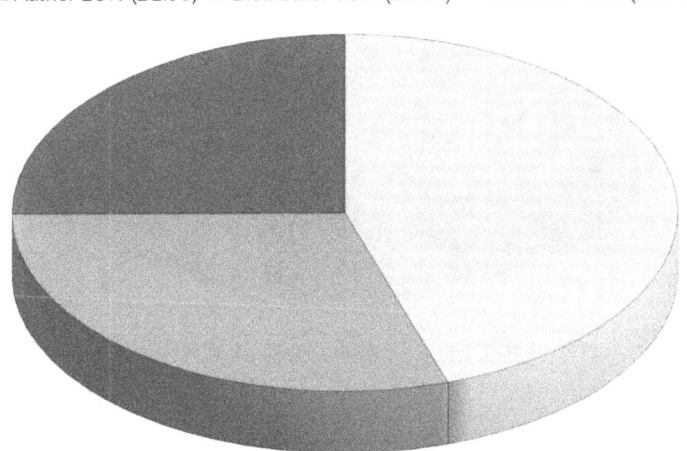

3.2 Money division for a £6 ebook, traditionally published author

An independent author's rate can vary by distribution channel and ebook price. For example, Amazon gives 35% royalties if the ebook is priced *below* $2.99 or *above* $9.99, but 70% for books priced $2.99-$9.99 (Amazon lists this in US dollars, but it is around £2.20-£7.37 in UK currency), which is where our fictional ebook falls. So, for each sale of a £6 ebook, an independent author receives **£4.20** (with no agent's commission to worry about). This is one of the reasons why some independent authors focus primarily on ebooks: it cuts out a lot of work and related expenses, whilst paying them a significant cut of every sale.

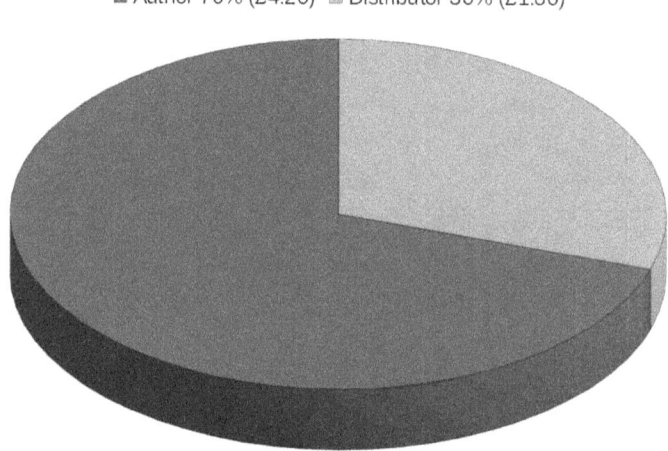

3.3 Money division for a £6 ebook, independent author

If the ebook sells ten thousand copies, the traditionally published author will receive £15,000. For the same number of sales, the independent author would receive £42,000.

Or, to look at it another way: if a traditionally published author needs to sell ten thousand copies of an ebook to earn £15,000 in royalties, an independent author would only need to sell 3,570 copies to make the same amount of money, all else being equal.

Royalties Versus Commission

I've been using the term royalties to refer to what percentage of the sales price goes back to the author, whether traditionally published or as an independent author.

However, to be technical, a **royalty** is a payment from someone who has licensed a copyright from you (e.g. the right to publish a book). So it applies to traditional publishing.

If you distribute an ebook to Amazon yourself, or through an aggregator like Draft2Digital, technically *you are still the publisher*. They are just distributors. So the terminology is really that they are taking a cut of the sale price as a **sales commission** and passing the rest on to you. So we talk about, for example, getting 70% royalties if we distribute a $3.99 ebook directly to Kobo. What's really happening is that Kobo are taking a 30% commission and passing the rest on to you. As you can see, the end result is the same, but it's worth being aware of this technical distinction.

The Long Tail

I mentioned the **long tail** in the "comparison of publishing options" table in Chapter 2. But what does that mean?

For some creative products, when they are new, they sell because of that novelty. It applies to music, films, and also books. In the first weeks, a book is more likely to be placed near the front of a bookshop, or even in the coveted window display. But before long it is ousted by new books, and placed on the shelves further in the shop, perhaps **cover out** (which means you can see the full front cover as an inducement to pick it up). Then it gets relegated to **spine out** (all the books next to each other so you can only see the spines – shelf space is at a premium, and this orientation lets you fit more books onto the shelves). Then it may disappear completely from some shops and only get ordered when a customer requests a copy (known as a **special order**).

For many publishers, that launch period is the one that determines whether they think they have a hit on their hands or not. If yes, they may well print more copies, and increase advertising spend. If not, they cease promoting it much: because they have new titles coming out, and the bookshops are returning copies on a sale-or-return basis. Only a teeny percentage of books make a big splash on launch. It's similar to the focus on opening weekends for blockbuster films, where film companies only care how much money it makes in an arbitrarily small period of time, even though the figures may have little to do with how much a film makes over a lifetime.

If you draw a graph with time on the x axis and sales on the y axis, it's common to see this:

3.4 The long tail

The lighter-shaded area, stretching off to the right ad infinitum, represents the "long tail" of low sales, but over an extended period of time.

What's interesting is that the sales in this kind of graph don't disappear completely. There is always someone who wants a copy of the book, perhaps from seeing a review. The longer a book is around, the more chance there will be connections to it, places where people have mentioned it. It may only be a dribble of sales compared to the initial release month, but they can continue indefinitely.

A further point is that, if the area of the graph equates to profits, then the area contained in a long tail can add up to more than the initial release, given enough time.

That's why too much focus on initial sales can be misleading, and not represent a book's total profit. Something with low but steady sales (as happens with sleeper hit books or films that attain a cult following) can add up to much more income over time than one with a blazing initial release but which soon fades into irrelevance. Think about how many films such as *Blade Runner* were initially seen as flops by the distributors, who were later proved wrong as the work's reputation grew over time.

Let's consider the situation of an author who releases roughly one book a year. (That doesn't mean they started it and finished it in one year – they may have been researching and writing it for a decade, but with multiple projects at different stages of completion the finished output might be one book a year.) After the boom of the release, sales slow to a long tail. The income is small. But if that applies to every book, even after they become part of an author's backlist (books have a long shelf life), then after ten years they'd have ten trickles of the long tail adding to their income. And, assuming their fame and the quality of their work grows, the long tails could also increase in value.

Suddenly a living income is possible.

Yes, it does depend on many factors. The books have to be good enough that people keep talking about them, recommending them, buying them, and generating interest in your new works. There needs to be some kind of continuing promotion of that backlist (though it's often said that the best promotion is releasing another book). But this is what long-term professional authors aim for. A book, and the author's brand, can exist for a long time. They are more of an oak tree than a cash crop, and as such it needs long-term love and support to grow.

The long tail of a backlist is what can keep an author afloat, whilst also levelling out the vast peaks and troughs of the annual new release. After all, we always have bills to pay. No electricity company will wait patiently until your next book is finished.

It's also why some authors focus on **series**, multiple books which are connected to tell a bigger story. A single book, unless it does something amazing, is a hard sell. But a series where sales of one book lead to many readers buying the next (called **sell-through**, or **read-through**) helps smooth this process along.

Financial Support

There is a question I get asked a lot by authors I have mentored. "Karl, you've read my stuff. Is it good enough that I can give up my job and follow my dream to be a full-time writer?"

I don't care how good the writing is (well, I do, obviously, in a different context): the truth is we all have bills. In recent years we've seen those bills increase massively, even as the companies make billions in profit. Many of us have dependents: children, cats, dogs, witches' familiars. We need food, water, shelter, electricity, and warmth. In an overpopulated world where space is at a premium and has a price tag attached, where we're all taxed and regulated and tracked and trapped in a capitalist dystopia, it is difficult to even live without money. So the idea of throwing away an income you may need in order to gamble on success at making a living with writing ... just, no. I don't want anyone to suffer for following their dream.

That's not the answer you want to hear, any more than it is for the people who ask me the question. But there's massive inequality in the world, and the super rich don't care about you. They won't hesitate to repossess your house, or put you into lifelong debt, or ostracise you from a societal system you didn't create or vote for. And if even some of my incredibly talented author friends struggle – well, it shows that most of us won't have people showering our path with gold. Making a living from writing is tough. Any financial security we can gain is important, especially when book sales fluctuate wildly, which is even more the case when you are first starting out. Writing full-time means money from your books is your primary income source.

As one of my traditionally published author friends (whose books I love) told me in an email recently: "This is a difficult industry to break into and there are unending barriers to success, let alone continued success. I used to be able to make a living doing this. I used to make a comfortable living out of it. Then I managed to scrape by for a while. Now… I'm part of a two income household and my contribution is not the lion's share. Beyond that I struggle to get published with my current publisher. I'm very lucky that they're willing to keep me around, but I know at any moment they could decide to cast me to the side."

So the answer is: take your time. A writing career is a marathon, not a sprint. Endurance and patience are more effective keys to success than betting your livelihood on a run of unknown duration and distance.

To be more specific depends on examining your own situation. To look at where you are with your writing, and be both honest and critical. Have you sold lots of books, won prizes, gained a solid international reputation, and have people clamouring for your next work? In that case you may be doing well enough to write full-time. You know your finances better than me.

But for many people it is a gradual evolution. It begins by writing in your spare time, driven by passion. You gradually hone your craft, and gain an audience. Once money from writing starts to come in, and it's fairly steady, then perhaps consider options for cutting your paid employment hours down. That gives you more time for writing, whilst also giving you the stability of some income. Believe me, the vast majority of authors receive money from other sources, whether it be part-time jobs, or through services related to their craft (e.g. editing books, teaching). And having that stable income from another source takes away a lot of pressure, and gives you more creative freedom to find your way, to be passionate about your work, to give it the time it needs to be the best it can be.

That's the approach I took. I was in full-time employment as a university librarian and teacher, and gradually cut my hours down to half-time, so I could do more writing. The feedback encouraged me, suggesting I could be successful. I took a huge financial risk when I left my job. I got a small voluntary severance, and combined it with my savings, eking it out for as long as possible during the transition.

So, following on from that: while you are working, save money whenever you can. The more savings you have, the more you'll be able to survive the fluctuations in income. Even when I worked full-time I didn't go on expensive holidays. My annual break was cycling over mountains and through valleys in Wales, and staying in a small family hotel for a few nights. Cheap as chips, healthy, and it provided me with lots of interesting experiences and inspiration. I've never owned a car (huge savings there): instead I always lived near my workplace so I could walk, run or cycle. I chose not to have children, which probably saved me more money than anything else. Rather than gym subscriptions I would exercise at home or go running and cycling. These things meant I could live frugally and save money even when my salary wasn't great.

As an aside, sometimes the combination of working part-time and writing part-time is not a transitional step, but actually the best endpoint. Not only is there less chance of money worries, thanks to some stable income, but the non-writing work provides interest and experiences that you won't get if you spend all day in front of a computer. Full-time authors often miss the buzz of daily interaction. Also, working part-time means when the writing hours finally arrive you are fit to burst with intense creativity, and achieve a lot in a short space of time. It can be fun and rewarding. And you are still a writer! You can tell people proudly: "I'm an author, and also a ... [martial artist / demon dentist / librarian / guitar repairer]."

Whereas having all day, every day, where you are expected to write … that can lead to difficulty in keeping the enthusiasm levels up, and creativity per hour can be less than someone squeezing the writing into a much shorter space of time. I'm aware of many authors who went full-time and found they actually became less productive.

Lastly: remember that goals are subjective, and different people have different aims. To finish writing a book. To be read. To find some fans. To share a story. To capture a moment, or even a life, in words. To say something important. To receive praise, or win awards, or get some good reviews. Success does not have to be financial.

Drinky's Digressions: Public Lending Right (PLR)

I mentioned in Chapter 2 that IP laws are complicated. Copyright isn't the only type of creator's right, there are many others, often added piecemeal over time. So in some countries there is also **Public Lending Right (PLR)**. It's a system set up to make payments when registered authors' books are loaned from libraries, based on the mistaken premise that these represent lost sales. In the UK the PLR system is administered by the British Library and you can register any title you've written which has an ISBN, in return for (possibly) getting payments if the book is borrowed in significant numbers from public libraries. In 2025 the rate paid for each loan of a registered work was 13.69 pence.

Personally, I think PLR is a waste of time and should be disbanded.

1. It is unnecessary admin for little gain. As we will see in the next chapter, there is a highly unequal distribution of income in our business, and PLR is no different, as it is structured to favour the authors who already sell a huge number of books. Those big-name authors with lots of sales get the maximum payment (£6,600 in 2024) and bulk of the money from the PLR pot, while lesser-known authors (who desperately need the money) usually get little or nothing. For them, the time applying, and keeping their account up to date, costs far more than any money ever made from PLR.

2. The world of libraries has changed. Loans from libraries are no longer an issue: the real issue is libraries closing down and having their services cut at a depressing rate. More than 180 UK public libraries have closed in the last few years.[38] Libraries are an author's best friend, and PLR is a bureaucratic relic whose time has been and gone. Do away with it, and give the money to struggling libraries instead. That would benefit authors (and everyone else in society) far more than PLR.

3. Issues with the British Library itself. Over the years I spent a lot of my own time trying to help the British Library (which runs the UK PLR system) in order to improve the experience for authors. I took part in consultations and informed them of issues with their clunky systems and policies. Unfortunately my suggestions were generally dismissed and ignored, and they took umbrage at me when I pointed this out publicly. An FOI request revealed they'd even considered legal action against me (using public funds). The British Library's behaviour here seemed

incredibly spiteful. After my negative experiences with them I wasn't surprised to hear that the British Library's security was inadequate and they were hacked in October 2023, with data stolen and their systems compromised (and it took them *a month* to email users about this, advising us to take precautions ... a bit late, methinks). If we hadn't had a PLR system run by the British Library, then there would be no PLR author data to steal in the first place.

"But if you dumped PLR, wouldn't we be worse off?"

Setting up piecemeal interventions for each industry is costly, complicated, and unfair. I'm more interested in systems that help authors with low incomes, but also help *everyone* on low incomes. It's why I've always been interested in the growing movement for a **Universal Basic Income (UBI)**, as has been championed by the Green Party for over a decade. The idea of UBI is that it's paid to all, free of increasingly harsh sanctions and conditionality. As a result it provides an income safety net which vastly reduces poverty, whilst freeing people up from financial struggles, precarious employment, and social exclusion, so that they have more options to take part in whatever they want: study and education, extra paid work, creative endeavours (hello authors!), democracy and community, being a carer, and voluntary work. If you lose your job or have a difficult month, you don't have to go through the time-consuming and potentially stigmatising process of claiming benefits: you're already being paid. And because you already were, you will also have been better off financially, and more likely to have been able to put aside savings.

You are less at the mercy of forces imposed upon you. Disparities in income would be lessened.

So, specifically in terms of authors: it would provide a guaranteed income so we could afford to write. With UBI authors would be far better off than they would have been with PLR, but so would *everyone else in the UK*. And this system treats everyone equally, in every industry, every creative profession. With political will from all the parties this is achievable.

Consider this topic the next time politicians clamour for your vote. The billions spent by the UK and US on invading other countries, maiming and killing their inhabitants, would be much better spent making life better for *us*.

My opinion on collecting societies is similar to that on Public Lending Right: rather than fill this book with my rants, you can read about what collecting societies are, and why I (as an author and also ex-librarian) object to them.[39] But, in a nutshell, I think they are guilty of: aggressive licensing; political lobbying for stricter copyright restrictions (which we saw in Chapter 2 is something I consider counterproductive to the creative industries); and illegally collecting money they aren't entitled to.

Wills

Your **literary estate** includes all rights to the creative works you have written: books, novels, novellas, stories, poems, articles, drafts, letters, and blog posts. It is your intellectual property.

Once you are selling books and making money, these manifestations of your ideas gain a financial value. As such it is definitely worth updating your will to include a section on your literary estate, and what happens when you die.

Someone needs to be assigned the right to make all decisions regarding publication, republication, sale, license or other exploitation of the works, and to be the financial beneficiaries from the sale of works and their rights. And you will almost certainly need to include an additional information sheet with details of the master documents, distribution choices, links, bank information, account passwords and so on.

I'm no will expert, so am just flagging it up as something to consider, rather than giving a guide to doing it.

Taxes

I am sorry to bring up such a painful topic.

If you make money from writing and selling books, then – whether you are a trade-published author or independent – you may need to pay tax. The procedures are different in every country, so check whatever rules exist within yours. There should be plenty of guidance on the tax department web pages. And I hope if you have the misfortune of needing to contact your national governmental money extortion organisation, they are easier to contact than the UK's HMRC, which I've always found to be painful since they are the opposite of customer-focussed.

(Obviously, now that I have said that, my tax bill next year will be in the millions, with no explanation as to how it was calculated. Oops.)

I'm going to give a few pointers for where I live: the UK.

If you are starting out, you won't set up a formal company – you will be what the HMRC classes as a self-employed "sole trader". This is someone who works for themselves, under their own name. As such, you will probably need to submit a **self-assessment tax return** at the end of each tax year (even if you have another job that is PAYE – Pay As You Earn).

I say "probably" because the rules often change, and at present you can earn up to £1000 without needing to complete a self-assessment tax return, but it may be worth doing anyway. Then you are ready for when you hit the big time! To register, go to their website[40] and follow the instructions.

The UK tax year (also called the financial year) runs from 6th of April to the 5th of April the following year. Yes, they do things like this to make life purposefully confusing. I recommend completing your self-assessment tax return in April or May each year, to get the pain out of the way as soon as possible.

Income is how much you earn. Expenses are legitimate costs in order to do so: courses, supplies, software, travel, professional memberships, postage etc. Always keep relevant receipts, either as paper or scanned images, and save digital receipts too. Expenses are deducted from your income to determine how much tax you will pay. This is known as *cash basis* accounting, and is likely what you'll use.

Keep track of author-related income and expenses using whatever system works best for you, such as a document or spreadsheet. Even a paper notepad plus envelope for receipts can work when you are first starting out. When you do a self-assessment tax return you total the amounts under different headings and enter them into the online form. It is fairly straightforward, despite the HMRC's attempts to obfuscate everything with confusing terminology.

This system works for hundreds of thousands of people but there are frequently rumblings that the HMRC wants to do away with it and "make tax digital" (even though it already is). The HMRC interpret this as forcing you to use paid-for software and services just to submit a tax return you could have easily done yourself for free, creating extra expenses and complications for businesses. They have already implemented this for people with large incomes. Let's hope the idiots pushing this system don't expand it to everyone else.

Income tax is paid based on the band you are in. If you earn enough to go into the next band (with a higher tax rate) you only pay that higher rate on *the amount over the previous band*, not your entire earnings. So, suppose the £12,570 to £50,270 range means you pay 20% income tax, and the £50,271 to £125,140 range means you pay 40%. If your income for the year is £60,270, you would pay 20% on the portion up to £50,270 (which would be 0.2 x 50,270 = £10,054) and 40% on the £10,000 you earned over £50,270 (which would be 0.4 x 10,000 = £4,000). Your total tax bill would be £14,054 – which is why it is important to set that money aside as you earn it, maybe in a separate bank account. So if I am always in the 20% tax band, I could set aside 20% of my monthly income. Then when it comes time to pay the HMRC, I already have the money.

The system where you pay in arrears based on what you actually earn is straightforward and error-free. However, if your tax bill is over £1000, the HMRC throw that out of the window and force you to pay not only the full amount of your tax bill, but extort an extra 50% towards next year's. They call this "payment on account". And from that point they'll do it to you forever, making you pay half of what they think you will earn next year, in advance. Since creatives and authors earn vastly different amounts from year to year, this painful imposition is even more stupid, and often means they are charging you money that you eventually have to claim back. No one ever said the HMRC were good guys.

Even if you earn over £1000 a year as an author, so have to do a self-assessment tax return, it doesn't mean you will actually pay tax. Tax is charged based on how much you earn, in various bands. The lowest band, called the standard personal allowance, is currently 0%. You're in this band if your total paid income (paid employment plus self-employment) is less than £12,570 a year (subject to change, but correct in April 2025).

Note that there's an additional wrinkle. "From 1 January 2024, digital platforms are required to collect and report seller information and income to HMRC."[41]

Yep, as part of spying on people, sites like eBay, AirBnB and so on will now send your income directly to the HMRC if you sell more than thirty items in a year, or the values of sales total £1,735. And even if selling some old possessions, it all gets added together with any income from writing, so could mean you incur a tax bill without realising ("My book sales only came to £900, so I don't need to register for self-assessment tax returns or pay tax"), and end up with a penalty for non-payment. So do keep track of the income from hobbies or selling unwanted items as well, to avoid an unexpected tax bill. Yes, rather than go after the big multi-million pound tax avoiders, the HMRC and politicians would once again rather go after the little people. I'm just flagging this up because it is worth knowing about, though come the revolution we can hopefully do things differently.

If you earn enough money, you may also have to pay Class 4 National Insurance Contributions (NICs). Even if you don't earn a lot you have the *option* of paying voluntary Class 2 NICs. You'd need to do that if this was your only income, otherwise you won't get credit towards your state pension when you retire. Whereas, if you write part-time and have a salaried job as well, you'll hopefully be getting your state pension credits from the latter.

The other thing to bear in mind is that book sales are international, and every country has its own tax laws. For example, the US may withhold taxes unless you are in a country with a tax treaty (such as the UK) and submit the relevant exemption form. Luckily the companies selling our books have made it much easier in recent years to deal with this. The days when a UK citizen had to register with US Internal Revenue and file scans of paper forms to acquire a US EIN or ITIN number are mostly long gone: nowadays it's usually just a case of ticking boxes on the distributor's site, sometimes in a section called "tax information" or "tax interview". It leads to a filled-in W8-BEN form that you can sign online, and which the service will keep on file so that you don't pay 30% tax to the US unnecessarily. If you use a company to distribute your books to other countries, ask them about these procedures.

Facts And Figures: How Much Do Authors Earn?

I'm going to include some survey data, so that this section isn't just my random ramblings. Note that for this section, all base figures are US dollars for ease of comparison, with converted and rounded UK GBP figures in square brackets (March 2025 conversion rates).

CREATe Authors' Earnings 2022 Survey (UK)

60,000 UK writers (traditionally published, independent and hybrid) were surveyed by CREATe.[42]

The median average income in 2022 was $8,600 [£6,650]. That figure was down 38.2% since 2018; and down 60% in the last 15 years.

Authors Guild of America 2023 Income Survey (US)

More than 5,500 authors took part in this survey, and it included both traditionally published and independent authors.[43]

Firstly, the results for traditionally published authors:

> "The median author income for full-time authors from their books was $10,000 [£7,730] in 2022, and their total median earnings from their book and other author-related income combined was $20,000 [£15,460]. Book income includes advances, royalties, and fees from licensing and subsidiary rights. Other author-related income includes work such as editing, blogging, teaching, speaking, book coaching, copy writing and journalism. When looking at full-time authors whose books are in commercial markets (i.e. excluding academic, scholarly, and educational books), the median book income was $15,000 [£11,590] and median author-related income was $25,000 [£19,320]."

Then for independent authors:

> "Where our 2018 survey found a median income of $13,700 [£10,590] for full-time self-published authors, that number for 2022 was $24,000

[£18,550], an increase of 76 percent. Interestingly, self-published authors' reported author-related income was primarily derived for their books, with very little from other writing related sources."

So, for traditionally published authors, we see an average of $12,500 [£9,660] for book sales, and a total of $22,500 [£17,380] when other income sources are included as well. That suggests that traditionally published US authors make $10,000 [£7,730] of their income from sources other than book sales.

Whereas the findings for independent authors $24,000 [£18,550] were mostly from book sales.

Their report also includes a bit of information about genres. (Spoiler: romance and romantic suspense authors made the most money.)

ALLi Indie Author Income Survey 2023-2024 (Global)

In Spring 2023 the Alliance of Independent Authors (ALLi) commissioned an independent global research survey of independent authors who spend more than 50% of their working time on writing and publishing activities.[44] They wanted to see how authors fared when the global trend is towards the devaluing of creative labour, with earnings decreasing across multiple creative industries.

This led to two reports analysing the figures (Indie Author Income Survey 2023 analysis rounds 1 and 2), and additional research projects called The Big Indie Author Data Drop, which collated information from multiple sources and organisations. The result is a wealth of interesting facts and figures on the current situation for authors, particularly those who are independent, though some of the data is relevant to traditionally published authors too.

I'll provide some of the key highlights from the various reports. Yes, I read them all so you don't have to (though I do recommend dipping in!).

First, those related to money:

- Median independent author income in 2022 was $12,749 [£9,850]. Whereas, if the mean average is used instead, the figure rises to $82,600 [£63.840], but the median is more representative as it isn't skewed by outliers such as the 1.2% of independent authors who earn over $1,000,000 [£772,840].

- Almost half of the respondents (43.8%) reported over $20,000 [£15,460] revenue. 28% earned $50,000+ [£38,640+]. Almost 18% reported income of over $100,000 [£77,280] per year.

- More than 2,000 self-published authors have surpassed $100,000 [£77,280] in royalties. (Source: Amazon, 2022)

- 60% of respondents indicated that their self-publishing income had increased in the past year. Average incomes of independent authors were also rising, with a 53%

increase in 2022 over the previous year.

- Like for like, self-published authors earn more revenue than authors who are traditionally published.

And some more general observations.

- Younger authors are making self-publishing their first choice.

- Independent authors often generate income from a multitude of sources, though the primary ones remain book sales.

- As we saw earlier with regard to creative industries, there is a highly unequal distribution of income. In 2022, the top 1% authors earned 31% of total revenues, and the top 10% earned 71% of the total revenues. Superstar authors with extensive networks receive a disproportionately bigger slice of the total net worth of writing, compared to the less established, more typical life of an author.

- Self-published authors made up over 50% of Kindle's Top 400 Books for 2023.

- Indie authors write most frequently in Romance (27%), Fantasy/Sci-Fi/Speculative (18%), and Crime/Thriller/Detective (15%) genres. Authors who write in these genres also earn a higher income than more generalist authors.

- 75% of book sales (fiction and non-fiction) were part of a series, by both unit and revenue. Readers love to binge-read their way through a series.

- Financially successful independent authors do three core things: they use professional editors, professional cover designers and they keep writing more books.

- 39% of Kindle royalties are going to indie authors, 32% to the Big Five, 15% to Amazon imprints, and 8% to other trad publishers. (Source: K-Lytics, 2022, based on the 30 Main Top-100 Category Bestseller Lists 2020-2022). This matches the estimate that books by indie authors account for 30-34% of all ebook sales in the largest English-language markets, as reported in Publishers Weekly.

- The ALLi report found a reverse pay gap by sex. In indie publishing women earn 40.9% more than men; in traditional publishing men earn 41.4% more than women. A separate study by FicShelf found that women wrote just 39% of traditionally published titles, but 67% of self-published titles (those figures matched ALLi's survey results). Women and LGBTQIA+ authors are more successful in self-publishing than trade publishing.

- From a choice of 19 success criteria, the top three selected by independent authors did not relate to money or sales. "Freedom and autonomy to set my own writing goals and challenges" rated the highest, followed by "Building a satisfied and loyal readership," and "Gaining enjoyment from the process of writing the book". They were followed by "Increasing the sales of my book/s," and "Building a long-term career as an author".

Top Tip: Pay Yourself First

Before becoming a professional writer, back when I worked full-time as a librarian, I knew pretty much what my income would be every month. It was regular. So I would transfer a fixed amount into the account used to pay bills, a bit to savings, and the rest was there to dip into.

Not so, the writer's life.

You may get all your income from writing and writing-related activities. Or you might have one or more other jobs. Writing may be something you do as a hobby in your spare time, while working full-time in another sphere.

Unless you make a lot of money from writing, it is easy to think, "I'll pay myself when I start making a profit … for now I'll just let the money flow in and out of the slush fund".

But there's something to be said for celebrating the income. For making it more concrete. For not seeing it as a shamefully low amount, but something that *is* an amount, and that will probably grow over time.

That's why I like the concept of Pay Yourself First. Whatever amount comes in that month from writing – whether it be £1,000 or £1.50 – you do something with it. And the easiest way is with percentages, since they're scalable to any amount of income, so work well with a profession like writing where it can fluctuate wildly.

The idea is that you decide on what you'll do with some of the money, then stick to it, regardless of the amount. Here are two example scenarios of how it might work.

Scenario A applies if your income goes into an account set up specifically for your writing business. In that case, at the end of each month transfer out a percentage as your personal payment. Maybe 50% of all writing income each month will get transferred to your personal account as "wages". What's left is available for business expenses, marketing, equipment purchase and so on.

Scenario B is where your writing income just goes into your personal account anyway. And you have another account which is a joint account with a partner, and that's used to pay for bills and shopping. In which case you could transfer a percentage of all income from writing into that joint account every month. (Obviously this requires an understanding partner who realises the figures will vary a lot.) You may also have a percentage that you put away as savings, or for a pension, or something else.

Yes, using percentages means manually totalling your writing income from all sources and doing a swift calculation, since – unlike fixed amounts – you can't set up an automatic transfer with your bank. But it normally only takes me a few minutes with a calculator to total the ten or so writing payments I get from various sources each month, since everything is recorded in my list of financial transactions that are used as the basis for my self-assessment tax return – every item of writing income, and every writing-related expense. It saves a lot of time later if you start off organised.

Whatever system you have, however you divide up the money, wherever it goes, the point is that you apportion writing income each month, however small it is. You *acknowledge* it. You are treating it like the professional income it is. It is a representation of people's enjoyment of your words, and that deserves to be celebrated.

My calculations have changed over time, but currently when I total my writing-related income for the month, I pay 50% of it into a joint account that is used for bills and the mortgage. I transfer 10% into a Triodos savings account (since Triodos do well ethically, compared to many banks). The last 40% is my own, to do whatever I want. Typically half of it is for business expenses, half for personal use, but I can be flexible there. This system works for me, but you'll develop your own.

What Should I Write To Make Money?

In one way, this is a misleading question. In another, it is vital. Let me explain.

For the first interpretation: some people look to see what's selling now, and then try to write the same kind of thing. That attempt to follow trends can be self-defeating. It's what many traditional publishers do. The problem is that, by the time the copycat books are released, trends have changed. And since so many other people will have also tried to imitate it, the book gets released within a tidal wave of derivative work. It's the kind of thing that happened with the great zombie revival of 2003. And there's an additional issue: if you're just writing something to make money, where's the passion? How good is the final book going to be? There won't be years of thought behind it, and careful crafting. That's why so much derivative work is average at best. The whole *point* is that it isn't trying to do anything fresh.

But I also said it's a vital question to consider. What do I mean by that?

There may be many things you could enjoy writing. And it's good to try them all. It teaches you different techniques and styles. Because I sometimes write suspense and horror, I'm able to ratchet the tension up even in non-horror novels. My interest in our literary history gives me an understanding of depth and theme that affects all my work. And so on.

Now imagine a Venn diagram. One big circle contains everything you would enjoy writing. The other big circle is what sells well. And the overlap? That's the sweet subset of writing to primarily focus on. Then you are truly writing things you love, with passion and craft. At the same time, you're writing books that have the best chance of finding an audience, so you can make a living from writing. That's my key guide for author profitability.

3.5 Author profitability diagram

When I say to identify what sells well, I don't necessarily mean mass market, mainstream fiction – it could be a niche genre, but with supportive and book-loving fans. Nowadays the market for books is so huge, and access to that market so open, that even niche books can be profitable. This is great in terms of catering to all readers, and can also be an avenue for fresh expression and new ideas.

If you've already published books and they aren't doing well, the first things that spring to mind as culprits are that the cover and blurb are wrong, or the book has a problem with the style or plotting. After that, it could just be that it isn't resonating with the readers in your target niche, or that niche isn't big enough. In that case you could try writing in another genre or subgenre, seeking that new sweet spot to dive into.

The last point here is less about *what*, and more about *how much*. Many of the richest writers are prolific. They know what their audience want, and they keep providing it, varying within a template. This is sometimes referred to as *rapid release*. It has a number of financial advantages, as it keeps the writer in the public consciousness, and buzz around one book is still going when the next one releases. Many independent authors say that the core secret to making $100,000 a year is to "publish great books, frequently". Some of them say four books a year is required to have a decent income and keep up momentum.

If a writer can do that, and do it well, and still love their calling, more power to them. It's not something I've ever aimed at, as I prize gestation of a story over time. On average I release a full length novel (or a few novellas) every year. However, it didn't just take me twelve months to write. There will have been years of idea generation, research, and thinking about the concepts. A year of writing and redrafting. Then a year of the book being edited, released, and marketed. But the system works because I usually have three books at three different stages of progress at a time – Book A at planning and ideas; Book B at writing and editing; and Book C complete and moved on to marketing and advertising. That's how I spend three years on a book, but manage to release one every year. When I need a break from writing Book B, I go back to research for Book A, or promotion for Book C, and so on. It's an efficient use of time that doesn't rush a book. They all get as long as they need to be nurtured into something for the discerning reader. I've always preferred quality over quantity, in every aspect of my life.

That's not to say that I haven't got faster. With experience, I am a more streamlined writer now. Some of my earlier books were actually things I'd been working on for over a decade, with multiple rewrites and restructurings as I studied the craft. The lessons learned mean I don't make the same plotting and writing mistakes nowadays, and each stage in taking an *idea* and turning it into an *item* flows much more smoothly. The next chapter will give tips on achieving that end.

Polishing The Draft

Chapter 4

We know the draft didn't pop into existence, all shiny on the writer's desk, a gift from the magic book fairies with a tidy satin bow around it. No, it took sweat, and years of thinking that borders on obsession, and research, and plotting, and agonising, and writing. All that effort has led you here, to a completed draft. And it needs more work.

The processes that refine a rough-hewn draft into a literary masterpiece include these stages from Chapter 1:

- 6 Rewriting
- 7 Developmental Editing
- 8 Copy Editing
- 9 Proofreading

Chapter 1 gave an explanation of the editorial stages (7-9), so I will just focus on the rewriting stage (6) where we self-edit a draft using a variety of techniques. You will revise and rearrange content, make cuts, alter the story flow, and improve clarity.

At heart is the principle that an author should always aim to make their book the best it can be. And even when we know there will be professional editing later – or if we submit work to an agent, publisher, or even beta readers – it is important to polish the manuscript before anyone else sees it. And if you pay for external editing later, the better quality the starting point, the smaller the bill is likely to be. If your book was important enough to write, it's important enough to nurture. And it gets easier with time and experience. Nowadays I make fewer edits as I am more efficient in planning, writing, and editing.

These tips are in no particular order. Your process and order of work will no doubt be different from mine. I just want to point out some ideas you might want to consider.

Read Through The Work Multiple Times

This is basic, but still needs stating. You will read the book, and mark things up for correction and enhancement. You will revise the text and end up with a new version. Then repeat the process, always looking out for things that can be improved. Repeat. Repeat.

Use other tips and techniques from this chapter in between reads, all as attempts to iteratively refine the work. If you just keep rereading with no real focus, there will be rapidly diminishing returns. The point of the other tips here is to give you a focus, and fresh input that can help you see problems that you'd otherwise keep glossing over.

It's also important to vary how you do this. I use three main techniques.

- Frequently I do the rewriting on my PC, since it is easy to drag paragraphs or sections around, highlight with notes, use find-and-replace, and jump back and forth through the whole document.

- Sometimes you need to get away from the screen, so print a draft out and sit in the open air with it. Mark it up with green and red pens, for ideas and corrections, respectively. Some authors prefer to use a print-on-demand service to do a single copy of the draft, and work from that. (Bonus to working with paper: I can do this in "Office B," my euphemism for editing in bed with a cup of tea on one side and my cat on the other.) If you're working on paper but need to write new material and there's not enough space, just write on a separate sheet. Put a code letter, number or symbol at the top of the sheet, and the same code in the main text at the point where the new material will go when you type it up later. You can also use codes to indicate where content should be moved somewhere else. The pages may end up looking like the scrawlings of a scientist driven mad by Cthulhu, but as long as they are readable by you that's all that matters. When printing I use scrap paper (any A4 paper where the back is blank), and print two pages to a sheet. It's important to think about environmental implications, as we'll see in Chapter 8: Distribution.

- An alternative is saving the file as a pdf or epub and putting it onto a portable device like an e-reader or large-screened phone. Again, you can read it in a different location then, and make notes. This option saves paper.

In each case you work on the nitty gritty of language at the word, sentence and paragraph level, but you may also be looking at the big picture. I usually have a separate sheet of notes about possible changes to make.

Correct Punctuation And Formatting Issues

We're aiming at good writing, perfectly presented, with no errors, so a lot of rewriting is an attempt to get nearer to that goal.

Correcting common issues is a surprisingly quick process, since a word processor will probably let you fix these across the whole document with its find-and-replace feature. Any good grammar and punctuation book will give you many things to consider and you will end up with your own list.

I'd just like to mention two. First is double spaces. Some people add them after a full stop (don't do that!) but in other cases they are left behind after deletions. I can't think of examples where you ever want a double space. So I open find-and-replace then search for two blank spaces, replacing them with a single space. Bang, done in seconds.

Also check you have used **dashes** consistently. Dashes are used singly to imply interruption, or in pairs to imply a digression (in the same way as these brackets do).

- The US uses unspaced em-dashes, also called em-rules. The name comes from the fact that the dash is the width of a capital letter M. To be clear, this—like a stretched hyphen—is what an unspaced em-dash looks like.

- In the UK we generally use spaced en-dashes, also known as en-rules. They are the width of a capital letter N, and this – yes, this! – is a spaced en-dash.

(**Spaced** just means something has a space on either side; **unspaced** means no space.)

A hyphen is not the same thing as a dash; hyphens are different characters with different functions.

Since en-dashes and em-dashes can be fiddly to input because keyboards don't have keys for either of them, it is often easier to type a double hyphen as a placeholder. Then you can use an autocorrect option to automatically replace -- with the correct dash as you type. Or you can fix them later by using find-and-replace to look for -- and replace it with the correct type of dash.

Drinky's Digressions: The Structure Of A Good Story

A good book needs solid and competent storytelling. Stories have a beginning, a middle, and an end. Great ones have a *gripping* opening, *unputdownable* middle, and *amazing* ending.

Much of the talk about plotting is related to the *middle*, and how it *connects* the beginning to the end.

- *The beginning* is important, but not in the way some people think. A good beginning is certainly not all the boring stuff that leads up to the story (sometimes referred to as **infodumps**). Cut as much of that out as possible. People want to be pulled into a character's *story*, not the character's (or world's) *history*. The true beginning of a story is the crisis situation, called the **inciting incident**; the thing that *triggers* the story. It's the bulldozer turning up to demolish a woman's home. It's being sacked for something you didn't do. It's the demon crawling out of the wardrobe into the child's bedroom. It's the moment when the man locks eyes with the person he falls in love with. It's waking to find yourself in a coffin. It's the point when *everything changes*, and your life can never be the same again. (Of course you can have a bit of stuff leading up to it, to establish the scene and create empathy with the character, to create context; just don't drag the back story on and on. Use your skills to keep any prelude interesting, lively

... and brief.)

- *The middle* is where momentum builds. I'll expand on that below, when discussing structures.

- *The end* is when things get resolved, for good or ill – what everything up to then has been leading to. If you do your job well then the reader will not be able to stop before they reach this point.

I'll give a practical example from my novel *Lost Solace*.

- We have an inciting incident: "Woman discovers a scary spaceship full of horrors; she overcomes her fears and boards it". Her life will never be the same again.

- Then there are a series of challenges of increasing tension and risk as she fights to survive and make her way to the command centre (with a goal that is hidden from the reader until the end, even though that breaks a key rule: but as I say to writers, any writing rule can be broken, *as long as the end result works*. That is always the key test. It's a good idea to write that down on a sticky note and keep it in full view while writing.).

- Then there is an ending, when we find out if she survives, and succeeds in attaining what she sought.

Stories have shapes. Stories can be plotted onto graphs. The story's plot becomes a visual thing. Before I go any further, it's worth thinking about this, and the best way is to watch this short and entertaining video: Kurt Vonnegut's talk about the shapes of stories.[45] I never tire of that. Then look at the description of Freytag's pyramid.[46] Okay, now you're an expert at visualising your story on a 2D graph. Well done!

Now let's take a step back and write down what happens in your story. There are many different ways of getting started with thinking about the plot points and shape. Some people follow a fairly traditional structure such as the Eight-Point Arc.[47] Others use systems such as the Snowflake Method.[48] I have also heard of authors who think of it as the Plot Pendulum: they keep actions and reactions swinging back and forth, further and further, so that the highs and lows for the main characters get more extreme as the story progresses.

The point is to come up with a structure that has increasing tension as the characters try to overcome obstacles in order to achieve their goals (survival, or a love interest, or a successful heist), but the world responds to their actions and new, greater challenges and threats are introduced. Characters make decisions, they perform actions, and the stakes get bigger. As an author, we can't make things easy for our characters if we want a compelling story. Pile on the challenge and see how the characters cope.

In simple terms this scale increases until the main peak where they succeed or fail. So at this stage you may well map out your plot points on a graph, with the X axis as time or advancement through the novel, and the Y axis as tension or challenge. This is a tool you can go back to at any point in a rewrite to help you restructure effectively, or check that things are going well.

The graph I visualise for most stories is like Freytag's Pyramid but with the peak pushed towards the end point. We want more build up and action than we do denouement. Also, the upward climb isn't a straight line – it is a zigzag or wavering line of emotional highs and lows as the characters have ups and downs. There will be twists, reveals, and moments of calm.

4.1 Story structure

The result should be momentum – a build up of tension and an increase in the stakes – that keeps the reader glued to the page, then a grand finale where they get their fix, then a bit of tidying up as the pressure is released ... and you're done. Although this sounds like I'm describing a thriller, it works for all genres. We always need characters we care about, and there always needs to be something getting in the way of what they want (otherwise it is not an interesting story).

Use Software Tools

Software tools can flag up potential errors, though you'll need to apply human consideration to understand the issues raised and weed out false positives.

What do I mean by that? Software can't understand context, so there's no distinction between *real* issues, and *possible* problems (that are actually fine in the way you have used language). For example, software might point out that you used "boiling hot" once with a hyphen, and once without. But, of course, grammatically it won't have a hyphen in the sentence "The water was boiling hot" but it will in "He poured the boiling-hot water," so that isn't a true inconsistency, or indicative of anything that needs changing. Hence the need to evaluate everything that gets flagged up by software.

Tip: in cases where you've used two different versions and they really are inconsistent, but where there is a choice, choose one and record your decision in a personal style guide. In future you'll stick to that version. E.g. the decision between "no one" and "no-one". I will discuss style guides at the end of this chapter.

Sometimes it is best analysing your book chapter by chapter rather than all at once, to avoid the reports becoming overwhelming (though the single-chapter approach will miss out on an overview of repetitions and echoes across the whole work; there are pros and cons to both methods). Here are three examples of software tools I have made use of.

- **Hemingway.**[49] It's free. You can paste a whole book into this, or do a chapter at a time.

- **Online Consistency Checker.**[50] Also free. It is handy for flagging up possible inconsistencies, though note that (as ever) some will be false positives.

- **ProWritingAid.**[51] A paid tool, but potentially worth it. I focus mainly on these reports: Overused; All Repeats (though I only check phrases longer than four words); Echoes; Cliches; Consistency.

Critique Groups

As a new writer it can be difficult to obtain informed feedback on your work. You're more likely to encounter only positive feedback from your mother, who says you are the best writer ever. (Her opinion may not be objective.) Once you have books out there, reviews help inform you of how your work is being received. Until then, feedback is usually paid, and expensive, so consider making use of writing and critique groups.

You may be lucky enough to have a local face-to-face writing group, or you could set one up. They can act as a like-minded and encouraging community, celebrating each other's successes.

If those are not options then many online groups exist which may be useful, such as Critique Circle[52] or Scribophile.[53] There are other feedback options, below.

Beta Readers

Beta readers are a possible additional layer of assessment, often used by independent authors but available regardless of your means of publishing.

Beta readers are a small and trusted group who read the work when the draft has gone through numerous edits and is just about finished. Then they give feedback. The key thing to realise is that they are not professional editors, they are fans, and their feedback comes before the professional editing stages. As such, a beta reader's perspective is different, and is more focussed on what they *enjoy* in terms of the story and characters, and whether the book meets their expectations.

The beta reader concept is similar to focus groups, seeing what people think of a product or creation. It's important that the beta readers are fans of the book's genre. And if the book is part of a series, it helps if the beta readers are familiar with the previous books. Often that's where beta readers come from: the super fans who want to be involved, who love the characters and worlds so much that they don't mind reading a less polished (but still good quality and complete) version of the story.

This process can be a useful chance to see things through fresh eyes, and to get an idea of whether this is a book people will buy and love and rave about, or if it falls short. If there are issues with the work then it can be an early warning, and there may well be ways to make the book more satisfying (without betraying your vision).

I've occasionally used beta readers, usually the fans I have the best connection with. Their feedback shaped some of my stories. Beta readers can also be used to give feedback on possible covers, taglines and blurbs (all discussed in later chapters), seeing which variants appeal to them most as readers.

How many beta readers? A single reader can have a skewed perspective. Gathering the opinions of more than one helps ameliorate this. And yet, you don't want too many, or the feedback might become overwhelming. I find about five is a good number to aim for.

What kind of questions should you ask? It depends on the work and what issues you think it may have. It's always useful to provide a questionnaire to guide the beta readers. Some possibilities:

- What were your overall impressions?

- Which bits of the book did you enjoy? What did you want more of?

- What did you dislike? Any bits that dragged, or were over-explained, clunky, or confusing? What did you want less of?

- How satisfying was the ending?

Why are they called beta readers? The first two letters of the Greek alphabet are alpha and beta: hence *alphabet*. (The next letter is gamma; so the Greek alphabet begins with a, b, g, not a, b, c: they have no letter C.) In the software industry the alpha phase is the first stage of software testing. After refinements and bug fixes, the next stage is beta testing. It is hoped that the beta testing will fix any remaining problems and turn the software into a "release candidate" (the stage after that is "stable release"). And in books it can be similar: the beta readers receive a work that has already been polished. The hope is that they don't identify new problems, but instead give it a thumbs up so the book becomes a release candidate ready for editing and publishing (and I guess the final item you hold in your hands – that lovely book which smells of tantalisingly fresh paper, a librarian's fetish – is the stable release).

Note that while some beta readers will generously post reviews of books they read, most authors keep a clear distinction between beta readers and their **review team**. The latter is comprised of superfans who love to spread the word about their favourite books via reviews, social media, and word of mouth.

It is important to show gratitude to anyone helping you out in these ways. Free copies of the books, and a thank you in the acknowledgements are both appreciated.

If you are just starting out, then colleagues, contacts or friends might be able to help fulfil this beta reader role until you generate a larger group of true fans of your work.

Writing Courses

Writing courses can be wonderfully intense creative experiences. Some are residential, and may be a week long, or just a weekend. Others are local, and you attend the sessions for that day.

I'm a great believer in their potential benefits, both for the freedom from distractions, and for being surrounded by writing and ideas. They provide the fertile soil that stays with you when you leave with so many new seeds to tend. A course isn't just about the five days you are there: the experience, skills and relationships continue.

Look out for courses that give you one-to-one time with a tutor so you can discuss your work-in-progress. You can then hopefully get feedback on both your writing style (by providing a sample), and the overall story arc (via the outline). Though note that residential courses can be as expensive as working with an editor, so weigh up the best use of your money, and look out for organisations that offer bursaries.

A writing conference can be another option, and may have more networking opportunities at the expense of writing opportunities.

If you're thinking of going on any creative course, identify what you hope to get out of it. Are you an unpublished author, and want to gain confidence, or learn the basics? Have you got a specific project you need to work on? Is there an area of weakness in your work that you would like to strengthen? You can contact the tutors in advance if you have questions. Everyone wants you to be on the course that's best for you. Having said that, I have yet to go on any writing course that hasn't had a broad range of ability within the group, and I've always seen improvement in my fellow writers. So everyone stands to gain, whether they treat the course as a "me-time" holiday, or as serious writing CPD.

My tips for attending courses:

- Prepare. Bring creative work or ideas with you, things that you want to write or edit in the time outside of the classes. Also note anything that's asked of you before coming, or that you have to prepare for a tutorial. Then you'll make best use of the time.

- Contribute to, but don't hog, discussions.

- Be critically supportive. There's no point saying flawed work is perfect; and no benefit from tearing into the work of others like a rabid dog. Learn how to start by identifying and praising good points, then suggesting a single idea for improvement, if any. Or even just focus on what you liked. It's a useful skill, and can apply to any writing groups you join. Basically, treat others how you would like to be treated. (A guide for life, right there.)

- Observe how the tutors do things, and learn from them.

- If it's a residential course and you like to be fit, then take running or walking shoes. Writing centres are often in lovely countryside. There's nothing worse than getting there, realising there are nice places to explore, but not having the gear. Remember: you'll be sat on your bottom nearly all day, so get out in the fresh air when you can.

- Attend the course expecting everyone to be your friend, and by the end of the course *they will be*.

Mentors And Support

A **mentor** (also called a **writing coach**) can be great for new writers, as it provides a knowledgeable person who can give personalised writing guidance and feedback, as well as answering the many questions that will crop up. If you've already written a draft then a competent mentor should be able to give you a manuscript appraisal, discussing the plot and structure, characterisation and pacing.

You'll want a mentor with a compatible style and personality, as well as industry experience. Sometimes a trial period can confirm those features. But mentors usually need paying.

It is always worth keeping an eye out for funded support for writers. I've known many poets and authors who applied for schemes that provided them with a mentor, or access to courses, or residential stays at literary centres. These grants are often aimed at new writers, and provide a means of getting extra feedback and help in the early stages of a writing career, when we need it most. So in my region of Scotland I can subscribe to the e-bulletin from the Creative Arts Business Network,[54] which lists funding and opportunities that could be worth applying for. There may be similar things where you live.

Read Aloud

Reading your work aloud – the whole thing! – really helps to pick up on awkward constructions, too-long sentences, and repetitions that you miss on the page. Note every clunky phrase and fix it until it flows like olive oil.

I started doing this when I was preparing my novels for audiobook versions, but now do it with everything I write. However, it does take a lot of stamina.

I remember one time when I had done all my usual checks and edits, but upon reading my draft aloud to myself – performing as if creating an audiobook – I picked up almost a hundred small changes. Most of them were not errors, just improvements. I'd missed them while doing edits on paper and on the screen, because my eyes had glossed over the issues – but, like Shakira's hips, my ears didn't lie.

There are also text-to-speech software options. I purchased a professional SAPI voice from Cereproc in a half-price offer, and used it with the free software Balabolka to generate an mp3 file of any document. The quality is excellent and I can listen to the book on a portable device anywhere (even walking or exercising) and make notes of phrases to change. Lots of improvements will be spotted this way. A final tip – I purchased a Scottish voice. The accent makes me hear the novel in a new way and it becomes unexpected and fresh, so that I hear the words spoken, not the words I expect.

Rinse And Repeat

None of those stages are one-offs. Some of them you will do multiple times across the whole work, or for specific problem scenes as you rewrite them.

To The Future!

The biggest problem with first books is that they are often not quite ready; there's good stuff in there but there hasn't been enough rewriting and editing in the rush to get them out the door. Established writers are better at spotting weak points but beginners don't have that experience yet: so make use of everything you can and invest in your book. We want our work to shine because our reputation, fanbase (and how quickly it grows), and future book sales all depend on it. Ratings and reviews hang around for a long time, and we owe it to ourselves and our readers to make a great first impression. Likewise, if you are seeking an agent or publisher, you want to present your work in the best light. For all those reasons and more, another pass-through of the work, or another quality check, can never go amiss.

Top Tip: Tips For Working With Editors

Many of these apply to all three kinds of editing.

Polish first. Make your work as good as possible before sending it to an editor. The self-editing tips in this chapter will help with that. The editor can then focus on bigger issues. Or, if they are paid by the hour, it can save money because they won't waste time fixing all the small errors you could have spotted. I've edited books for others that are a joy because they are so well-polished that I can focus on more complex issues of style, structure and character.

Be consistent and provide information. Language is flexible, and there are many options to convey information. An important aspect of good writing is ensuring that you are always consistent. Will you use serial commas? Will you end words with –ise or –ize? What are your preferred spellings: no one, noone or no-one? How do you treat large figures, and when do you use words (twenty-five) versus numbers (25)? If you change these things randomly, editors will waste a lot of time fixing discrepancies.

And that is where following a **style guide** comes in, as it will provide guidance and consistency. If you use a particular style guide then let the editor know whether it's Hart's Rules, the Chicago Manual of Style, Guardian Style, New Oxford Style Manual, or something else.

Since I have never yet found a style guide where I agree with all of its pronouncements, I have gone down the route many authors take, and created my own style guide which has developed over time. I supply that to copy editors and proofreaders.

If you don't have a fixed style yet that's fine, but I'd recommend that if anything of this type comes up in queries from your editor, then once you make a decision, *record it*. Pop it into a document called "my ultimate style guide". After working with a few people you'll have a comprehensive and shareable list of your editorial preferences. Further, it will soon become a subconscious part of your writing, aiding consistency.

Get a free sample. This applies only if you are paying for the editorial service yourself. Most editors will edit a sample of your work for free, usually a few pages, and provide a quote based on that. It helps to illustrate their quality, and establishes if they are the right editor for the job (and also, from their end, the sample helps them decide if they want to work on the rest of your book).

If, after due consideration, you don't agree with their suggested changes, or you don't feel like you'd enjoy working with them, then go elsewhere. It helps if author and editor think along the same lines, and their styles and temperaments match. And if the editor made suggestions where you can see that your work would be improved, and you feel like there is professional compatibility, then you'll be off to a great start.

Partial edits. Another option (if you are footing the bill) is to pay for a *partial* edit. You could save a lot of money by getting an editor to just edit a few chapters. Whatever repeated issues they pick up on – mistakes of style, grammar, sentence structures, overuse of passive voice, speech tags, punctuation – you can go through the rest of the manuscript yourself fixing those, before submitting the full thing. Then you'll really understand that issue, and be less likely to make the mistake in the future. Also, any future editorial work won't require the same little things being pointed out again and again.

Likewise you could get an editor to just look at the areas you feel are weaker, such as the opening of your novel. I did this once with a short story collection where I knew most stories were good since they'd been polished in the past, or published already. However, other stories were brand new, more experimental, and I was less sure about their strengths. In that case I paid a substantive editor just to work on the new stories.

Genre. Some editors specialise in particular genres, subjects or styles. They are more likely to know the tropes and expectations of the genre than one who is a stranger to it. Likewise, editors have specialisms in terms of writing – one may be great at dialogue, another at structure, another at developing mood. This is where an editor who is also an author can be a big help.

Nationality/region. If your editor is in a different country (e.g. UK author but US editor, or vice versa) then make sure they are familiar with your country's spellings and idioms. If the book's content is heavily tied to a region or subculture where there are all sorts of nuances of language or dialect, it might be advantageous if the editor is familiar with that area.

Editorial variety. There are benefits to sticking with the same editor over time. They get to know you and your style, there is trust, a communication shorthand develops, and the writing can be taken to the next level. It may become cheaper as you internalise what they have to teach, and they know your work won't contain basic errors any more.

There are also benefits to working with different editors. In those cases a new editor can be refreshing, as they pick up on different issues, and guide you to new techniques and story improvements. It's like having multiple teachers.

Don't look at it as just one book. Expanding on the last point slightly: when you work with an editor you are not just working on that single book. You are learning things that you will take forward and apply to future works. That is an additional value.

Realise that you need more editing at the start of your career. Early in your career, money spent on editing is an investment in your writing future. When I left paid employment to become a full-time writer I invested most of my savings in my business, from buying ISBNs and software to going on writing courses and setting aside the money for editing and proofreading costs for a number of books.

Over time an author's style and writing improves, especially if they've worked with good editors, until they end up with first drafts that need far fewer tweaks. I work on the assumption that an author needs to write five novels, in a reflective way that involves feedback from others, to become really proficient in the *craft* side of writing. The *art* side is a different matter, but in both cases good editors speed up the process.

Editing costs can go down over time as you become a better writer.

Related to this growth in skill, there is nothing to stop you going back to previous books and revamping them after you have more titles under your belt. I've done that with my early works, applying new skills, choosing new covers, reformatting interiors, and writing new blurbs. A lot of the rewriting was easy because I had learnt more in the interim, having worked with other editors.

Multiple edits. The three types of edit must be separate stages. They can't be done in one go because you will make changes as a result of the editorial feedback, and you may well introduce new errors or problems.

The traditional editorial order I presented earlier (developmental > copy edit > proofread) is sensible: there's no point in an editor spending a lot of time correcting typos in sections that they are recommending for deletion and rewriting.

Using different editors for each stage provides the best recipe for success. Each one is a fresh pair of eyes, with their own skills and preferences. A single person will never find all the typos, errors and potential improvements in a book.

FORMATTING

CHAPTER 5

Let us assume you have a completed book. It is quality work, well-written, engaging, and should resonate with readers. That gives it the best starting point for success. Now we can move on to the stages that turn the polished ideas into a finished item.

In this chapter I'll provide more information about the tasks involved in formatting the text for a printed or electronic book, which is stage 10 of those listed in Chapter 1. Even if you're having a book published by a traditional publisher, it is useful to understand the conventions, processes and options. For my own part, I am fascinated by this kind of thing.

When I use the term **formatting**, I mean it to encompass **typesetting**, which is the more traditional name for preparing a manuscript for printing. Nowadays all books start as digitally formatted documents.

Getting formatting right means a book is pleasant to read and doesn't distract you from the text. Get it wrong and it would look amateurish and difficult to read. We want the reader's first impression to be one of confidence: "You're safe in my hands, I know what I'm doing," and that comes from both content *and* presentation. You can't go wrong if you follow standard conventions of layout for chapters, images, tables, headings, paragraphs, and running heads, but you will go wrong if you don't. It's hugely important, and yet is one of those things where – when done well – the work that has gone into it isn't noticeable, because everything is in the correct place.

I'll be focussing on books you look at to read: ebooks and print books. There are also narrated audiobooks, which are a different beast altogether. Note also that I'm basing this on the conventions relevant to the language I write in (UK English). Things are different in languages where text is read from right to left, for example.

Some book designers would swap the order of this chapter and the next one, preferring to design the book cover first, and then the interior. As the book designer Michelle M. White told me: "I always design the cover first because I like to carry the design throughout the interior in some way for a unified package. I have a system in place for adjusting the spine width in just a few minutes before outputting final print files." There are pros and cons to both methods, and you are welcome to read Chapter 6 before this chapter.

While reading this chapter I recommend collecting a pile of books from your shelves to refer to. Look at how they are laid out. Conventions should stand out clearly then, and make more sense.

Front Matter Versus Back Matter

Front matter is everything that comes *before* the first chapter of the book. Title pages, copyright pages and so on.

Back matter – sometimes called **end matter** – is everything that comes *after* the final chapter, such as acknowledgements, previews, a call to action, and information about the author. Hopefully your readers loved your work, and back matter is your chance to get them to do something while they feel enthusiastic.

The chapters in between front matter and back matter are known as **body matter.**

Some elements can only go in one of those locations: for example, the title page is always front matter. Some can go in either place: a list of other titles by the author can go at the start or end of a book – or both.

The order back matter items are placed in is not fixed. Also, all of them are optional. That is not the case with many front matter items.

The Main Types Of Front Matter

Praise For ...

> **Praise For Cold Fusion 2000**
>
> "I was captivated by this intelligent, witty love story."
> **Hair Past A Freckle**
>
> "A novel of incredible genius. At times sad, but also full of hope and with a promise of new beginnings."
> **Cover To Cover**

5.1 Detail from an example "Praise for" page

Some books have testimonials at the start. It could be "Praise for [author]" and include quotes about the author's writing or impact in general, or it could be praise for the book itself – editorial review-type quotes. In that case the heading might be "Praise for [title]" or even just the title of the book. In both cases there might not even be a heading at all and the page begins with the first testimonial.

Some use a style where everything is centred, with the short quote in quotation marks, and the source in bold below. Others lay the quotes out as block paragraph text with a space between each quote.

Title Page

5.2 Title page

All books must have a **title page**, and it is the first important page you see. It will include:

- the title of the book (and any subtitle);
- the author's name;
- the publisher's name (imprint) and **colophon** (logo).

A good title page is the welcome mat to a book. It is an opportunity for decoration and visual interest, especially elements related to (or extracted from) the cover. As such, one element of good book design is to make sure the title appears with the same layout, font and decoration as it has on the cover, which ties the interior to the exterior of the book.

For a print book, whose interior starts as a pdf file, this could be done with text in the correct font: as long as the fonts are embedded in the pdf, they will display perfectly. That won't work for ebooks though, as the fonts displayed are determined by the device or software.

The other way is to display the title as an image extracted from the cover file. Many cover designers will provide a separate graphic file of the title (or title and author) for this exact reason, especially if it includes any additional decoration. It may be referred to as a "transparent title file". This method works in print and ebooks.

The elements should all be centred. The font size is likely to be around 40 points. Note: **points** (abbreviated as pt) are a standard measure of text size, and nowadays a point is defined as $\frac{1}{72}$ of an inch, which converts to 0.353 mm.

The subtitle will be smaller, perhaps 18-20 pt, and maybe also in italics. The size of the author name is often determined by the name's length (longer names = smaller font) and how famous the author is (Stephen King might get the word KING on its own line, for example). The publisher name will be a lot smaller, perhaps the size of the text in the main body of the book, or a point smaller.

If the book's title is displayed in the same font as the cover title, then whether or not it is in all **capitals** (also known as **upper case**) will be determined by whether it is in capitals on the cover.

Copyright Page

5.3 Copyright page

This goes on the reverse of the title page.

It contains a copyright notice, bibliographic data, and legal information.

The **copyright notice** includes the author name and year of publication e.g. *Copyright © Karl Drinkwater 2025*. If there is a major revision you can record the copyright notice as follows: *Copyright © Karl Drinkwater 2020 (updated 2025)*.

Bibliographic data is information about the book (*biblos* in Greek): the ISBN, publication date, edition information, and publisher details. The publishing information is mostly concerned with the edition held in a reader's hand, but it is standard practice to also include details of any previous editions or publishers, along with the publication dates and ISBNs. This makes the publication history clear. It is useful to list the ISBNs of all formats available: ebook, paperback, audiobook, large print, hardback etc.

Legal information governs what readers are allowed to do (or not allowed to do) with regard to the text, along with any disclaimers. Note that the legal information is often dubious, saying things like the book can't be resold (sure it can). Or "No part of this book may be reproduced in any form or by any electronic or mechanical means, including information storage and retrieval systems, without permission in writing from the publisher and copyright holder" – also untrue, most countries have laws that allow a certain amount as fair use.

Another example is the disclaimer that "This is a work of fiction. Any resemblance to actual persons, living or dead, events, companies or locales is entirely coincidental." That is almost always untrue. I picked a random book off my shelf with this disclaimer: and yet the book does mention real world places, people, companies and events.

A slightly more honest form of wording would be: "This is a work of fiction. Names, characters, places, and events are a product of the author's imagination or used in a fictitious manner." The fictitious manner part is an argument that even when the real world is mentioned, it's not the *exact* real world being referenced, but a fictional version.

Copyright pages often group information in blocks. For example, ISBNs may be blocked together, then a gap, then the next block of information. This helps readers parse a complex page.

Text may be smaller than in the rest of the book, e.g. 10.5 pt if the rest of the book is 11 pt. It is also common to align text to the bottom of the page rather than the top: the only page in a book to be laid out like that. Sometimes text is centre-aligned rather than left-aligned.

The copyright page (like the title page) must be included. All other sorts of front matter and back matter are optional.

Drinky's Digressions: Proving Copyright To Amazon

Sometimes whole books are illegally copied and uploaded for sale, perhaps with different titles, covers, and fake author names. That can make it almost impossible for a publisher to spot. Ripping off books is a big industry, and obviously none of the money goes to the real author, even when Amazon is informed of pirated books and (eventually, maybe) blocks them.

Amazon is doing something about plagiarism, and that's good, though their methodology leaves a lot to be desired.

When Amazon finds books with matching content, its automated systems have no way of knowing which is the real author and who is the pirate, and so it may flag both up as needing to prove creatorship. And that's when you get one of the dreaded emails saying you have to prove you wrote the book (within a few days) or it will be withdrawn. Worse, they will only accept certain forms of evidence, which may not even exist. As you can imagine, this causes terror for many authors. This is what one of Amazon's emails looks like (I received this one in 2020):

> "During our review, we found content within your book that's available from a different publisher. We need you to confirm your publishing rights before the book is made available on Amazon.
>
> [List of titles published by Karl Drinkwater]
>
> To publish the book(s), reply to this email and send documentation and/or verification showing you hold rights to the content. Please submit any documents you have, along with an explanation of any previously published books within 5 days. If we do not receive the appropriate documentation, the book(s) will be set to "Blocked" and will be unavailable for sale on Amazon.
>
> Acceptable documentation may include:
>
> • A letter from the previous publisher reverting rights back to the author

• A signed copy of the agreement between you and the author
• A signed copy of the agreement between the author and the previous publisher
• A signed letter from the previous publisher indicating that they do not object to your edition
• Documentation showing the previous publisher holds nonexclusive rights
• An email from the address listed on the previous publisher's official website indicating that they do not object to your edition
• If previously published through KDP or CreateSpace; an email from the address listed in the previous KDP/CreateSpace publisher's account indicating that they do not object to your edition
• If the author has an official website, an email from the address listed on the author's official website indicating that they do not object to your edition

Examples of documentation we cannot accept include:

• A personal statement by you that you have the publishing rights
• A copyright application for which registration has not been confirmed
• Contracts that have not been signed by all parties"

But that list of documents Amazon accepts? Most don't apply if you are an independent author-publisher. In fact, your only option then is the final one, so I hope you have a website and own your own domain, and have set up email accounts from it, and can email them from that address. I'll discuss websites as part of your author brand in Chapter 9: Marketing, but it shows there can be other advantages to setting one up properly.

Note that they give you five days to reply, yet my distributor told me "They have been taking 7-10 days to review such issues" – so sometimes Amazon haven't dealt with the evidence until after the deadline, meaning the books could be withdrawn by the automated systems before anyone at Amazon even reviews the submitted evidence.

The mention of my wonderful distributor is key. The books the email referred to were sent to Amazon via the aggregator Draft2Digital. As such, I didn't have to deal with this alone – they stepped in and vouched for me as the author of those works, sending more evidence than Amazon had requested, including legal documents. They were incredibly supportive. It's an advantage of distributing to Amazon through an intermediary, rather than going direct.

Even then, with all that support, Draft2Digital told me: "The amount of proof you've provided was MORE THAN ADEQUATE to determine you own the necessary rights to the content being published, so the fact that it took a month to resolve, and two dozen emails between the two of us to Amazon customer support seems unnecessary. I cannot apologize enough for the headache, stress, and frustration this has been."

Of course, while Amazon can demand all sorts of information, your rights are not reciprocated. Any requests from an author asking who has copied their work, or what triggered the issue, will be ignored. "For security reasons, we can't provide details about our internal procedures," Amazon will say. You will never know if someone has plagiarised your books or if it is caused by a bogus copyright challenge from a third party, or even if it was something as innocuous as one of your stories appearing in an anthology or magazine elsewhere. Without details you have no opportunity to follow up on it and have rights-infringing works removed from other vendors. And if someone has been selling copies of your books, any profit from the illegal sales is kept by Amazon.

If you ever get hit by one of these requests, either directly, or via your publisher or distributor, then there is useful guidance from ALLi.[55]

Drinky's Digressions: Convenient Fictions

A note on **publication dates**. Usually they are just listed as a year, e.g. 2025.

This gives you an idea of how old the book is.

So if a book comes out in January 2025, all is well. The publication date will match the current calendar year for a full twelve months, looking like it is fresh off the press.

However, if a book comes out in *December* 2025, after a few weeks it will seem like it is a year old to potential purchasers in 2026. "That book is from last year, I'll get this other one, it is more current." Of course, in reality, the book is only a month old.

This is why I generally don't release books between October and December. I get on with my next book, and release the finished one in January of the next year. But the book industry often adopts a different approach, which is worth knowing about: if they publish a book at the end of a year then they sometimes set the publication date as the next year, so it looks like a "just released" book for a full twelve months. This is something car manufacturers do as well, and it is also standard for magazine publishers who release the "June edition" of a magazine in March or April so that it can sit on the shelves for longer before it looks out of date. (Originally magazines had the correct month; then only one month added; but the procedure started an arms war as every publisher tried to make their magazines look current for longer, so nowadays it can be many months ahead of reality, and the date on the magazine's cover is a total fiction.)

Joel Friedlander, the book design guru, once told me: "For a book coming out in November or December, I usually advise people to use a January publication date, since it's mostly a 'convenient fiction' and will keep your book feeling fresh for the entire year. September? I don't think I would. October is where it gets hard to decide."

Dedication

> *To Mum, for supporting me in my reading, writing, and passion for things that stagger and moan in the darkness.*

5.4 Dedication

A **dedication** is when the author dedicates the book to a person, place, thing, group or even concept: "To Billie, I couldn't have done it without you," or "To Beauty, who art my eternal inspiration".

It's an old-fashioned practice from the days of rich patrons sponsoring poor artists, or from sycophants sucking up to titled nobs. Rarely are they of interest to the reader, which is why I avoid them in my own books nowadays, though I have read a few creative ones over the years.

Sometimes bold or italics are used for this kind of content. It may also be indented like a block paragraph (which I'll discuss later). They are often placed a third of the way down the page, but there is scope for variation here. These pages have a lot of blank space around the limited amount of text.

Table Of Contents

> ### CONTENTS
>
> Transmission (Part 1) 1
>
> If That Looking Glass Gets Broken 5
>
> They Move Below 9
>
> Creeping Jesus 29
>
> Just Telling Stories 39
>
> Claws Truth Forebear 61
>
> Breaking The Ice 95

5.5 Detail from an example table of contents

A **table of contents** (**TOC**) helps the reader find the chapter or section that they are interested in.

A TOC in a print book will look slightly different to a TOC in an ebook. Both will list the chapters and sections, but in a print book the TOC will display the page number where each begins, so you can flick to the correct page. Whereas ebooks do not have page numbers, so the TOC entries will instead act as links to jump straight to the appropriate place.

Navigating through an ebook is more clunky than being able to riffle through a print book's pages, so an ebook will *always* have an inbuilt TOC at the start, which can usually be called up at any time by a navigation button.

However, although all ebooks have a TOC, not all print books do. And there's a reason for that. A novel is something you are expected to read from start to end, as the story has a logical progression. As such, it is standard for a printed novel to omit a TOC. Whereas you *will* have a TOC for non-fiction, poetry, and short story collections.

The TOCs in some books (primarily non-fiction) have extra entries for subheadings within chapters. These may be indented to differentiate them from main chapter headings.

For non-fiction it is important to choose chapter titles that help a browsing potential buyer quickly understand what content is covered. Avoid titles that may be jokey and fun but not serve your readers well in terms of explaining what the chapter contains.

Maps And Contextual Material

In some novels (especially in the fantasy genre) a map at the start of the book can be useful to readers. There are no fixed rules on exactly where it is placed, but obviously at some point before the main body of the novel begins, and ideally in a place that is easy to flick back to. That's why I've sometimes seen them on the inside of the front cover.

Some novels might have a foreword, preface or timeline at the start. Or, if it is a book in a series, possibly a half page of catch-up, summarising events so far. Personally, I always favour making sure anything important becomes clear just by reading the novel, but opinions on this vary.

Epigraph

5.6 Example of an epigraph introducing a chapter

A standalone **epigraph** is a kind of thematic quotation from a real or fictional source, and is intended to set the mood.

The source usually appears on the next line after the quote, introduced by an en-dash or em-dash. Or, instead of a dash, the source might be right-aligned or centred, and displayed in capitals, bold or small caps (which I will explain later in this chapter, at Top Tip: Indicating Special Types Of Text).

Beware of using song lyrics without permission: big music companies can be litigious. See my note about using lyrics in Chapter 2, "Can IP Law Go Too Far?"

If the book has a single epigraph then it goes after the TOC (if there is one), on the right-hand side, so that it acts as the start of the book. However, in some books every chapter is preceded by an epigraph.

An epigraph usually appears a third of the way down the page.

Half Title

5.7 Half title

Half titles contain the title of the book, nothing else (no author, no publisher) – so, kind of like *half a title page*. As with a title page, the title type may match the cover fonts.

Half titles were often placed before the proper title page (in which case they are sometimes referred to as a "bastard title"), but since they have no information that the title page doesn't have, they are redundant nowadays, and their use is fading out.

One exception is when they go before the title page and have a list of "other titles by the author" on the back.

Occasionally, where books have extensive front matter, a half title could signify the end of the front matter and the beginning of the first chapter or section.

There is another situation where they can be useful, though, and it relates to this question: what follows the copyright page? Pick up some books from your shelves and check.

You may find that the paper facing the copyright page has a dedication. Or it may have an epigraph. If the book is divided into parts, then there may be the name of part one there, a major subdivision of the book. If the book is non-fiction, or a short story or poetry collection, then there may be a table of contents facing the copyright page.

But what if none of those are appropriate?

The space opposite the copyright page probably isn't empty. Since the first chapter of a book has to start on the right (I'll explain recto and verso placements in print books soon), that would mean a whole blank page doing nothing, which would be a waste of money and look rather bare. Book designers like to put *something* facing the copyright page.

It probably isn't the beginning of the book, either. Starting chapter one directly facing the clutter of the copyright page is something publishers usually avoid. It is generally seen as messy, and looks wrong, as if something is missing. They like to have some content which acts as a divider between the front matter and the start of the book proper.

And that's when a half title can be the perfect spacing element between pages, where it serves a useful function in saying "That's the end of the front matter, now settle down and read the book". It's almost like someone telling you the name of a bedtime story before they begin reading it.

When used in this way, the back of a half title is blank, and the opening chapter begins on the next page. There is no page numbering on a half title – page one would be the opening chapter or part.

The Main Body Of Text

The main body of the text – **body matter** – goes between the front matter and the back matter. It represents the content people are paying for, and is made up of a number of chapters, and possibly parts.

Part Title

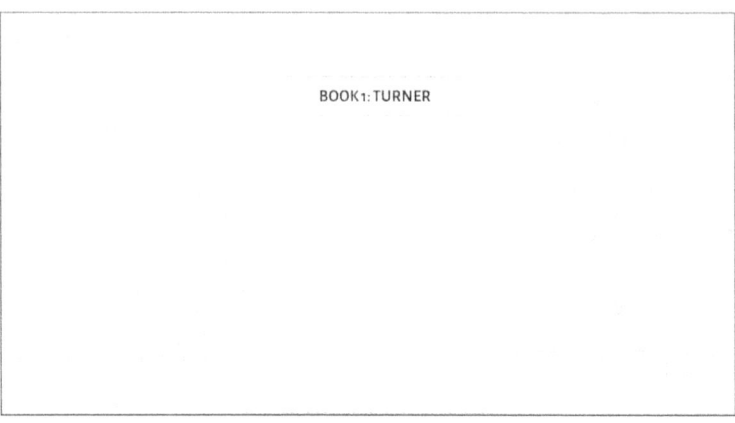

5.8 Part title

Books are divided into chapters. Some books are also divided into *parts*, which are major subdivisions of the text which group related chapters together. Parts are indicated by a **part title**.

Parts often indicate a radical change in fiction – a big jump of time, place, perspective, or escalation. They are not necessary, but may be useful in some stories. Parts are also used in non-fiction works. Finally, with a compilation of previously separate books, a part title can indicate the title of each book, to divide them.

Part titles could be called Part One, Part Two etc, or divided as "books": Book One, Book Two. They may also have named parts (like chapters): "1978" or "John's Story" or "Death By Summer". These two systems can be combined: "PART FOUR" on one line and "2027, Tokyo" on the line below, for example.

Usually a whole page is dedicated to the part division. It may be embellished with graphics to make it stand out. The back of the page will be blank.

Traditionally, part titles will appear in the table of contents, if there is one, but they won't always display the page number on the part title page itself. That's just because some people prefer how it looks without, and that tradition stuck.

The text of the part title is often bigger than a chapter title, but smaller than the title on the title page. Part titles may be in capital letters (caps) or small caps – even when chapter titles aren't – to make it stand out more, and show it is an important book division in the hierarchy. Some have a horizontal line above and below the part title, or may use bold or italics. They're usually centred.

Part titles can also include quotes, like the epigraph. Or the quotes can appear at the head of every chapter.

Chapters

5.9 Example of a new chapter's first page

The main body of most books is divided into **chapters**, as a way of grouping material on the same topic together in non-fiction, or presenting a story mini-arc in fiction. In a short story or poetry collection, the chapters will be separate works. These chapters provide the bulk of the content; they follow the front matter, and precede the back matter.

Chapters usually have a name. In non-fiction it will indicate something about the contents of that chapter. In a short story or poetry collection it will be the name of the story or poem. In fiction, it may be an indicative title, though hopefully not one that acts as a spoiler. That is why many authors choose ambiguous, moody or thematic titles – ones that make sense in retrospect, but don't ruin the fun of reading the chapter.

In some fiction books chapters have a number instead of a name (they may be called Chapter One, Chapter Two etc, or even omit the word Chapter altogether) which reveals another reason why a TOC in fiction is unnecessary – with chapter names like that, a TOC would be of limited use, making the book look boring. It's also fairly common to have a chapter number *and* a name.

Note that a fiction book might not have chapters at all, and could be one long narrative. That is more common with novellas.

In terms of formatting chapter numbers and names, there are lots of choices in how they appear and how they are combined. Even when chapter numbers are used they can be written as a number or a word, and may or may not have the word "chapter" in front. So many combinations! And the chapter element and title elements can appear on one line, or on separate lines; the chapter number can go above or below the title, if both are used. Look at a selection of books for examples of the many layout options. Some examples of possibilities:

- The Awakening
- 1

- One

- Chapter 1

- Chapter One

- 1: The Awakening

- One: The Awakening

- Chapter 1: The Awakening

- Chapter One: The Awakening

A chapter may have its own subtitle, in terms of indicating the place, time or character that it relates to. It may also include an epigraph. Either way, the book should be consistent – always use them, or never use them.

If the book is divided into parts, page numbering (and the table of contents, if there is one) begins with page one being the part title. If there are no parts, then page one is the first page of the first chapter.

Subheadings

5.10 Example of a subheading in fiction

Subheadings are mostly used in non-fiction, to break a chapter into smaller topics or highlight a new idea: as I've done with the subheadings in this chapter. Some fiction books use them too, particularly if shifts in time, place, or perspective, might otherwise be confusing.

They should be smaller and less bold than a chapter heading, but larger and more bold than the main text. So something like 16 pt font size with an 18 pt space afterwards (0.64 cm). Even if I centre chapter headings, I tend to left-align subheadings, which keeps them more connected to the paragraph that follows.

Note that a subheading should never appear on its own at the bottom of a page, separated from the line that follows it. It should always be followed by at least two lines of text.

Some non-fiction books use multiple levels of subheading, though that can be confusing.

Subheadings, especially top-level subheadings, may be included in the TOC (often indented below the chapter name they appear in). Other design styles exclude subheadings from the TOC.

The Main Types Of Back Matter

Acknowledgements

5.11 A sample acknowledgements page

Authors use **acknowledgements** to thank people who helped in the process of writing and publishing the book, or who acted as inspiration and support. Some publishers put this at the start of the book. Americans spell it "acknowledgments" (no second "e").

Previews And Teasers

These are suggestions for further reading by the same author which the reader might enjoy. At the simplest level it might be a cover and the blurb for another book, with the page headed "Read next," "Further reading," or even just the book title. That promoted book might be the next in the series, or another book in the same genre by the author. The page may include some testimonials or review quotes.

Some take it further, and include the first chapter of another book as a taster. This is often frowned upon, particularly in print books where the reader is paying for the pages, and doesn't want to pay for what is essentially an extended advert. Even in ebooks they can be annoying, because they mess with the estimate of how much of the book is left to read. It can also be associated with attempts to pad a book in order to get extra payments from Amazon if the book is enrolled in KDP Select, (where the author is paid a small fixed sum for every page read by subscribers).

Call To Action

A **call to action** (**CTA**) is when you try and persuade a reader to *do something*. This could be inviting them to sign up to a newsletter, to buy the next book in a series, sign up to a course (for non-fiction), or to leave a review of the book if they enjoyed it. Note that if you are traditionally published, you may have no control over elements like this, and it is more likely that any links and sign-up options will be for the publisher's own mailing list, not yours.

CTAs aren't just in books, but also social media posts, websites, newsletters and adverts. We've all seen "Buy now! / Share this post! / Book your place! / Sign up to my newsletter!". These are a form of CTA, too. Those website pop-ups seem naggy and rude to me, though other authors swear by them.

For a CTA to work most effectively, it must be concise and clear, and presented in a way that attracts attention.

About The Author

5.12 About the author

Keep it short but interesting. It may include relevant links such as the author's website, or social media profiles. It could include a "Praise for [author name]" section, though that can also appear as front matter, or even sometimes on the back cover or dust jacket flap. I will talk about author bios in more detail in Chapter 9: Marketing.

Other Titles By The Author

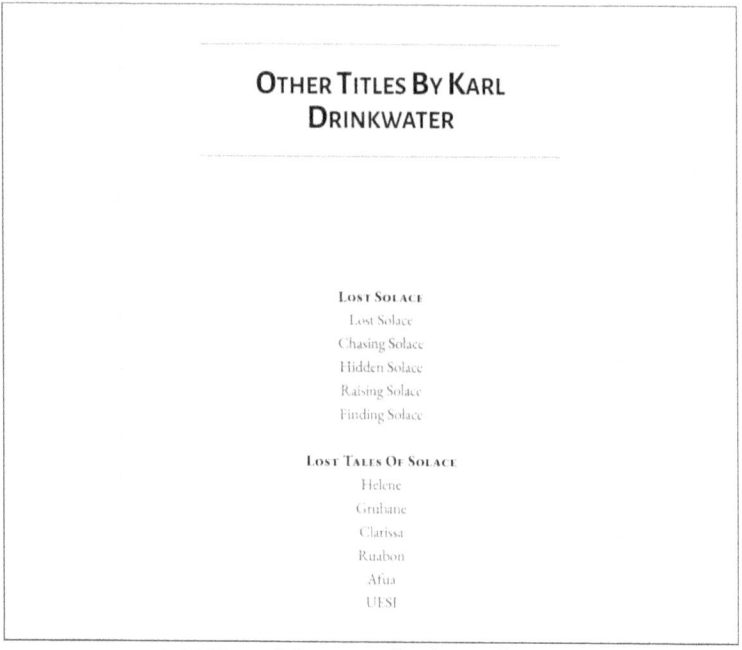

5.13 Detail from an "Other titles" page

Sometimes headed "Also By [author name]". It could be a single list if the books are all standalone, or they may be grouped under headings if there are multiple series or genres. This should be updated from time to time (even in earlier books), so that the list includes all the books you've written: which an impressed reader might want to seek out and buy.

Some publishers put this before the title page.

Author's Notes

5.14 Example "Author's notes" page

I'm fond of including a little behind-the-scenes story, such as why I wrote the book, where the idea came from, or interesting experiences while writing. Some call these **afterwords**.

Other Types Of Back Matter

Other types may include book club discussion questions, a glossary, index, bibliography and appendices.

Drinky's Digressions: The Art Of Book Design

Book design is about the interior layout; the exterior packaging (the book cover); and the relationship between them. Book design, like writing, has elements of both craft, and art. Without the experience and knowledge (craft) you would make errors due to lack of understanding. Without talent (art) you will create things that are pedestrian, not exciting or original. You need both. Then you have professional results, but created with an eye that is individual to you. Because writing, and book design, both require *choices*.

As such, there is often a lot of freedom in how to go about it. And so, when looking at a book, should there be more, or less, spacing somewhere? Should the margins and headings be bigger, or smaller? What about font choices and font sizes? For many things there is no right answer apart from: if it works, it is good. Sometimes you have to follow rules as a starting point, then examine the appearance. Do the results please you? If so, you're good. If not, tweak. Does it look too cluttered? Add more space. Continue until you have something that works well, even though your selections may be different to those made by another creator.

This is easy to confirm. Pick ten books from your shelves. The order of front matter might change. The position of headings and how much space follows them might change. Some books have half titles, some don't; some have them before the title page, some after. There will be different fonts, line spacings, proportions, and heading styles. How many words are there on a page? (Multiply the number of lines by the average number of words on a line: one book I checked crammed 520 words on to a page, while another had a more spacious and relaxed 264 words.) Check whether there are running heads at the top (I'll talk more about these soon), and what information they display and how it is formatted; whether page numbers are at the top or bottom of the page, centred or outer corner. Examine how much white space there is around the text. Do chapters always start on the right, or do some begin on the left?

Once you know the craft, art comes to the fore, and we get self expression within boundaries: whether that's writing a poem, or designing a book the poem will be included within.

Printed Books: Additional Considerations

I'm interested in books: both the knowledge and stories within them, and their existence as physical artifacts. If you are reading this, then you might well love books, too.

A lot of work goes into making a printed book, and there are many considerations. And yet, when it is done well, the average reader won't notice all these decisions, such as carefully selected spacing, alterations to deal with widows and orphans (explained later), and non-breaking spaces to prevent connected elements from becoming separated. These adjustments are all aimed at the goal of best fitting text onto an unchanging physical page in a visually appealing way without drawing attention to any difficulties, just as someone enjoying a story shouldn't notice all the elements of craft that went into writing it.

The considerations I'll discuss in this section are industry-standard *conventions* (rather than *rules*), but they are often based on good reasoning – for example those aimed at making a reader's life easier, such as page numbers – so it is wise to follow them. People have expectations of what a book looks like, built up from the reading they have done their whole lives, and if you don't fulfil their expectations they will assume it is a mistake or ignorance on your part.

Page Size (Trim Size)

Printed books have a physical size. Three dimensions (width, height and depth), plus weight. The thickness of a book is determined partly by its cover, but mostly by the page count multiplied by the paper thickness (higher quality paper is more substantial).

The width and height of a page are known as the **trim size**. When books are printed they come out on big sheets of multiple pages that are cut and trimmed (hence "trim size") to the correct dimensions, then bound together in the correct order.

There are lots of trim sizes, and I'll list some of the most common in the table below. They are described in inches (width then height), with converted metric sizes in mm, rounded up or down. Sometimes people use slightly different dimensions and names to refer to the same thing.

The proportion of width to height determines how elongated or square the book is. This is known as the **aspect ratio**, and I'll explain it in more detail in the next chapter, when talking about ebook covers.

Note that many printed book considerations don't apply to ebooks. The latter use reflowable text and user-selected preferences, so the designer doesn't have – or need – control over these elements. For example, trim size is irrelevant to ebooks, as ebook text will flow to fit the size of the screen. We'll look at ebooks specifically later.

The trim size (along with other settings, such as font size, line spacing, and margins) determines how many words can fit onto a page. In turn, it affects how it feels for a reader to hold the finished book: some are chunkier formats, some are more slender. The advantage of smaller sizes is that they may be easier to hold and to carry around, making them popular with readers, where large sizes might be seen as "indoor" reads only (as one reader told me: "bigger trim sizes are far too big to put in my bag").

Note that trim size affects cost. The downside of smaller sizes is that they can be more expensive since there are fewer words per page, so more pages are needed, which (in turn) increases the cost for the reader. Of course, sometimes publishers try to mitigate the cost of popular small sizes by reducing the font size to cram more words onto the page. But this can make reading difficult for many people, creating a new problem, so is not an ideal solution.

As an experiment, I formatted a standard novel-length work of 62,000 words in a variety of trim sizes, noted the page counts, then checked what the base cost of that version would be with a print-on-demand distributor.

Here's a list of some common fiction trade paperback trim sizes along with how that size is often referred to. From my experiment I have included the base page count and cost (2024 prices) of the same book formatted at that trim size, and you can see how the cost goes down as the trim size increases. With some of the smallest "mass market" trim sizes such as those used for supermarket bestsellers (not included in the chart) I ended up with an eye-watering 456 pages / £5.52 to print each copy!

For each one I will list its name(s) in bold. Then the size in inches / millimetres. Next will be the page count / cost for my test novel in this trim size. Lastly, any notes.

- **"Novel".** 5 x 8 inches / 127 x 203 mm. Test size and cost: 318 pages / £4.19. Notes: used for compact paperbacks and novellas.

- **B-format (UK), and Large Crown.** 5.06 × 7.81 inches / 129 × 198 mm. Test size and cost: 323 pages / £4.24. Notes: often used for literary books, especially in the UK, and Penguin Classics. The weird inch measurements in decimal is because they were originally described as fractions: 5 ⅛ × 7 ¾ inches.

- **"5.25 x 8".** 5.25 x 8 inches / 133 x 203 mm. Test size and cost: 299 pages / £4.01. Notes: Used for novels and memoirs.

- **Demy / C Format (UK) / Digest.** 5.5 x 8.5 inches / 140 x 216 mm. Test size and cost: 264 pages / £3.67. Notes: Common in both the UK and US.

- **US Trade / American Royal / octavo.** 6 x 9 inches / 152 x 229 mm. Test size and cost: 229 pages / £3.34. Notes: General fiction. For longer books and hardbacks. Popular in the US, rarer in the UK.

When formatting a print book in software, the page size *must* be set the same as the trim size that will be used in printing it. Any mismatch will cause problems. And it needs deciding early on, as it affects so many other things such as cover dimensions, interior templates, and optimal image sizes.

As an experiment, take the books you gathered earlier, and sort them into piles of the same size. Non-fiction trim size standards are different from fiction, so put non-fiction books in separate piles.

Now measure the books and note the width and height of the cover, plus how many books of that size there were. Compare the results to the table above and see if there were any non-standard sizes. What was the most common size? What was most comfortable to hold and read?

My print books are all published at 5.5 x 8.5 inches. To me it's the ideal size. Sure, I can appreciate the other options, but since I grew up in the eighties, I've always fancied Demy more. (Groan.)

Verso And Recto

In an ebook you generally only see one page at a time – the one you are reading. But a printed book uses paper, and the sheets of paper have two sides. When you open a book out (called the **spread**) you are therefore looking at two pages: one on the left, one on the right. In printing terms, the page you see on the left of the spread is the **verso**, and the page on the right is the **recto**. Recto means "right," and verso means "back" – so the verso is always the back of a recto. It's easy to create a mnemonic to help you remember, e.g. Value Reading! = verso recto; or just remember recto = right, and verso = the re*verse*, or the back of the recto. Verso pages are always even numbers, and recto pages are always odd numbers.

The first page of the book will only have the recto on the right, and the interior of the cover on the left. When you turn the page you will reach your first spread with the recto on the right and verso on the left.

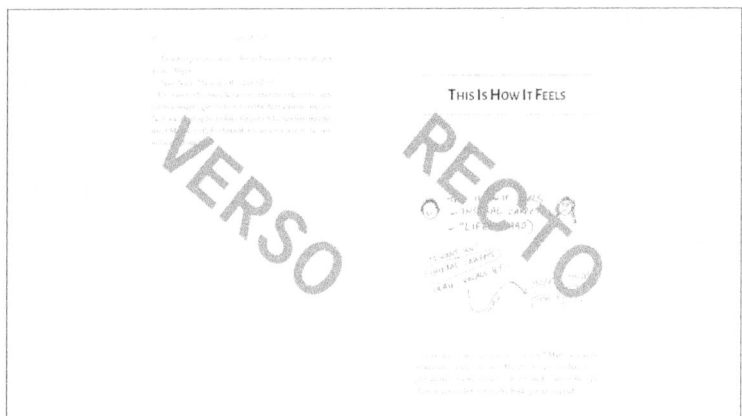

5.15 Verso recto

We've already seen that books have front matter, main content, and back matter. In an ebook they all just start on a new page, but in a print book each type of content may have its own rules as to whether it begins on the verso or recto.

- Title pages (and half titles) are always on the recto.

- Copyright pages are always on the verso, on the back of the title page.

- Dedications, epigraphs, and tables of contents are always on the recto.

- Part divisions always begin on the recto.

- The first page of the first chapter always begins on the recto, an odd-numbered page.

- Every item of back matter always begins on the recto.

After the first chapter, the other chapters can follow one of three systems.

Option one is where a new chapter always begins on the recto. This has a luxurious appearance, and is often used in premium editions such as hardbacks, or in shorter books (if you are cynical, you might claim that publishers are inserting blank pages to make the book look longer). The downside is lots of blank space on the facing verso: increased page counts (even if they are blank) add to the unit cost. An example of this layout from my bookshelf: *For Who The Bell Tolls: One Man's Quest for Grammatical Perfection* by David Marsh (non-fiction).

Option two is to just let a new chapter begin on the next page, regardless of whether that is the recto or verso. This saves paper, possibly up to twenty pages in a standard novel. This is a commonly used system for short story collections or books with many chapters, and in general paperback fiction these days. I favour this approach. An example of this layout from my bookshelf: *One* by Conrad Williams (mass-market fiction).

Option three is to begin a new chapter on the same page as the previous one ends, if there is room. This isn't used often, but I have seen it in mass-market or budget paperbacks with large word counts and lots of chapters. They also tend to have a smaller text size. Those books are more about cramming the text in and reducing page count (and therefore printing cost) and can look rather cramped. An example of this layout from my bookshelf: *A Fire Upon The Deep* by Vernor Vinge (a 580 page sci-fi novel).

Fonts And Typefaces

Generally a **font** is a specially designed set of letters in a unified style on a computer, whereas a **typeface** is used in printing. But since books are always designed on computers nowadays, many people use the terms interchangeably. So, for example, Times New Roman can be both a font and a typeface.

An ebook reader usually lets the owner set the font (so the font used in the book's master file is irrelevant), but in a print book the decision is made during its design. The font choice (and point size) has implications for readability and mood. It also affects page count, since some fonts have wider letters. And as we saw, page count affects printing costs.

Fonts can be divided up in many ways, but I think of them as three main types. Serif, sans serif, and decorative.

- **Serif fonts** have tiny tails and extensions at the end of strokes. They derived from the style of handwriting. Examples include the aforementioned Times New Roman; also Palatino, Baskerville, Book Antiqua, Bookman Old Style, and Garamond. Serif fonts have a traditional look, and some people find them easier to read. They're often used for print fiction interiors.

- **Sans serif fonts** are fonts that don't have those little extensions (sans means "without"). The letters are bare and unadorned. Examples include Verdana, Arial, Libre Caslon, Tahoma, Calibri, or Liberation Sans. Sans serif fonts look more modern in their decoration-free simplicity. Some people find sans serif fonts easier to read. Yes, you may have spotted that the same advantage applied to serif fonts. Some people are passionate about which type of font is easier to read, but as with many things, we all have different preferences and perceptions.

- **Decorative fonts** (also called **ornamental fonts**, or **display fonts**) are those designed for special situations. The fonts that look like they are blood-spattered, handwritten (**script fonts**), made of trees, or include sparkles. These are often not as readable as plainer fonts. This category can also include emotive fonts: those that strongly imply a mood, such as the light font that implies wistfulness; the broad bold font that implies strength; or the child-like curves of a playful font.

For the main text in a book, always use a serif or sans serif font. However, for book covers (and possibly then using the same font on the title page and chapter titles), decorative fonts can be wonderful, especially if they match the mood. For example, a script font might work well for chapter titles in a historical or romance book, but probably not for sci-fi. Some book designers suggest that if a serif font is used for the main text, then headings look nicer in a sans serif font (and vice versa).

> Example of a serif font.
> Here is another. Compare the letter "i" with the sans serif font below.
>
> ———
>
> Example of a sans serif font.
> Here is another. The letter "i" doesn't have fancy tails.
>
> ———
>
> EXAMPLE OF A DECORATIVE FONT SUITABLE FOR HORROR.
> Also a script font, like handwriting.
> Good for book covers, not for reading lots of words in!

5.16 Serif, sans-serif, and decorative fonts

Another way of dividing fonts is whether they are monospaced fonts (often abbreviated to mono in a font name) or not. In a **monospaced** (or **fixed-width**) font, characters all take up the same amount of horizontalspace, even the letters *w* and *i*. If you type ten random letters or characters, then another ten on the line below, both lines will have the same total width. Whereas in a **proportional** (or **variable-width**) font, the letters and spacings have different widths, and a letter *i* would take up a lot less space than a *w*. Monospaced fonts were based on the way typewriters worked. They would definitely not be used for main text, but can be useful for special purposes, as discussed in the Top Tip below.

```
Monospaced (or fixed-width) font.
Letters take the same amount of horizontal space.
Here's another example.
Even i and w are the same width: iwiwiwiw
```

Proportional (or variable-width) font.
Here's another. Note the different widths of i and w: iwiwiwiwi

5.17 Monospaced versus proportional fonts

Since you may, like me, sometimes buy new fonts, it's worth being aware of a few things. Firstly, fonts might be offered in .ttf (True Type Font) or .otf (Open Type Font) file formats. Generally there is little difference between them, so don't worry about which you buy, though .otf is often slightly better for swashes and glyphs which are additional decorative elements (especially useful for book covers). Both formats should work on any operating system.

Another thing: a font that comes as a single file will just be the standard characters. If you use bold or italics then the software will try and create them for you, but the end result is an approximation and won't be as good quality as a font that comes with separate files for regular, bold, italics, and bold italics. If you buy a font and it comes as separate files called something like "font regular.ttf," "font bold.ttf," "font italics.ttf," "font bold italics.ttf" and so on then that's good – it means the font is specially designed to have proper bold and italics, thanks to building them as separate styles. When you install them all it will still appear as a single font in your word processor and graphics package, but when you apply formatting like bold and italics you'll get a better-designed result.

Also, when considering a font, make sure it works with any special characters you will need. I had issues with a version of EB Garamond that didn't have characters such as ŵ – an absence which caused problems when displaying Welsh dialogue in my novel Turner!

What is the ideal text size? Point sizes 10-12 are seen as acceptably readable, depending on the font. And the font chosen is a key element, since (with the exception of the monotype fonts I mentioned) all fonts vary in letter widths. One of my book interiors used EB Garamond and came to 618 pages. As an experiment I switched the font to Libre Caslon, and the book grew to 715 pages. Same font *size*, but changing to another font added almost a hundred pages to the page count (though the Libre Caslon version was lovely and readable). If using Libre Caslon I would drop the font size a point to compensate for it, since the page count affects print costs. Though a font should never be so small it is difficult to read – space is your friend in all elements of book design and it is important to find a balance. As a rule of thumb, a line of text should have between 60 and 72 characters, including spaces, for maximum readability and spacing.

Font choice is incredibly important, especially for book covers, and yet also difficult until you have a lot of experience. I remember seeing a meme that reinforced this. On one side was a sticky note with the words "I will always find you" in a deep pink, curly font, with hearts as the dots above the letter i's. Ah! Such a lovely note about always being there, always having your back! Then the same words appeared on another sticky note, in a jagged, slashy font: "I will always find you." Suddenly it was a stalker's threat, and the pink was reinterpreted as the red of blood, even though the actual colour was the same. Just changing the font can alter our perceptions of a message.

Top Tip: Indicating Special Types Of Text

Sometimes there is a need for special display of text such as extracts from a letter. There are formatting options to call out this type of thing, beyond just bold and italics.

- SMALL CAPS. Capital letters (**caps**) are also known as **upper case**. Non-capitals are known as **lower case**. **Small caps** are so called because they are capital letters in place of lower case, but at half the height of a full capital. As such they look softer than using ALL CAPS, and less like shouting. Compare THESE SMALL CAPS with NORMAL CAPITALS. Small caps are useful for indicating a new section or chapter, when the first 3-5 words can be put in small caps. I sometimes use them for a sign in a book, e.g. "The notice read 'KEEP OUT OR DIE!'" I've also used them to differentiate things like AI speech in a sci-fi novel.

- `Monospaced text` (discussed earlier) can be handy to indicate memos, computer text, and newsprint.

- If the main book is in a serif font, then sans serif can be useful for indicating texts, chat messages, neatly handwritten notes and so on. Or vice versa, sans serif to serif.

- **Block quotations**, where the text is set inwards from the left margin, can be handy to indicate a letter or note. Block quotations may also have different line spacing from the rest of the text.

- **Script fonts** are useful for indicating handwritten notes. Take care to use a font that is clear and readable.

Running Heads

This refers to a section at the top (head) of the page which is used to display useful – or not so useful – information in some books, both printed and electronic. Reminders as to what book (or section of a book) you are reading, and who wrote it. In theory, like the TOC and page numbering, they can help orientate the reader.

Some readers and authors see running heads as fussy, distracting or pointless. Many modern novels don't bother with running heads at all, for a cleaner look, but they remain common in non-fiction.

If you examine the pile of printed books you gathered earlier, fiction and non-fiction, you'll find great variety in whether running heads are used or not, what they display, and how it is represented. Look inside the books, revel in the feel of the pages, the smell of paper, and the presence or absence of squiggles at the top of each page.

You only have two running heads – even and odd pages – but there are many options for the combinations of information they might display. Here are some, in the order verso / recto.

- **Book Author / Book Title.** A common option (especially in the US) is to have the author of the book on every verso page, and the title of the book on every recto. Personally, I can't see the point of repeating them on every page. You can just look at the cover of the book if you forget what you are reading.

- **Book Author (or Book Title) / Story (or Chapter, or Poem) Title.** In a single-author book where the chapters have different titles, or in a short story or poetry collection by a single author, you could have the author name or book title on the verso, then the chapter name, short story or poem name on the recto. In my opinion only one of the running heads is really useful, and the other exists just to create visual equality. (I have also seen books that reverse this and have the chapter title on the verso and book title on the recto.)

- **Story Author / Story Title.** If it is a short story collection by different authors, then the verso running head may be the name of the author of the current story, and the recto running head its title. Both running heads have useful information. In a similar way, if the book is a non-fiction collection of essays by different writers, the chapter's author could appear on the verso, and the essay title on the recto.

- **Book Part / Chapter Title.** If the book has parts (whether it is fiction or non-fiction), then we might have the part of the book we're in on the verso, then the chapter name on the recto.

Sometimes one of the elements is in capitals or small caps: often the verso element. The recto running head may use italics if displaying a chapter or short story title. But those are not set in stone. There is no standard as to whether running headers should be all caps, small caps or title case; bold/italics or not. I've seen every permutation.

5.18 Example of running heads in a short story collection (in this case showing book title / short story title)

The text in running heads is typically one or two point sizes smaller than the main body text. If a story or chapter's name is too long to fit in the running head, it can be shortened.

Note that any text which appears at the bottom of a page (such as a page number) has the charming name of **running feet**.

Display Pages

Display pages include front matter such as the title and copyright pages, half titles, dedications and epigraphs. They are also pages where a chapter or part begins, or the first page of any front matter or back matter. Blank pages also count as display pages.

They have special rules of minimal ornamentation, so running heads don't appear on display pages.

Page Numbering

All printed books have page numbers. They're a convenience for the reader. Even if there isn't a table of contents to relate it to, page numbers let you keep track of progress, or refer to a location. Without page numbers that would be almost impossible.

Page numbers can go at the top of a page (which is then called a **folio**), or at the bottom (a **drop folio**). They can be centred, or go on the outside edge of the page (far left for the verso, far right for the recto) so as to be easily visible as you flick through the book. If they are at the top of a page, they can be combined with running heads (if used). When a page doesn't have a printed page number it is called a **blind folio**.

As with running heads above, page numbers aren't generally shown on display pages. If a page number is desired there, then it would always be a drop folio at the bottom (even if the rest of the book has folio numbers at the top). However, in non-fiction books, where the reader may be navigating the book by the page numbers in the ToC, it is often convenient to have the page number at the bottom of the opening page of chapters.

Page numbering begins with the first page of the book proper. Probably chapter one, but it could be a dedication or epigraph, or even just a page stating the part of the book (if it is divided into parts). So most front matter is not part of the page numbering system. The title page and copyright page, for example, won't have a page number or be included in a TOC.

Non-fiction with extensive front matter may separate it from the main content and include page numbers, but in that case they are lower case Roman numerals (i, ii, iii, iv, v etc), with the main book still beginning as page one (1).

As with all these things, flick through a selection of books and see which systems they adopt, and which seem most pleasing visually.

Obviously a running head takes up space (both the line it appears on, and the blank area around it) and means the main text has to move further down the page. This is why the running head sometimes includes the page number on the outside edge of the pages, so that we do not also lose space at the bottom of the page where the page number normally appears. In my tests I found having a running head, and separate page numbers in the running feet (rather than having everything in the running heads), adds about eleven pages to the length of a standard novel.

Page numbering is irrelevant to ebooks.

Chapter Headings

Chapter headings in print books may be in the same font as the cover title, which looks good and helps to unify the design of the book. This is easy in print where the same font can be used; not so easy in ebooks, because the font of an ebook can be changed by the reader. To achieve the same effect in an ebook the chapter name needs to be turned into an image.

Note: that tip applies any time you need to do something fancy with text in an ebook. Newspaper cuttings, handwritten notes, charts, tables of data and so on: make them images and they then work in both the print and ebook versions.

Chapter names can be in all caps, or just title case. It's purely a stylistic choice. If the chapter names are in the same font as the cover title then I emulate what was done on the book cover regarding capitalisation, as I would with the title page, because in some display fonts the capital letters look different from the lower case letters.

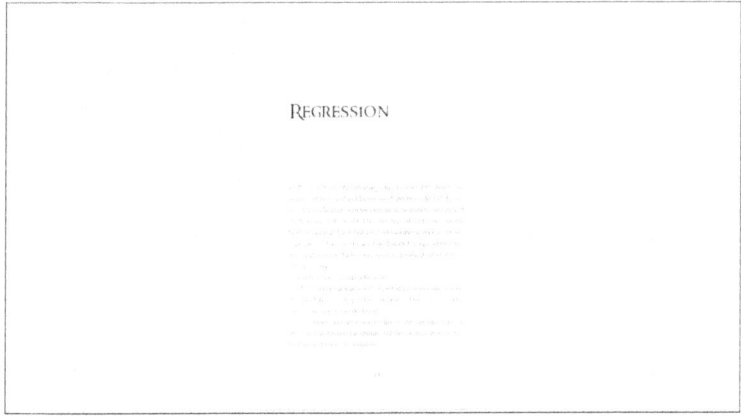

5.19 *Example of a chapter heading which uses the font from the book's cover*

Chapter headings may be centred or left-aligned.

I often choose 24-28 points as the font size. Chapter headings will have space below them before the main text begins. I favour 48-84 points (1.69-2.96 cm) of space, but have seen larger gaps such as the main text beginning halfway down the page. However, when it is back matter, the spacing between the heading and the text may be a lot less, perhaps as little as 15 pt (0.53 cm).

Margins And Gutters

Words in a book don't go right up to the edge of the page. If they did, you wouldn't be able to see the words under your smudgy fingers as you read. So there is a margin of blank space around the block of text. This also serves as a frame for it, which is aesthetically pleasing.

How big should the margins be? It's subjective, and also affected by the size of the pages (the trim size), the genre, and the quality of the book (mass market versus luxury).

When you hold a printed book open, it may look like the margins are equal on all four sides, but that isn't true. Bear in mind that pages need binding together. Where they are fixed to the book's spine you have an area that isn't fully visible. For that reason the margins on the inner side of each page need to be bigger, to take account of the way the book folds and gets bound together. This wider margin where pages curve in to meet the binding is known as the **gutter**. Verso pages have a wider margin on the right, and recto pages on the left, so that the text appears centred on the page when the book is bound together. I often adopt an inner margin of 2.34 cm and an outer margin of 1.90 cm, but many trade books are less generous with space. The more pages there are in a book (or if the paper is particularly thick), the larger the gutter may have to be.

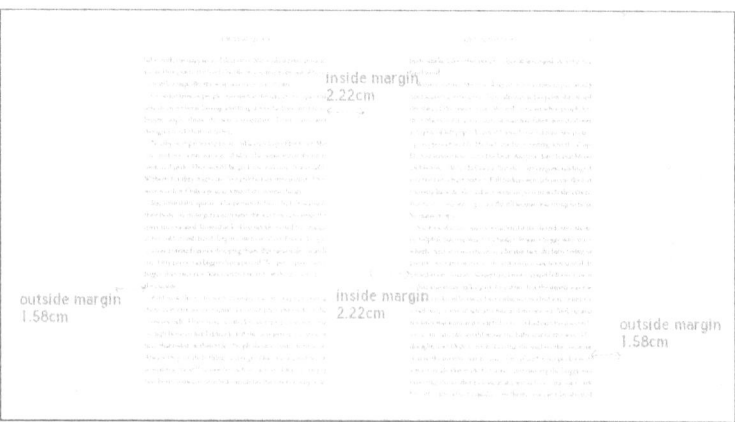

5.20 Margins and gutters

Margins are irrelevant to ebooks, since they are determined by the software or ereading device.

Alignment And Hyphenation

Words have different lengths and appear in different combinations, so it's rare for them to line up evenly on the page.

As a result, both fiction and non-fiction are usually fully **justified**, meaning both the left and right sides of the text are a neat line, creating a block of text on each page. That is achieved by altering the spacing between words, so there are bigger gaps between words on some lines. Usually that isn't noticeable, but when a line includes a few long words, it may lead to exaggerated and noticeable spaces between them.

Left alignment is less common, where spaces have fixed widths so you end up with a ragged edge to the right of the page.

5.21 A fully justified layout

In both cases, **hyphenation** can help. Most software will offer an option for it in the settings or in style menus. When enabled, if a long word would get shifted to the next line and leave a large gap, instead the word is broken in two (between syllables), and half of the word moves on to the next line. A hyphen at the end of the first part of the word indicates that it is joined to something following. Although you'd think this might be distracting, it is standard to use hyphenation in publishing, and in most cases you don't even notice that the word runs onto the next line because we're used to it.

Hyphenation helps even out the gaps and create a more uniform appearance to the blocks of text. It also makes slightly more efficient use of space, which has a positive effect on the number of pages. If I turn on hyphenation in one of my sixty thousand word novels, it removes around two pages from the page count. Over a bigger book, the effect would be more noticeable.

The trick is for the software to use the bare minimum hyphenation to smooth the text out, without going overboard. And in that manner, not all software is equal, since the logic as to where a hyphen would be acceptable varies. I used to find that Microsoft Word added far too many hyphens, often in ugly places or breaking up even small words unnecessarily. Whereas Draft2Digital's tools applied to the same book were more restrained.

There can be downsides to hyphenation. For example, if the book has web addresses then they will be treated as words by the software. If it is a long web address (as many are) then it increases the chance of it becoming hyphenated and running over two lines. And, because the web address has to be typed in if someone with the print book wants to visit that website, it can be unclear whether the hyphen is part of the web address that needs typing in or not. So hyphenation may need to be removed from some bits of text, which can be fiddly.

One more point. If hyphenation is turned on in a document then it can cause issues if you copy and paste the text into another program or run it through other software (such as the free ebook conversion tool Calibre). Sometimes the end-line hyphens become part of the text, breaking up mid-line words for no reason. As such, I think it's best to avoid hyphenation during the writing of drafts. It's something that will only be applied by whoever formats the final version of the book prior to publication.

Printed poetry isn't bound by these rules. The lines of a poem can be centred, left-aligned, or even arranged in shapes on the page. Poetry does what it wants, as punk as ever.

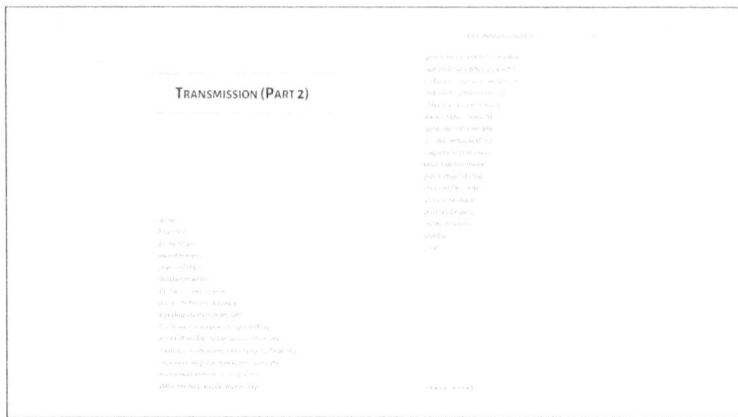

5.22 Poetry, left-aligned

Hyperlinks

In an ebook you can easily create a link to a web page. Someone taps or clicks on the highlighted text and it will open a browser and go to that web page, if it is an Internet-connected device. As such, the links can integrate smoothly with the text, so if an author mentions **their wonderful website** then the bold bit – which might also be coloured blue and underlined – will take the reader there. There is no ugly web address visible. (The downside to people reading ebooks on a phone or tablet is that you have no way of knowing where a hyperlink will take you – whereas on a desktop computer, hovering the mouse pointer over a link will show where the link will take you without you needing to click on it. It's one of the flaws of touchscreen systems.)

Obviously, printed books can't have hyperlinks. (I've tried pressing my finger against a web address in the paperback version of this book, and nothing happened.) Instead you have to include a visible web address, which the reader would type into a browser. For example, if my website is http://karldrinkwater.uk then I could have this text:

"Visit my wonderful website at karldrinkwater.uk for more information."

There's no reason to include http:// or https:// at the start, since no one has to type that bit in – the browser will add it automatically. Likewise the www. in many web addresses can be removed, and any forward slashes (/) at the end. Always truncate web addresses to the smallest and tidiest one that works – if in doubt, test the shortened web address in a browser. And if the web address is one of those awfully long ones which can't be truncated, consider using a link shortener to create something that is humanly typable. Sites like tinyurl.com can give an alternative web address that points at the original.

Of course, you could have visible text like karldrinkwater.uk (without underlining) for print *and* make it a clickable hyperlink to that address for the ebook, so that it works in both, but it is more standard for the base documents for an ebook and a print book to be separate files. Each format has different requirements and it's difficult to create a single source file that works for both.

Footnotes And Endnotes

These are both ways to include a digression, clarification, reference or some other aside related to the text, but without breaking the flow of the main work. Both types of note apply mostly to non-fiction.

- **Footnotes** go at the bottom of the page, in a section that expands upwards as more words are added. Footnotes are usually in a smaller font size than the main text. They may be separated from the text by a space, or by a short line at the left margin.

- **Endnotes** can go at the end of each chapter; or they can all go together in a special back matter section (sometimes called Notes).

5.23 *An example of footnotes*

If there are few notes, and never more than one per page, then it is fine to use just an asterisk to indicate them. If there are multiple notes on a page, then they need to be indicated with superscript numbers or letters, which look like this[1].

When they go in footnotes or at the end of a chapter, the numbering (or lettering) starts again in each chapter. If the notes from all the chapters go into a single back matter section, then the numbering won't reset each chapter, but increases throughout the book.

Line Spacing

How much space should there be between each line of text? Too little and it feels cramped; too much and it can massively decrease how many words fit on the page, with the result that more pages are needed in the book, which adds to the printing cost per copy. Too much space also makes it harder for the eye to find its place when reading from one line of text to the next.

When printing a letter to an agent or publisher it is standard to select luxurious **double spacing**, where the blank space between lines of text is the same height as one of the lines; but that is rarer in a published book that may be a hundred thousand words long.

I favour line spacing of at least 17 pt (0.60 cm) but it depends on the point size of the font; a rule of thumb is between 1.2 and 1.6 times the point size.

Paragraph Spacing And Indents

The standard style in fiction is for the first paragraph of a chapter to be flush left with the margin, but for each paragraph after that to have the first line indented. An indent of 0.5 cm looks about right. There are no extra gaps between paragraphs; the spacing between paragraphs is exactly the same as the spacing between lines within a paragraph.

Fiction may also delineate that first block paragraph in additional ways to make it stand out even more. Sometimes the first three to five words appear in small caps. That is clear, has no downsides, and even works fine in ebooks.

5.24 Fiction chapter opening, and paragraph layout

Other times, the first capital letter is large and stretches up (**raised cap**) or down (a **drop cap / initial cap**) two or three lines. Drop caps and raised caps make a bold statement. The letter may even be illustrated or in a fancy font, especially if the designer wants to adopt an older-style look, as might be the case in a fantasy or historical novel.

5.25 The same fiction chapter opening, but with a drop cap

Although drop caps look nice, it can become awkward when an opening paragraph is only one line, or begins with quoted speech: suddenly the opening quotation marks feel like spare parts, especially if the first letter is an A (which is why I have seen books using this system omit those opening quotation marks; but that creates a different problem, when the reader only realises partway through the sentence that it is quoted speech). Drop caps can also have problems in ebooks. As such, I recommend the small cap system, or using neither.

Non-fiction can use that same style as fiction (and often does) but it has another option used only for non-fiction. This non-fiction style tends to have a gap between paragraphs (e.g. 6-10 pt / 0.21-0.35 cm), and also doesn't indent the first lines. This creates multiple blocks of text on the page. Non-fiction doesn't have a drop cap when a new chapter begins, or use small caps.

5.26 Non-fiction chapter opening, and paragraph layout

The non-fiction style is often used on web pages, so many people see it more often than the fiction style. As such, they occasionally format fiction that way, which is either a dead giveaway of someone who doesn't know the basics of book design, or because the work is aiming for a particular effect where each paragraph is almost a separate thought bubble (as with *The End We Start From*, by Megan Hunter).

The ultimate sin is to use both systems at the same time. Yes, I have seen books where this was done (indented paragraphs *and* gaps between them), and they look awful, like a Frankenstein's monster of formatting with the story continually falling away into the gulfs between paragraphs.

Scene Breaks

Scene breaks are sometimes referred to as **section breaks** or **text breaks**. In fiction, it is common to use a scene break to indicate a change of time, location or viewpoint.

The simplest form is to just have a gap between the final paragraph of the previous section, and the first paragraph of the next. I favour a space of 36 pt (1.27 cm) for maximum clarity.

The first paragraph following a scene break is usually treated the same as the one that opens a chapter: so in most fiction, it will be flush left with no indent, followed by an indented paragraph.

5.27 Scene break, delineated by a gap

This system works best if combined with the style where the opening paragraph of a chapter has the first three to five words in small caps. Why? Because if the scene break occurs at the bottom of a page, it is easy for the reader to miss the fact that the next paragraph does not have a first line indent. They may think this is just a continuation, and that can be confusing when the place, perspective or time have changed. Small caps (or a drop cap) are an extra visual indicator that something has happened, that there's a "new start".

Note that, with this system, the gap between sections is *not* created by pressing Enter three times! If you did that then when a scene break occurs near the bottom of a page it may push blank lines to the top of the next one, meaning the text there is shifted down. Instead, the gap is governed by **styles**, and rather than a *normal indented* paragraph style, a *new chapter/scene* paragraph style is used. One of the great things about creating the gap with styles is that when the scene break occurs at the bottom of a page, the next section would still begin correctly at the top of the next page. I'll discuss styles in more detail when I talk about word processors.

Another system for indicating a scene break is to include a visual element. That may be as simple as blank lines with

* * *

between them, centred, just like that.

Or a fancier symbol can be used (called an **ornamental break** or **fleuron**), such as:

> When the time came to take a handful of clumped earth from the mound and throw it onto the coffin, Sam had to borrow more tissues. That was her *gran* in the box. Mamgu would never talk to Sam again. Never cheer her up and tell her everything was okay. Never need help getting a jar open. So many nevers.
>
> ❃
>
> Mark Hopton held a striking bunch of black and yellow flowers. Life wasn't fair. Why did all the good ones go first?
> Today was Sunday 21st May, year 2000. Eighteen years ago there had been such a hopeful beginning. It never grew to be an adult. Mancunian potential killed in its prime.

5.28 Detail showing an ornamental scene break

The symbol can be related to the theme, so a book called *Autumn Falling* might have a symbol made up of a line of leaves, for example. A horror book might have a smear of blood, a romance might have a soft curve. It could even be an element of the cover imagery.

Using *** or a symbol is a clear way of indicating a scene break, and shows up more clearly than space alone if a section ends at the bottom of a page.

Note that it's always fine if an ornamental break falls at the bottom of a page, but it's frowned upon by some designers for it to appear at the *top* of a page as the first element. So, in a way, scene break symbols can be thought of as joined to the text preceding them (the opposite to subheadings, which are inseparably joined to the text following them). If the symbol does appear at the top of a page then these designers will adjust the text spacing to avoid this situation. As with all elements of book design, creating the appearance of seamless and effortless perfection actually takes a lot of work, and each change can impact on other parts of the book.

Of course, some designers don't mind when a scene break appears at the top of a page. They perhaps view the symbol as a liminal marker existing *between* two sections and not having a strong connection to either.

One more thing: as stated, scene breaks are a convention of fiction. And that's part of the reason why fiction follows the style of indented paragraphs without a space between them – when a space *is* used, it indicates this structural element of a scene break. We already saw that non-fiction uses a gap between paragraphs as its standard format. That's one of the reasons why it doesn't make sense to use that layout for fiction: scene breaks would lead to a massive gap between paragraphs (in order to distinguish it from the normal gap). And in non-fiction, when some kind of break for a new section is needed, there is a simple answer: a subheading, which wouldn't normally be used in fiction. Fiction and non-fiction have different layouts for a reason.

Straight Quotes And Curly Quotes

When typewriters (and therefore keyboards) were designed, they had one key for a single quote, and one for a double quote. The **straight quote** characters stamped onto the page were small vertical lines, whether they were the opening of a quotation, or the closing of it.

"What a joy!" 'I love tofu.'

However, published books have extra effort put in to make them attractive and readable. Hence we have **curly quotes**, where what looks like a tiny 66 opens a quotation, and a tiny 99 closes it. Well, that's if you use double quotation marks for quotes. If you use singles, it is a 6 and a 9.

"Hi!" 'Go away.'

```
"straight double quotes"
 'straight single quotes'

 "curly double quotes"
  'curly single quotes'
```

5.29 Straight versus curly quotes

Whether you use double quotation marks or single ones, a quote within a quote uses the other type. So these are both correct:

"The axe murderer said 'Chopity chop!' as he chased me down the stairs."

'I love the way you say "cherry roulade" in that seductive voice of yours.'

I favour using double quotation marks as the default for speech, so they don't get mixed up with apostrophes.

In general, software makes quotes curly via a smartquote or autocorrect system. It tries to guess from the context if it is an opening or closing quote, or an apostrophe, then replaces it with the curly variant. Although often right, it can also get it wrong, since there is no set of automated rules that govern every situation. I'll discuss why that is in a digression below.

My suggestion is to use autocorrect for the draft, since that will get most of them right and save time later. But turn the feature off while preparing the final version of the text, so that autocorrect does not make unwanted changes. At this stage we don't want a single character in our book changing without us initiating it!

Instead, at that point, go through the text and *manually* replace any quotation marks that are wrong with the correct symbol, using insert or command codes. I'll discuss one method later in this chapter, in the section Top Tip: Shortcuts For Special Symbols.

Drinky's Digressions: Quotation Symbols In Other Languages

Note that in other languages totally different symbols may be used, as I discovered when my books were being translated. For example, the French use **guillemets** with a **non-breaking space**

(I'll explain what that is later) between the marks and the text. So whereas we would write:

"I am tired," she said.

in French it would be:

« Je suis fatigué, » dit elle.

Germans might use inverted guillemets without a space; or *die Anführungszeichen*, where the quotation marks at the beginning are at the bottom pointing to the left, and the closing ones at the upper end of the last word point to the right. So both of these can be seen in German books:

Dann sagte sie: »Ich komme nicht mit!«

Dann sagte sie: „Ich komme nicht mit!"

Drinky's Digressions: Why Can't Software Get Curly Quotes Right Every time?

Programmers try and create complicated rules based on particular word or letter combinations in conjunction with punctuation and position, but they often get it wrong. No set of rules covers every situation in standard English, let alone when you throw in dialects, translations, degree marks, primes and double primes (for foot and inch marks), programming code, or speculative fiction that uses different punctuation in names and languages. The punctuation rules vary by country, time period a work is set in, style guide used, choices within the guide, stylistic issues, and what is being quoted. Those choices mean the same sentence can be written multiple ways, and that's before anyone does anything inventive with language.

Even straightforward situations like an apostrophe of omission at the start of a word will often be incorrectly replaced with a single curly open quotation mark by most software. So this is correct:

It might be years 'til we meet again.

But many word processors will turn the apostrophe around into a single quote and leave this incorrect text:

It might be years 'til we meet again.

(Whenever I see that mistake in a book I know there hasn't been a competent proofreader involved.)

The problem is, communications always have an element of *context* that a human can understand immediately, but software cannot. For example, if I was creating a book about writing I might include examples of common punctuation errors. Software would change the examples to "fix" them, thinking they were mistakes, and thereby mess them up.

Consider the following:

What the 'ell are you doin'?

Have you seen the sign 'obey all laws'?

You can immediately tell that in the first example we're dealing with two apostrophes of omission, but the second should be single opening and closing quotation marks (if you use Oxford style single quote rules). But software won't be able to tell the difference and will treat both the same.

Here are some other examples that software and fixed rules probably won't be able to parse correctly, but a human could work out. See if you can determine which of the neutral quotes (') should be open quotes ('), apostrophes ('), or close quotes (').

- 'Twas was a bit of a shiner, wa'n't it?'

- 'Dulcetta was a 6'4" catwalk model 'til that fateful day.'

- The handwritten message read 'stealin' from the jumbo Pick 'n' Mix at Woolworths will get 'em shot'.

I agree that those were extreme examples, but I've encountered software like Microsoft Word, or Atticus (which I will discuss at the end of this chapter) get far simpler examples completely wrong. In fact, errors made by Atticus in 2022 forced me to spend months painstakingly checking every apostrophe and quotation mark across more than 600,000 words, manually fixing all the ones they had got wrong. I still have painful memories of that, which is why I favour writing first drafts in offline tools where I can back things up easily, and nothing is done to the text unless I choose to do it. Smart quotes must always be optional in software, so you can turn off autocorrect during the editing stages of a book.

Widows And Orphans

Widows and orphans are metaphors for the same concept: words separated from the rest of their paragraph and looking all lonely.

A widow is the last line of a paragraph alone at the top of a page. An orphan is the first line of a paragraph all on its own at the bottom of a page.

Except I've seen texts that describe widows and orphans the other way around, and say widows are at the bottom of a page, orphans at the top. People will argue about it, which is stupid when the metaphor of separation applies equally to both, so use whichever interpretation you want. I prefer to just think of "top orphans" and "bottom orphans" which is unambiguous.

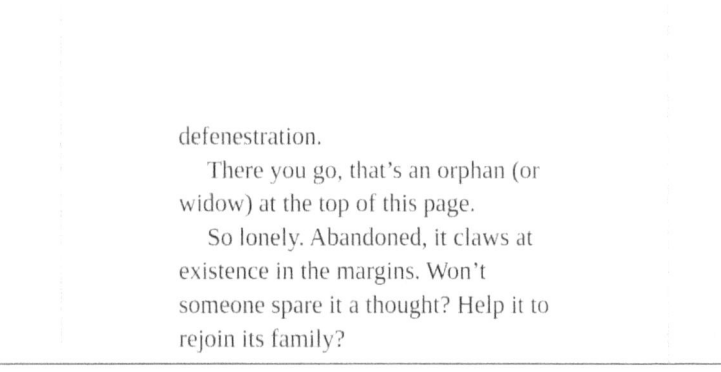

5.30 *Widows and orphans*

Widows and orphans are seen as signs of poor layout. A designer will alter spacings and other elements in subtle ways that shouldn't be noticeable to the reader in order to make sure that instead of a single line at the top or bottom of a page, there are two lines (or three lines). This can be done automatically by software.

However, doing so can mean some pages have fewer lines in the text block (since widow/orphan lines are moved to keep them with their paragraphs). This means the bottom of text blocks may be at slightly different levels, so the books are no longer **squared off**. And for some designers, that is worse than widows and orphans! So this is a design issue to be aware of, and it's a good example of the compromises that must be made. It's unlikely that anyone can avoid widows and orphans *and* still keep squared off pages, unless they do an enormous amount of manual formatting and respacing. And, of course, if the interior ever changes (e.g. some typos are fixed, or words added and removed, or chapter title design altered) then all that manual formatting is wasted and must be done again.

For me, life's too short. Decide whether you prefer squared off pages, or pages without widows and orphans. Then accept the compromise. Most readers won't notice either way.

Images

Some of the points made here will also apply to images in ebooks.

Colour. Colour printing is expensive. So if you have images and charts, then whether they will appear in colour or black and white (**mono**, from monochrome) is a key consideration.

Sometimes you need colour. Maybe it's a children's illustrated book with colour images, rather than line drawings. Maybe a recipe book with tantalising photos.

If there are colour images, it may require special paper to present them in the best light: an example of knock-on considerations, which affect book production, cover design (remember that spine width is determined by page count multiplied by paper thickness), and cost.

If you are an independent author then it is worth looking into how your printer will deal with it. For example IngramSpark have two prices, one for colour interiors, and one for black-and-white interiors. But if you even include a single colour image, you get charged the full colour price for *every* page, even though most have no colour on. Ouch. Whereas BookVault (which I will cover in Chapter 8: Distribution) have a more advanced system, and if you include a single colour page you only get charged for the one colour page.

Whether something prints in colour or mono is determined by the settings chosen when uploading the book, not by the content. Images in the master file pdf can be colour – they will just be printed in greyscale if the book is set up as black and white only.

For quality mono printing, any colour images should be converted to greyscale and optimised, with the levels of grey adjusted for proper contrast. This is important for clear photos as well as infographics and charts that were originally colour.

I use colour images in my master file because I generate both the ebook and print book interiors from the same master, and in ebooks it makes sense to always use colour – it is free! Then for print I sometimes create a second set of images if greyscale isn't clear enough. In that case I might increase contrast, change colours to bold black, or even convert the image to a line illustration. It is a case-by-case decision.

Transparency. Not all image types can deal with transparency. If you take, for example, the publisher's colophon (logo) that might appear on the title page, then as an image file it might be a central logo with white space or transparency around it. In a printed book it could be any acceptable format e.g. png or jpg. If there is transparency around the logo (possible with a png file), then in a printed book the transparent area won't be printed. Great, that's what we want. The reader would just see the logo. A jpg file can't contain transparency, so the same logo in that format would be surrounded by white instead of transparency. But that is also fine! *When a book is printed, anything in white will be treated as transparent.* You'll just see the paper there, in exactly the same way.

And if you use those same images in an ebook, then as long as the ebook is read with a white background to the text, both logos will appear the same. But the joy of ebooks is that users can change the settings. So if the reader chooses a sepia background, or a black background (with white text – night mode) then the version of the logo that is a png file with a transparent background will look as expected – a logo with a transparent background.

But the jpg version with a white background will look like a logo in a white rectangle. So, while for printed books it doesn't matter whether an image is a png or jpg, in an ebook where there are image elements you don't want to be visible, it is better to use a png file and make those areas transparent.

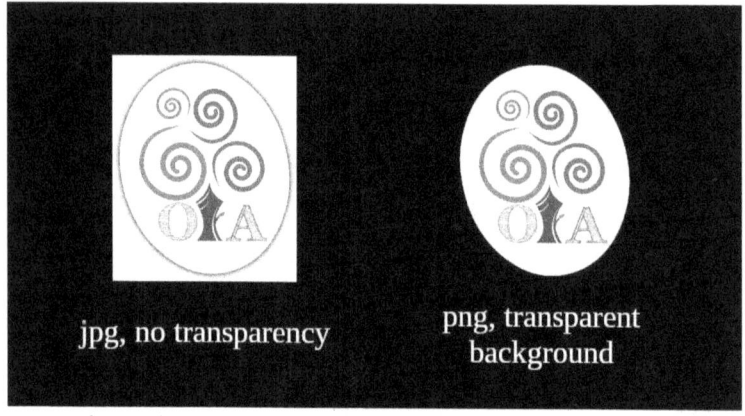

5.31 *The difference between an opaque jpg, and a png with transparency, when viewed against a non-white background on an ereader device*

File size. If you are going to include images in a book then you always start off with the best quality images you can. This also means they will be larger files, taking up more disk space. You can downgrade images (shrink them, or lower their quality) later, if required; but if you start with a low-quality image you can never put extra detail back in. So start with the best.

Printed books – both the text and the images – should be at 300 **DPI** (**Dots Per Inch** – or, more accurately, 300 **PPI, Pixels Per Inch**). The high quality images can make the master pdf file huge. But that's standard, and important for the quality of the book. When someone buys a paperback, the size of the original file used to print it is irrelevant.

However, ebooks are distributed from servers to devices every time someone buys or downloads the book. The bigger the file, the longer it takes to download, and the more storage space it takes up on the device. And one of the biggest contributors to file size is the images within a book. Further, Amazon charges a distribution fee based on file size that eats into your royalties.

For all these reasons it is better to do extra work on the images in an ebook, such as reducing their DPI so that the file sizes are smaller. When done well, there is no discernible decrease in quality, and yet the file size could be reduced by two thirds.

As an experiment I took one of my books which included images. At full resolution (greater than 300 DPI) the ebook was an eye-watering 77 MB (megabytes). At 220 DPI the file size dropped to only 8 MB. The quality to the naked eye looked about the same, even though the end file was ten times smaller. Whereas dropping the image DPI to 96 meant the file was only 1.6 MB, but the images were exceptionally blurry.

When compressing images, be aware that you are more likely to notice the loss of quality in things that should be crisp, such as text or line art; it is less obvious in a photo image packed with detail. Also, the former type of image is less in need of compressing in the first place, as a line drawing with no shading will be smaller (more compressible due to lots of areas of the same colour) than an image where every pixel is different from the next (e.g. a busy photo).

Since jpg images are always compressed, they work well for photos with lots of detail where you won't notice the inevitable smudges that come with compression, but for an image composed of a stark diagram with text I would avoid compression if possible (and use the png lossless format rather than a jpg).

The image dimensions in pixels, the format (png, jpg), and the level of compression, all determine the final file size. It is always a balancing act to keep size down, but image quality up.

Positioning. In print books an image can appear anywhere on the page, and have text wrap around it. In ebooks it is best to have images in their own paragraph, and centred.

Full bleed. This applies only to print books. Bleed is a buffer area used when images go right up to the edge of a page. A full-bleed image is one that fills an entire page. Since paper cutting isn't exact, we make sure the image is bigger than the space needed, even though some will be cut off. That is better than distracting white lines at the edge if a book is cut slightly larger than the image. The software and printing service you use will determine how full bleed is dealt with.

Print size. There is a useful way to calculate the resolution an image needs to be, in order to print at a certain size on the page.

Books are printed at 300 DPI. Anything (such as an image) below 300 DPI will start to look blurry. Above 300 DPI will result in a larger file size, but no increase in quality. So it is most efficient to make images 300 DPI to begin with.

How?

1. Decide on a rough measurement of the image that you want on the page, in inches e.g. "2.2 inches wide, 3.8 inches tall".

2. Multiply each dimension's inches by 300 (for 300 DPI) to get the ideal size in pixels (px). So 2.2" x 3.8" = (2.2 x 300) x (3.8 x 300) = 660 x 1140 px. (If you work in centimetres, multiply the desired CM width by 118 instead of 300.)

You can also do this calculation in reverse to find out for a given image what its largest print size would be at 300 DPI.

1. Suppose you have an image of resolution 1200 x 600, and want to include it in a book. (Again, the first number is the horizontal measurement, the second is the vertical: x then y.)

2. To find out how much space it will fill on the page, I have to divide each side of the image by 300 to find the print size in inches.

3. 1200 x 600 px, divided by 300 = 4 x 2. So it will be printed as a crisp 300 DPI rectangular image at a maximum size of four inches across and two inches high.

(Yes, you may need a calculator for some of these spacial sums.)

Ebooks: Digital Files

A lot of the conventions of print formatting don't apply to ebooks. Page numbers, fixed fonts, running heads, even layout can be irrelevant since many options are decided by the reader, and the software or device being used. Still, it's worth looking at some of the special considerations for the electronic versions of our books.

Fixed Versus Flowable Layouts

There are two styles of ebook. Fixed layout, and flowable layout. Most e-readers or e-reader software can deal with both.

A pdf is a good example of fixed layouts. They capture exactly how a page would look if printed out, with the fonts embedded within the file to ensure perfect reproduction. If you are reading a pdf on an electronic device then you can't change the layout, but can zoom in and out. Fixed layouts can work well for things like graphic novels, visual encyclopaedias, or text with multiple columns, text boxes and images, as you'd find in a magazine or cookbook.

Epub files are a good example of flowable formats, and are much more standard for fiction. There won't be fancy columns and layouts, primarily just text. The number of words you see on the screen and how they appear are determined by the reader's choices in font, size and spacing. Even orientation (portrait or landscape) and colour background can be altered by the reader, such as sepia colours, or completely reversed so they have white text on black (good for reading in the dark – not as bright as a white background glaring into your eyes).

Flowable ebooks are like web pages. That's because they almost *are* web pages. We may see a single epub or mobi file on our device, but really it is a package (akin to a zip file) containing a lot of other files in xhtml, css etc. It's possible to open up the archive and view the contents, if you have some know-how. The files inside the epub will be a mixture of content (the text) and formatting (codes to say if a word is italics, bold, a heading etc). It's why flowable ebooks are so flexible, since the e-reader or software can override style elements for the user, letting you set your own preferences and read in the way that is most comfortable to you.

Note that epub as a format can also be used for fixed layouts, like pdfs.

Drinky's Digressions: Reports Of Mobi's Death Have Been Greatly Exaggerated

Epub is the widely-accepted standard for text-based books, and even many with images.

Amazon used to have its own ebook format, called mobi. In 2023 they switched to epub. This led to many people in the book profession declaring that the mobi format was dead and no author ever has to bother with it again. One article said: "Since mid-2022 you can no longer add your own mobi files to your

Kindle." Another told me "There is no longer any reason why you would ever need a MOBI file...ever." And another news piece said: "Kindles will now support ePub files. They will also, interestingly, stop supporting mobi files."

I raised an eyebrow at all that.

I have a Kindle Fire HD ebook reader (an unrequested gift – I don't buy things from Amazon). I transfer ebooks to it via USB, because it is far more convenient for me. The Kindle is already plugged into my PC when charging, so I just drag the files over as if it is an external drive. It takes seconds, and since some of the books are over 20MB so are too big to email (e.g. graphic novels, image-heavy non-fiction), drag-and-drop is the only way to transfer them. I never use the clunky email-to-Kindle feature that involves slowly emailing books from your PC to a distant server, which then sends them back to your house and onto the device that was sat next to you all along! But the key point is that, despite Amazon saying mobi is no more, and people repeating it without any research, *if I put an epub file on my Kindle then the device can't read it.* If I put a mobi file on, it can.

All that has happened is Amazon's email-to-Kindle service switched from mobi to epub, and new devices will be able to read epub files. For anyone with older devices like me, mobi is certainly not dead. Amazon hasn't updated my model to work with epub files, and never will. I have friends in the same position as me, even though their Kindles are a more recent model than mine. So there are obviously Kindles that do still require mobi files, and cannot read epubs.

As such, when I buy ebooks direct from authors or sites such as Humble Bundle, if the ebooks are only in epub format they are useless to me. My device can only read mobi and pdf files, so I only buy ebooks in those formats. It's also why, when I sell ebooks direct to fans or include them as Kickstarter rewards, or provide ebooks to beta readers and reviewers, I always let them choose the format they want: epub, mobi or pdf.

Drinky's Digressions: DRM And Piracy

For me, **DRM** means **Digital Restrictions Management**. DRM uses hardware or software to try and limit what a consumer can do with something they've bought. It stops you copying, converting or editing files, can destroy or change content, and can downgrade signals. It is always anti-consumer, and turns a purchase into a tentative loan of unclear duration.

This is part of the reason why consumers often see ebooks as secondary or poorer-quality choices, because they are more ephemeral, due to DRM. We've all heard tales of ebooks disappearing from Kindles when on holiday due to regional restrictions, or accounts and books being deleted by Amazon. See *Microsoft's eBook store: When this closes, your books disappear too*[56] as another example. In the digital audio arena whole swathes of music just disappeared when DRM-including formats stopped being supported. All songs bought on MSN Music and Yahoo! Music were lost forever when the services closed. Why would I buy something that can be taken away from me at any point?

"But don't you need DRM to stop piracy? Look, this naughty site is offering my book for free!"

The irony is that DRM is easily removed if you have the know-how, so criminals aren't inconvenienced by it. DRM doesn't stop pirates. In fact, it increases piracy, as it means the DRM-free pirated version of media is more attractive than the buggy, problematic, and devalued neutered version.

And that site? It probably doesn't even have your book. Scam sites scrape metadata (see Chapter 7) from Amazon and other places, pretend to offer the books for free, but then ask for payment details "as a security measure". Anyone entering those details or creating an account will just find themselves being scammed, a victim of identity theft, money stolen, or ending up with malware on their PC. Or all four.

The only people who suffer from DRM are paying customers, which is the opposite of what it is intended to do. I have many examples of how DRM has blocked me from doing things with books, films and software I have bought. I remember a publicly funded ebooks scheme in Wales where Adobe DRM on the ebooks meant that library users (such as myself) couldn't read the ebooks on the most popular ebook reader, the Kindle.

When you buy ebooks (or games, or music, or software) it may or may not have DRM, and it isn't always easy to tell in advance as the vendor or manufacturer are unlikely to be honest and open about it. It's why you can't search an ebook store (or game store like Steam) for DRM-free products.

The only people who benefit from DRM are the companies that design and sell it. And obviously they spend a lot of money trying to mislead people into thinking that it works, that it doesn't have downsides, and that you need it.

DRM says "I don't trust you" to the customer. It is an awful statement to begin any relationship with. Have you ever been in a shop where they watch you like a hawk? How does it make you feel? What about when you go into another shop where you're trusted, with a "take a penny, leave a penny" pot, or where they don't mind if you pop back later with the 10p you were short of? I know which shop I would prefer to go back to. I remember when you'd buy a DVD and were forced to sit through an unskippable five minutes of video clips accusing you of being a potential criminal, and making you wonder why you bothered buying it in the first place.

Publishers should focus on the customer, and getting new books into as many hands as possible. Since DRM causes problems for consumers, whilst also antagonising them, whenever there is a choice of whether to add it or not, my advice is *don't*. Selling things which are inherently broken is not a good business practice.

Sure, some people will always share stuff illegally, but DRM won't stop them. Likewise there are always honest people who want to support creators and buy their stuff. Adding DRM will only discourage them and cheapen the offering. They won't be able to back up the content they bought, or convert it to a different format that is more convenient for them.

The music industry gave up on DRM and switched to selling mp3s, and people bought more than ever. Tor stopped adding DRM to their ebooks in 2012 and are still a hugely successful publisher. GOG doesn't allow DRM on any of the games they sell, and people still buy them.

If something has DRM (including online account activation) then I am 99% less likely to buy it. If it doesn't have DRM, I am 99% more likely to buy it.

Don't worry about piracy. It isn't a threat to most authors. Obscurity is.

Formatting Tools

If you're submitting work to your agent or publisher, there's no need for fancy formatting. You will just write the book in word processor software, then provide them with the document according to their specifications. They may ask for double spaced, or a certain font and size, or whatever. Just do that. And if the book is eventually published, then other people with deal with formatting. For you, this section won't be relevant (though it may be informative).

But if you are an independent author then you'll need to organise book formatting. Ebook; perhaps print; most likely both. For example, print-on-demand services require a pdf file of the book's interior, and a separate pdf file for the book's cover, both correctly formatted and sized, with embedded fonts and images.

A key consideration for independent authors, which applies equally to cover design (the next chapter) is this: are you money-rich and time-poor? For example, maybe you work full-time in a well-paid job, and have little free time to write. Well, in that case it probably makes more sense to pay a professional to do tasks like book formatting.

However, if you are time-rich but money-poor, *and* good at learning new skills, with a creative eye and technological know-how, then you have the option of learning to do it yourself.

Bear in mind that these aren't skills you can acquire in a weekend. It's like learning a language, and requires lots of time investment and practice. Software can shortcut some of the work, but as with cover design there is still lots to learn about industry standards, software, design choices, and file formats.

Because I am interested in all this from the days when I did a publishing module on my librarianship MSc (Master of Science postgraduate degree), and have always been a tech geek, I studied and practised. I learnt book formatting. I took courses in design and layout. I read books, did tutorials, and watched videos. I undertook graphics training: both the software, and the overall design philosophies. I studied rights and licensing. Gradually the mysteries become clearer. Though, as with most skills, it isn't a case of "do it once and that's it forever". You need to keep up to date, to be aware of changing trends and new developments. Basically, you have to be *really* interested to make it worthwhile.

If this is something you might want to do, then let's move on to some software that can help to format ebook or paperback interiors to industry standards; especially if there are options to make a book interior beautiful, rather than just functional. And even if you're not an independent author, some of these tools are worth looking at if you are interested in book layout. They can be fun to play with and master, providing new formatting options for tidying and sharing your work.

Word Processors

Ah, the humble word processor. A tool every author should have.

Nowadays it is possible to write and edit documents online, but I always favour a locally installed, offline word processor on my PC. Then, even if there are Internet access problems, your work is unaffected and nothing is lost. It also makes it much easier to be in control of versions and backups. If anything goes wrong it is down to you, not a service that crashes, gets hacked, and suffers from broken updates or loss of connectivity.

But first, word processors. My tool of choice is Libre Office Writer. It is free, fully functional, reads and saves in many formats (including docx, epub and pdf), defaults to 300DPI for images (the industry standard), and is available for most operating systems. It's part of the Libre Office suite,[57] so you also get spreadsheet and presentation software. I'll be honest: although I used to own Microsoft Word, since I switched to Libre Office I have found myself to be more productive, and less likely to battle against the software. I have no idea why people would pay for Microsoft Office nowadays when something better is available for free, but it's your choice. And there are hundreds of other word processors out there, so use whatever you have available. As long as it lets you format text, you're golden.

Ideally, the tool should let you use headings. When writing a draft I use summary headings for scenes and sections, as my own aide-mémoire. They make it easier to create and edit your manuscript, and even to reorganise it: word processors should let you view a navigation pane where you can move a heading somewhere else, and all the content below it moves with the heading. That saves a lot of copying and pasting, and enables you to quickly try out different structure options. The headings get deleted in the final version, when the book is ready to go for external feedback.

One thing to understand is that proper formatting in a word processor should be done by **styles**, which I mentioned briefly earlier. Styles are pre-configured commands that format selected text in specific ways, such as changing font, size and position. They exist to make formatting simpler, and are easily applied: highlight some text and choose a style. The words are then automatically formatted in that pre-defined style.

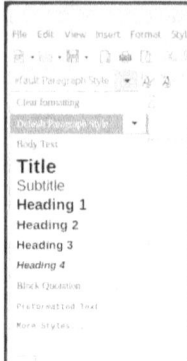

5.32 Detail showing a drop-down styles menu

Styles save time. You can set a *paragraph style* where the first line is indented (never indent paragraphs using the Tab key or spacebar!). Then have a *new section style* where it is not indented, but where the paragraph is preceded by blank space to indicate the change of location, time or perspective. A *chapter heading style* would insert a page break before it, so it appears at the top of a fresh page. An *indented quotation style* could be used to highlight longer quotes, and so on.

Styles can even link to each other. I set mine up so that I begin a new chapter with the heading style; when I press Enter at the end of the line it switches to a non-indented first paragraph style; and when I press Enter at the end of that, it becomes an indented paragraph style, and stays like that for each subsequent paragraph until I tell it otherwise.

The secondary advantage of using styles is the power to change things. Suppose I've formatted my book a particular way, and then I'm told by an agent that they want different indents, fonts, spacing or sizes. Rather than manually having to change every paragraph, I can just alter the style, and the text updates immediately. So, for example, if my indented paragraph style has the font of Times New Roman size 11, double line spacing, and an indent of one centimetre, I can just change the style to Garamond 12, one-and-a-half line spacing, and an indent of five millimetres (all of which takes me about five seconds), and the whole document is immediately updated: everything using that paragraph style adopts the new settings. It is well worth getting to grips with styles: understanding and editing them, and even creating your own.

"Hey, Karl. That sounds good and all, but I can't be arsed learning much about styles. I wouldn't know where to start. Can't you do it for me?"

Well, in that case you can make your life easier and buy a template. I built my own in Libre Office Writer, but companies like Book Design Templates[58] will sell you one which has all the styles set up already.

If you try and do everything in a word processor then you will likely need *two* master files, one with styles set up for ebooks, one with styles and layout for print books. Then the printed book master file can have running heads, page numbers, and fancy fonts, and the ebook can omit them. Yes, two documents means that if any content changes, you have to update both of them.

The alternative is to use specialist software tools, which I will get to later in this chapter.

Drinky's Digressions: Hidden Code

Text can be *plain text*, which means just characters but no formatting; or it can have *formatting* applied (styles, bold, italics etc). The formatting is defined by hidden codes, which are a type of metadata.

So there is the formatted text you *see*, and the hidden code *underneath*.

A fun experiment I used to do was to copy and paste a single sentence from Microsoft Word into a HTML editor. The visible text would look the same. But when you switched to the HTML view there would be 4-5 lines of gobbledygook made up of unnecessary formatting codes.

Here's a quick example. I copied this text from a web page:

Author: the writer of a book.

When I pasted it into a word document it looked the same. *On the surface*. But when I examined the code in a HTML editor, it wasn't just the words being copied, but formatting styles too:

```
<p><span          class="kY2IgmnC-
mOGjharHErah"     style="-we-
```

```
bkit-line-clamp: 3;">Author: the
writer of a book.</span></p>
```

Suddenly, the 29 characters I wanted was really 109 characters of code; it had more than tripled in size. That extra formatting information added bloat to the content, but could also cause huge issues with presentation. Whereas if I pasted the same words as plain text, and looked at the HTML, it was perfectly clean. Just the words.

That hidden code can add up to a lot of junk, and if you copy and paste text from different places (e.g. web pages, or one document into another) then the negative impacts of the hidden code increase massively. Many times when I've heard authors complaining about printing errors from pdfs or display errors from their ebooks, it has almost always been down to hidden formatting codes created by copying and pasting text from different sources.

It is better in terms of document size and stability to strip all formatting from pasted text, and there are many simple ways to do it. I created a custom keyboard shortcut in Linux which does that for me, meaning no hidden formatting ever finds its way into my documents when I copy and paste. You may find that the keyboard shortcut Ctrl+Shift+V works for you. However, do note that, unfortunately, bold and italics (as types of formatting) will also get stripped out in plain text, and need to be put back manually.

Top Tip: Shortcuts For Special Symbols

Keyboard shortcuts are great. I save a lot of time every day running things on my PC without touching a mouse. Some shortcuts specific to text are invaluable tools. For example, a soft return (Shift + Enter) makes the text move to the next line without starting a new paragraph. It can be a handy way to break up long chapter titles, for example, or to lay out poetry.

It is worth learning how to insert special symbols, especially for those that aren't on keyboards. Every operating system has at least one means of doing so, and the software you use may provide extra options.

I use Linux (Mint Cinnamon variety) on my PC. Linux is a free operating system, and I find it vastly more user-friendly than Windows. Many special characters just require me to use the AltGr key (the right Alt key on my keyboard) and then another key.

"" [double curly quotes] = AltGr+V or B

'' [single curly quotes] = AltGr+Shift+V or B

^{123} [superscript numbers] = AltGr+1 or 2 or 3

€ [Euro symbol] = AltGr+4

° [degree symbol] = AltGr+Shift+0 [zero]

© [copyright symbol] = AltGr+Shift+C

However, an alternative way to get symbols in Linux is to press Ctrl+Shift+U, then type the number of the unicode character I need, then Enter. It's the only way to get these three easily:

Ctrl+Shift+U, 2013 = En-dash –

Ctrl+Shift+U, 2014 = Em-dash —

Ctrl+Shift+U, 2026 = Ellipsis …

Ctrl+Shift+U, 00a0 = Non-breaking space. You can also get one in many word processors by using Ctrl+Shift+Space.

Yes, I have all these codes memorised, since I use them so often!

There's a list of unicodes for different characters,[59] and this works for any of them. You can then add Trademark symbols and so on.

Many of the special characters I have given shortcuts for may be known to you, apart from **non-breaking spaces**. These look like a space to a reader, but they stop the two elements on each side of the non-breaking space from being split up at the end of a line. For example, with the International System of Units (SI) it is standard to use a non-breaking space between the measurement and the number: 12 km. 7 a.m. 13 lbs. 100 kg. 10 m. 10 V. The non-breaking space stops you having the number 10 at the end of a line and the letter m or V on its own on the next line, as could happen if you used a normal space. Another example, from when I discussed quotation symbols in other languages: French uses a non-breaking space next to its guillemet quotation symbols so they don't get separated from the enclosed text at end lines.

Other Tools

You could do everything in a word processor. Or you could do the formatting in a more automated tool, as discussed in this section. Note that none of these are recommendations, nor is the list comprehensive: I'm just covering a few of the tools that are available. I'm still waiting for a DRM-free offline tool that does everything I need and performs reliably. I'd happily pay for that.

All of the resources listed below will produce a distribution-ready ebook and interior print file. One of the key advantages of these tools is that you have a single version of the book's main text, and can produce both print interiors and ebooks from that same content. I've put them in alphabetical order, not order of priority.

Atticus[60]

Atticus lets you format text into both epub (ebook) and pdf (print) formats. The tool is online, which has pros and cons, as discussed in the word processing section above. It's part of why I'd never use it to write a first draft, only to format a finished manuscript written in other software. It has a one-off fee but it's not expensive, nor is Atticus overly complicated, and it will produce a formatted book. Do be aware that it is buggy, though, and features might be removed or break at any time. And there is no way to backup or restore the books yourself.

Draft2Digital[61]

Draft2Digital lets you format ebooks and print books for free, even if you don't use them as a distributor. You need to create an account to do this. There are limited customisation options, though that isn't a negative if you are new to this, and just want to create an attractive book with minimal fuss. Draft2Digital built in some handy automations, such as hyperlinks which work normally in the ebook, but get automatically turned into footnotes in the printed book. Even Atticus doesn't have this feature.

Jutoh[62]

Commercial software for Windows, Mac and Linux. Mainly focussed on creating ebooks, not printed versions.

Reedsy[63]

Reedsy has a book editor. You need to create a Reedsy account to use it, and some say it has limited design options, but it is free.

Scrivener[64]

This is more complex than the other tools, because its focus is planning, writing *and* formatting, hence including project outlines and note tools. It is paid software, and you'll need to deal with licences (DRM) to activate it. If they do a major update, you need to buy a new licence if you want to access the updates. There is no Linux version.

Vellum[65]

More expensive than Atticus, and restricted to people who use Apple computers. However, it has a good reputation and is well established. You will need to deal with licences and software activation (DRM).

Finally: Proof The Print!

Whether the book is an ebook or printed book, always read the proof copy carefully for any errors that have crept in, such as weird formatting in the ebook, or incorrect spacing and printing errors in the paperback. For checking the print version a physical copy is best, but a pdf proof of the interior can be a good (free) alternative.

This is the checklist I use when proofing a paperback copy.

Book Cover

- Layout – check nothing is too near the edge (or even running off it); all elements should be nicely and evenly spaced.

- Is text clear and readable?

- Make sure any quotation marks and apostrophes in the tagline and blurb are proper curly ones rather than straight ones (see earlier section *Straight Quotes And Curly Quotes*).

- If the book is part of a series, check key elements on the cover align with others in the series.

- Check the spine text is nicely aligned and central (though novellas may be too narrow to have anything on the spine).

Title Page

- Should begin on the right (recto).
- Check the elements are correct.
- If it is a book in a series, it should make that clear, and say what number it is in the series.

Copyright Page

- Always on the rear of the title page (so it is on the left, verso).
- Should be bottom-aligned, and in smaller text than the rest of the book.
- Check the details are correct.
- Make sure the ISBN matches what is on the back cover.

Table of Contents (TOC) or Half Title

- There should only be a TOC if it is a short story collection, anthology compilation of books, poetry, or non-fiction.
- The TOC should begin on the right (recto).

- Check the TOC page numbers match the actual book pages.

- In books without a TOC, there should be a half title instead – just the title of the book, beginning on the right.

Chapter Starts

- The first chapter should begin on the right side (recto). Chapters after that begin on either side, so there should be no blank pages until the back matter.

Images

- Check any images in the book look okay.

Multi-book Anthologies

- If it is one of these, check that each new book has its own title page on the right before that book begins.

Running Heads

- There should be a centred book title at the top of left pages, and the chapter name at the top of right pages. Both have page numbers at the top outer edges.

- There shouldn't be running heads on the first page of a chapter or in the book's back matter.

Body Of The Book

- The first paragraph of a chapter – or a new scene after a section break – should be flush left (not indented). The following paragraphs are indented.

- The text should be justified (straight lines on the right-hand side).

- I use hyphenation, so check that it is applied correctly. Most pages will have hyphens.

- Subheadings: if the book uses them, they should never appear on their own at the bottom of a page, separated from what follows them.

- If there are sections in Welsh (or another language), check that special characters such as ŵ appear correctly.

- Find some examples where text is in italics, check it looks okay and isn't overlapping with punctuation such as quotation marks.

- Skim down the left side of each page to spot any widows or bits on their own line at the ends of paragraphs. E.g.
   –"
   may end up on its own line, or
   …"
   (I don't mind word widows that are single words – it's just these symbols that look weird on their own.)

- While skimming through the book, check that there isn't a single line of text (a widow or an orphan, as

- discussed earlier) at the top or bottom of a page.

- If you use endnotes or footnotes, check that they are all present and correct.

Back Matter

- All back matter should begin on the right side, so there may be a blank page on the left.

- I usually just have these: About The Author; Other Titles; Author's Notes.

- Check any important web addresses are visible (not just hyperlinks that won't show up in print).

- Is the list of books in Other Titles up to date?

There may be other things to look out for, but this is a starting point. Obviously, where you (or your publisher) have made different choices about things like running heads and page numbers, you'll need to update the list accordingly.

Cover Design

Chapter 6

A Book Cover's Purpose

A book cover is the first thing a reader sees. It needs to be distinctive and appealing enough to grab the reader's attention and tempt them to pick up the book (or click on a link) and look inside, to find out more.

As such, a book cover is for the *reader*, not the author.

It should communicate as precisely as possible the genre, and can hint at other things such as themes, setting, and dominant mood. This can be done partly though words, but also via:

- the images chosen and the style applied to them: the grunge of horror, versus blurs representing speed in thrillers, versus the bright postcard cartooniness of cosy mysteries;

- colour schemes: horror may be in greys, blacks and reds, but a romance might use bright pastel colours;

- fonts chosen: fantasy might have ornate fonts that look like polished steel, versus the battered and spiky fonts implying horror or thriller, or the whimsically curved fonts of light romance. Likewise the fonts for non-fiction are carefully chosen to imply seriousness, stability, fun, or anything else relevant to the topic.

When done well the cover should be like a film poster, where you can glance at it and already have a good idea of what genre the film is from the complex shorthand techniques intended to convey that information to us.

The final design should be clear, with text elements easily readable. A strong cover helps to sell the book, whereas a weak cover will hurt sales.

If you're trade published you'll likely have no say in the cover, but if you publish independently then you'll probably hire someone to design it.

Remember that working with a cover designer is a two-way process. When you give them a description of a scene in minute detail, down to the exact design on the background teacup, and the designer says that's not necessary, and that it is better to give a general idea – they're right. We can't be too precious about it. The cover is meant to pull in new readers, not act as a catalogue of a scene full of details that will mean nothing to the reader that has yet to read the book – and, in fact, will put them off even buying it if the cover is overcomplicated. So yes, the cover may introduce the protagonist or other characters, or some aspect of them, such as the cigarette and handcuffs of a chain-smoking detective, but it needn't reproduce every freckle.

Top Tip: Be Specific About The Subgenre

Subgenres are different specialisms within a main genre, and each subgenre has its own audience. So we know romance is a massive genre. But within that could be "steamy romance" where the book includes sexual encounters, or "chaste romance" where it doesn't. And the book cover can indicate that in many ways.

If I focus on a broad genre I am familiar with – science fiction – there are many subgenres. For example, *space opera* covers might be indicated by a spaceship, and one or more characters wearing futuristic clothes, with a hi-tech or space scene as the background. *Military sci-fi* covers are more likely to show multiple spaceships in combat, or armoured space marines waving their big phallic guns. Whereas a cover showing a run-down (but futuristic) urban city, with a character hooked up to some kind of computer, tells us we're dealing with a *cyberpunk* novel.

Imagery Composition

A book cover's imagery could be based on illustrations, abstract patterns, or photographs. It might show people, scenes, objects, or just be symbolic. There will probably be a uniting colour theme. The imagery should capture the mood and contents of the book, but only in a vague and tempting way. And there should be adequate space for the typography, which is the other key element I'll discuss soon.

Sometimes the imagery (especially in particular genres) can be separated into foreground and background. So the background could be coastline, or clouds, or a blurred cityscape, or hills and a castle; the foreground might be a car on a road, or a person, or a group of people. The foreground is the part that attracts the eye. In many cases a cover will be composed of different images composited together, and merged foreground and background images is one of the most frequently used ways of creating a book cover.

There should always be a clear focal point to draw the reader's eye, whether it be the title, a character, or something else appropriate to the book.

Drinky's Digressions: Original Or Expected?

A book cover designer is not necessarily aiming at beautiful art. Many designers say covers shouldn't be unique; instead, they should follow the expected template of the genre. I have to admit that I only partially agree with that.

Copying a style exactly can lead to bland and derivative repetition. That applies to text and stories as much as book covers. It can be the plague of traditional publishers who make decisions based on what sold well last year, creating me-too bandwagons that are always behind the trend. It's why suddenly zombie books and TV shows and films were everywhere, until you're so sick of them you feel like you're one of the living dead yourself. If I look for a psychological thriller and every book has the same yellow text and visual design, it bores me. When everything is vanilla, how do you choose between things? Instead I'll be drawn to the thing that looks different, interesting, perhaps hoping the writing and plot is also somehow fresh and different rather than same old same old.

As with any guidance, bear in mind that it is all subjective. Any rule adopted by everyone ends up becoming staid and predictable (which includes writing: don't get me started on how many stories the concept of Chekhov's Gun has ruined).

The trick is to reinforce the message of what kind of book it is, whilst also promising something that isn't generic and copycat. It's a fine balance, but you don't have to slavishly copy the way everyone else has done it.

You must never mislead readers. If *misery lit* is presented with a *romance* cover, romance readers will be upset by the dark content. People are rightly annoyed if they expect one thing and are given another, even if both are good quality. The cover must give the right message for the genre. But within that broad area, there are millions of delightful alternatives.

Top Tip: Examples Of Quality

Buy a stack of books in your genre, or get them from a library. Ideally the books should be both recent and successful. Read the books, but also analyse everything about them: the interior and cover design, blurbs, and reviews (what people did or didn't like). This can be really useful in terms of giving you pointers for designing and marketing your own books to the same audience.

Then take it further. I have a folder on my computer called "covers I love". Whenever I see a book cover that strikes me as amazing, or which acts as a perfect example of wonderful font placement, visual effects, colour choices, design, or anything else that gives it impact, I save a copy of it to my folder. There are subfolders for different genres, or text effects and layouts, or even just where the back of the book cover is perfectly designed. When I need inspiration, I browse these exemplary images. I regularly add new ones, and delete those which are starting to look tired or overused, so that my folders always include up to date and inspiring examples.

I recommend doing this, and beginning today.

It helps keep you informed about current practices in your genre. More importantly, it provides a way of communicating desires if you hire a cover designer. You may not know what the fancy curves in the corners of that historical book are called, or the name of the effect that gives the cover a certain appearance, or what the name of a font is: but if you can point to examples then you have an easy way to consolidate and share your thoughts.

"I like the colour scheme of this, the layout of this one, and the font choices of the third: is there any way to combine those general ideas, but replace the sword with an amulet?" If you will be traditionally published, then you could also make suggestions (though the bigger the publisher, the less likely they are to pay attention).

For those reasons, you could keep any images that catch your eye even if they aren't book covers. They all enable conversations about preferences and ideas in visual ways, and can still be useful if you want to brief a cover designer.

Note: this is not copying. It is just using the best as inspiration. It's no different from saying you want to try and write a book with the whimsy of writer A, the wonderful plot twists of author B, and the believable characterisation of author C. Emulating achievements and combining ideas isn't the same as passing off someone else's work as your own (which would be **plagiarism**).

Typography

Typography refers to the text on the cover, and – along with the imagery – is one of the two key elements. Getting typography right is difficult. Often more difficult than working with imagery. When it is done well, typography is not just words filling a space: it indicates mood and content, and is integral to the whole design.

So what text will appear? Some, or all, of those below.

- Title and author. You can use ALL CAPS or Start Case (where all words have the first letter capitalised) – it depends on the font and genre. Some genres even use all lower case. The only overriding concern is that it is large, legible, and well laid out. Less important words may be smaller than the main ones. Never put "by" before the author name.

- A subtitle, if there is one.

- A **tagline** (also called a **strapline**, or **hook**), is a super-short temptation, an intriguing few words to attract the right audience. For example "In space no-one can hear you scream" from Alien immediately suggests sci-fi and horror. I'll discuss taglines below.

- Endorsements / puff quotes / testimonials. More on these below, too.

- If you're a bit pretentious, it might also say "A novel". (Believe me, when it is with all the other fiction in a bookshop or online vendor category, people won't have been confused about whether "The Awakening: A Novel" was a novel or not.)

- **Series statement**. If the book is part of a series, there may be a line indicating that, and what volume it is within the series, e.g. "Lost Solace Book 2". Though, if the books can be read in any order (e.g. a crime series where each book is an unrelated case), the book number may not be relevant, and might even put people off if they think they must read all the previous ones first. Basically, if the order is relevant, always put the number. If the books in the series are standalones, it is fine to include a general statement such as "A Mandy McCloofeinder Detective thriller" or "The Omega Bomb Series".

Text has a hierarchy of prominence, so the book's title will be larger than the subtitle. Usually the title is bigger than the author's name until you become super famous, like Stephen King, and then the author name is the largest element.

Text must be clear. There should never be busy imagery behind text, as it would make it difficult to read. Look at a few books from your shelf to see how the text is often placed in front of image parts that contrast well, and aren't distracting.

The book cover is an ideal place to use ornamental fonts. They should still be readable, but it is less of an issue for a couple of words than it would be if the whole book was written in that font. Other times it can be a normal font with graphical effects (appropriate to the theme) applied: grungy distressed effects on a font for a horror book; extra ornamentation for an ornate fantasy; waviness to imply uncertainty, or water, or ethereal qualities. The font can be plain or textured, such as polished steel on a militaristic sci-fi book. Once text is built into a cover it can be manipulated and individualised like any other graphical element.

You can use serif or sans serif fonts – but look at what other books in your genre do, first. For example, sci-fi books almost always use sans serif fonts for the title (and all in capitals).

Some great book designs only use two fonts: one for the title, which has the most impact, and another font for everything else. Three different fonts at most, to keep the design unified.

Taglines

Taglines are optional, but most books have one on the cover.

Here's an example where the punchy tagline works brilliantly, and immediately makes me ask questions about the book, which is already taking me partway towards a purchase. It's from the cover of *The Sisters* by Claire Douglas. The cover shows the title, and underneath are two pairs of shoes. Below one pair it says: "One lied". Below the other: "One died".

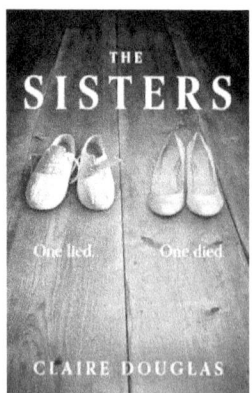

6.1 Cover of The Sisters by Claire Douglas

No nonsense. It is clipped, confident, and stylish. We have juxtaposition and intrigue. What was the lie? Did it cause the death of the other, or was it related to that tragedy? Further, the tagline layout is integral to the whole design of the cover, and its relationship to different parts (the title, the pairs of shoes) which makes everything clear. Even the shoes chosen, in contrasting styles, tell us about the main characters and their differences.

Here's another good one, that achieves a similar effect. On the cover of *The Beautiful Dead* by Belinda Bauer, the tagline tells us:

He might kill her.

She might let him.

The first line brings in threat, and an indication of a protagonist. The second line adds mystery and surprise. What situation could lead someone to let another person kill them? Our brains begin to whir.

6.2 Cover of The Beautiful Dead by Belinda Bauer

As with the first example, breaking the hook over two lines means the second sentence appears after a pause, allowing it to undercut or reinforce the first line. You see, there's a lot of thought about every element of a book cover.

Likewise, the tagline may reinforce the main image cover, or contrast with it. As one example, my first book had the tagline "Some islands don't welcome visitors". That would have one interpretation on a cartoonish cover, implying comedy mishaps, maybe a humorous travel book. However, when the cover shows a blood-spattered man with a chainsaw, the context of the image forces a different interpretation on the tagline. In both cases the way it works with the rest of the cover can help to define genre at a glance.

Note that taglines don't need a full stop at the end.

Drinky's Digressions: Puff Quote Proliferation

Endorsements or "puff quotes" may be found on the front cover, and sometimes on the back cover, too. (Occasionally inside as well. Traditional publishers obviously love them.)

Their value is debatable, but in moderation they aren't a problem. A single one can work nicely on a cover, especially if it tells you something about the genre, treatment or topic, and isn't just generic, "Wow, it was a good book!". Though I still think testimonials are less effective than a good tagline. And when overused they can definitely become irritating to the reader.

I recently came across an extreme example. I won't name the book or publisher, but the book's title was ambiguous, just the name of an animal. The front cover imagery was cartoony pictures of a bird and a mammal. There was no tagline, and I had no idea what the book was about. However, the front cover was packed with the bad kind of puff quotes that tell us a work is "a masterpiece" or "brilliant," but not *why*. So now I knew some newspapers liked it, and another line told me it had won a major literary award (which is no guarantee that I'll like the book, and sometimes actually means the opposite).

"No fear," I thought, turning to the back of the book. "I'll read the blurb!"

I found a blurb made solely of two ambiguous lines that still didn't give me any indication of the type of book it was. Then sixteen more lines of newspaper endorsements. I opened the book, expecting a proper blurb to be inside in some crazy avante garde publishing decision (since this can happen sometimes with hardbacks that have a sleeve, but not usually in paperbacks). But inside there were just three more *pages* of quotes telling me how great the book was. That's it. I still had no idea if the book was a story from the perspective of the named animal, a kid's book, a thriller, misery lit, or horror. The twenty-three puff quotes were all I had to go on. I think this is a perfect example of how not to do a book cover (and interior), where all the basics of helping a reader know what a book is about were thrown away in place of a single-minded shotgun blast of strangers' views.

Ebook Covers

I'll start with these because they are simpler than print book covers, as we'll see.

Ebook covers are a jpg or png file (though if the latter, they shouldn't include transparency). They are always rectangular and in **portrait** orientation (images that are taller than they are wide), rather than **landscape** (wider than they are tall). The ebook cover image is what will appear as a **thumbnail** (small version representing the book) on vendor sales sites such as Amazon, and at full size on e-reader devices and ebook software.

The actual pixel dimensions of the image are not fixed. Over time, services will require higher resolution images, because the screen resolution of digital devices also increases. It's generally better to aim high, then scale down if required. That's a useful guide for all graphics work: you can remove detail from a picture if it isn't needed, but you can't easily add it in. Think of a photo at a low resolution of 800 x 600 pixels. It only takes moments to rescale it to 640 x 480 and will look just as crisp, only smaller. Whereas if you enlarge it to 3200 x 2400 you will have a huge, blurry mess.

Aspect ratio refers to the relationship between the dimensions of one side, and the dimensions of another; width and height. We're used to seeing it when discussing screens on TVs, monitors and phones. 16:9, for example, means that for every 16 pixels along the horizontal edge, there will be 9 pixels on the vertical edge (which gives us a wider landscape orientation). An aspect ratio of 1:1 would be a square (as used on audiobook covers, where 3000 x 3000 is the current standard).

Aspect ratio is not the same as resolution, or the number of dots in an image. If an image is 160 x 90 pixels then it has an aspect ratio of 16:9. If the image is 1600 x 900, it also has an aspect ratio of 16:9, but a hundred times more pixels. So aspect ratio governs only the shape and proportions, not the end resolution.

Every ebook reader has its own screen size, resolution, and aspect ratio. But it would be a pain to have to create multiple book covers, one for every device. So designers generally settle on an aspect ratio and pixel size that most closely fits the greatest range of services. Where it isn't a perfect fit the image might become slightly stretched or have a tiny border applied, but neither is a problem, and most people won't even notice. If in doubt, aim at a tall rectangle with roughly a 2:3 ratio (e.g. 1700 x 2550 pixels).

Conveniently, that's similar to the proportions of a 5.5 x 8.5 printed book cover.

Since the ebook cover may be displayed as a tiny thumbnail, always check that your cover is still clear, even at a small size. Similarly, cover art with light backgrounds can seem to disappear against a white background, e.g. on a vendor site which displays the cover thumbnail. If you have this kind of cover then a narrow (2-4 pixel) grey border helps define the cover boundaries on the screen.

Print Book Covers

Print books have additional elements which don't apply to ebooks: a rear cover and spine. If the front cover is the eye-catching part, then the back is the informative part. It includes the book description, a barcode (in the bottom third), and may also include things such as genre information, price, publisher, (brief!) author details, and maybe endorsement quotes.

The print book cover will generally be a pdf file, and will be sent to the printers along with a separate pdf containing the book's interior.

If you take a printed book, open it out and look at the cover, you'll see that on the left is the back cover; then there is the narrow area of the spine; then the front cover on the right. This is called the **cover spread**, or **full cover**. That's exactly how a pdf for a print cover is laid out. You can see the three parts joined together in this image of the wraparound cover:

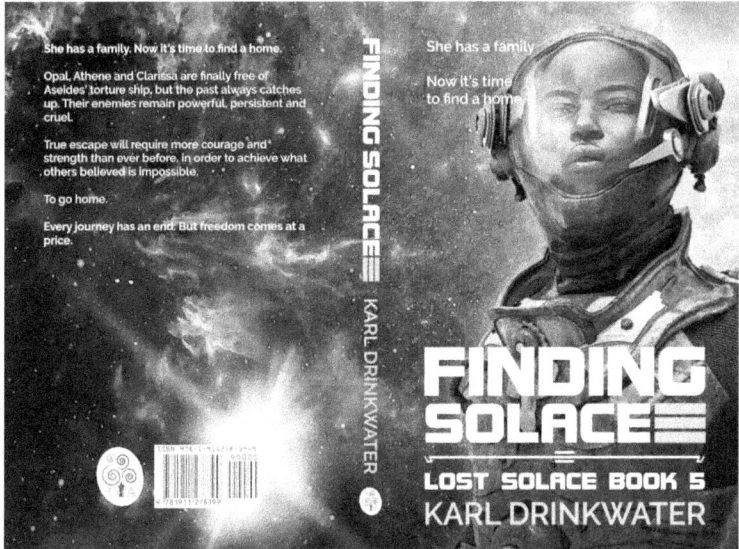

6.3 Spread of a paperback cover

Usually there will be a master file for the ebook cover (from which the jpg or png can be exported) and a separate master file for the print book cover (from which the .pdf can be exported). An alternative is the system I use when I design book covers. I use a single master file, with dimensions that work for both types of cover. I can export the full print wraparound cover, but also perfectly crop the front cover element, which is used as the ebook cover.

Note that electronic screens define colours using the RGB (Red Green Blue) additive colour model.[66] Printing uses the less vibrant CMYK (Cyan Magenta Yellow Key) subtractive colour model.[67] Some people export a CMYK pdf for the print book cover, but I have always used RGB for everything, and not had any issues.

I categorise book covers two ways. One is the style where a single cover image wraps around the front, back and spine, usually with less busy areas which provide good contrast for the text elements. The other style is where the front cover is basically the ebook cover, and the spine and back are not part of a continuous image. The former is more complicated to do but unifies the cover and is much more attractive. The latter can look like a budget cover. I see the two types in both traditional publishing and independent publishing.

When a cover is being created, the cover designer should record all the steps taken, to make sure elements are replicated consistently for a series or brand. Font type and sizes, colophon and ISBN placement, title and author placement, colour schemes, filters applied and so on. Using guides and positioning tools, it is possible to place elements with pixel-perfect accuracy.

The most common paperback binding is called **perfect bound**, where pages are folded, stacked and glued to a wraparound cover. The cover image is printed straight on to the card that will form the cover.

But there are also hardback books, which have two main types of cover.

A **casebound hardback** (or **case laminate**) is where the cover is laminated cardboard (the **case**) rather than thick paper, so is more substantial. Instead of printing onto the board, the cover is printed onto paper and then stuck to the case. The image is folded over the board to the inside, then plain paper stuck down to cover the joins. When designing these covers they will have extra image areas to account for the folding over.

The other type of hardback has a **dust jacket** (also known as a **book jacket**) which folds over either a casebound cover, or one with a plain cloth finish. This removable wraparound dust jacket has flaps to hold it in place – again, this has larger dimensions than a normal paperback cover and is much wider to account for the folding areas, so needs to be designed appropriately. Dust jacket flaps can be used as a place for information such as book descriptions or an author bio.

Lastly, materials and finishes are relevant. A book could have a **matt** cover (non-shiny) or **gloss** (shiny). Matt is most common in fiction, gloss in non-fiction. The cover may have raised or indented areas you can feel (embossed if raised, debossed if sunken), or additional coatings such as metallic foil effects or glitter (though they have recycling implications, as we'll see in Chapter 8, in the section on The Environment).

Spine Considerations For Printed Books

The spine is always the narrowest element of the cover. Since bookshops and libraries may put the books on shelves spine-out to save space, this might be the only part that a potential reader sees, so it should be clear. It will have the book's title, the author name (or just their surname), then the publisher colophon or initials. The text will be rotated ninety degrees clockwise to fit it on, so people have to tilt their heads to the right to read it. Note that if the book is thin, with not many pages (which can apply to some novellas) there might not be enough room to display any spine text.

Don't forget about the spine when working out the size of the cover spreads. As we saw in the previous chapter, books are printed at 300 DPI. That applies to both the print interior, and the book covers. On a computer, in resolution terms, a dot is the equivalent of a pixel (px). The size in inches is determined by the trim size chosen of the book (discussed in Chapter 5); and the trim size, combined with knowing it will be printed at 300 DPI, easily lets us work out the resolution for the front and back cover elements.

An example will help illustrate this.

If a book's trim size is the fairly standard 5.5 inches wide and 8.5 inches high, then by applying the sum from the previous chapter's Images section, we know the resolution of the front cover element must be:

5.5 x 300 = 1650 px in width

8.5 x 300 = 2550 px in height

We know the cover has a back as well as a front, so let's double the width, to get an image size of 3300 x 2550. (The height doesn't change.)

But that isn't the final resolution, because we've missed out the spine.

The spine is tricky in terms of cover design because it sits *between* the front and back covers. Unlike an outer edge which is more easily tweakable, any change to the spine area will move all the elements of the front and back covers too.

The spine's width is determined by the number of pages in a book, multiplied by the thickness of the paper. (And as we know, the number of pages is determined by the word count in conjunction with design choices such as font and font size, spacing, and margins.) This is why the final print book cover cannot be finished until the interior of the book is formatted so that we know the final page count. Up until that point an estimate has to be used, which will be modified later.

Although it is possible to calculate the spine width manually once you have all the information, it isn't usually necessary. The printer may well provide a template for the designer, with the correct spine size and margins, showing which areas are safe to print, and which borders might get cut off in the printing process (*bleed areas*). No vital information should be placed in those regions.

Here is an example of a template for a book cover. This one was generated by BookVault.

6.4 Print cover template

The final dimensions for one of my standard length books might be 3553 x 2628; a novella with a narrow spine might be 3445 x 2628. The two books are the same height (2628 pixels), but the different spine thicknesses is what makes the difference to the final image widths.

The centrality of the spine is why you can't make big changes to a book's interior that will affect the number of pages without also modifying the cover file to accommodate the increase or reduction, by extending or shrinking the spine width. And because the spine is in the middle of the image, it has knock-on effects on all the other cover elements, which then need repositioning. As you can imagine, this is not a trivial task.

A change of up to ten pages and you can probably get away with using the same cover file, but beyond that it will need alteration.

ISBNs And Barcodes

Most (but not all) books have ISBNs. An **ISBN (International Standard Book Number)** is a unique product number that identifies a *title* and a *format* in the distribution chain. Lost Solace has an ISBN for the paperback, one for the hardback (a different format), one for the ebook, and one for the audiobook. If there was a large print edition, that would require another ISBN.

If you know the ISBN and present it to a librarian or bookshop, they will be able to look up the details and order a copy of the book. An ISBN is an unambiguous identifier, whereas the author and title may lead to a wide range of results, and it may not be clear which edition or format is required.

The numbers in an ISBN aren't random: they encode useful information. It's a secret power of publishers and librarians to be able to read and comprehend it.

Here's the thirteen digit ISBN for the Lost Solace paperback: 978-1-911278-11-5. Sometimes you'll see ISBNs without hyphens as they aren't necessary, but they are a handy way of separating the meaning of each block of numbers.

- 978: just a prefix showing that the ISBN refers to a book (it may be 978 or 979)

- 1: indicates the country or language. 1 = English language

- 911278: a code unique to the publisher or imprint. So this number always indicates Organic Apocalypse.

- 11: a unique identifier for the particular title, format and edition. So this was the eleventh ISBN used by Organic Apocalypse, and applied to the paperback of Lost Solace, first edition.

- 5: the check digit – a final single number that confirms the ISBN is formulated properly (i.e. not mistyped) when a calculation is applied. If I mistyped any of the numbers, the check digit would indicate an error had occurred.

A printed book has a barcode on the back. That is just the ISBN in a form that a digital scanner can read. The ISBN block also includes the ISBN in a form a human can read, in case they need to type it in or write it down. Many publishing and distribution companies provide a template which has the correct ISBN barcode already on it, or they indicate where it should be placed. Beware of companies that try to charge you extra for something so simple as a barcode of your ISBN.

An option with barcodes is whether to include the book's price in the barcode or not. In theory it can be a convenience, so that when the barcode is scanned in a shop it identifies both the item and its price. However, it can also cause problems if the price ever changes: then there would need to be a new barcode and new cover containing the up-to-date price. It can also be problematic if the bookshop wants to charge a lower price, for example selling off remaining copies cheaper, rather than return them: then they have to put stickers over the barcodes. As such, I recommend *not* including prices in book barcodes.

Drinky's Digressions: When Do I Need A (New) ISBN?

If a book is only being printed for a few people, and isn't being distributed through bookshops and libraries, then it doesn't need an ISBN at all. Some independent authors distribute solely through Amazon, as we'll see later: they often don't bother with ISBNs either, and just use the Amazon-assigned ASIN (internal Amazon stock code). But if a book is to enter the main worldwide distribution chain, it definitely needs an ISBN.

Once an ISBN has been assigned, it is permanently attached to that title and format. If a book's title changes, that requires a new ISBN. If there was a major revision, that would require a new ISBN. If the binding or trim size changed, that would require a new ISBN. And a translation would require its own ISBN. Basically, the ISBN points to a specific edition, and someone should get the exact one they order. But small changes to content don't need a new ISBN. And nor does a change of cover or blurb.

Premade Versus Custom Covers

Independent authors usually commission a cover specifically for their book. Hiring a professional costs, but the results can be worth it.

Look at the cover designer's portfolio to assess the variety of their work, what moods and genres they can create covers in, and how much the imagery grabs you. And some designers are surprisingly affordable, such as GetCovers.[68]

But if you are starting out, or it's a minor release, or you only ever plan to do a couple of books, it can be an option (and a lot cheaper) to buy a **premade cover**. This is where someone's come up with a design, imagery and placeholder text. You buy the premade and they change the text to be your book's title, your author name, your tagline and so on. Then the book cover is removed from sale so no one else can buy it. (Of course, that doesn't mean component images from stock photography and graphic sites won't be seen on other books – see my digression on Stock Repetition later on.)

If you want to try premades, choose a site with high-quality covers, which has something fitting the spirit of your work. Premades are usually not a good option for a series, where you want consistency. If you do consider a premade cover but think the book might become a series, it is worth asking the designer if they would be willing to work on future books in the series, to the same template, in order to create a series brand.

Some possibilities (not recommendations, just examples of what is available): BookCovers.com;[69] BookCoverZone;[70] DarnGoodCovers;[71] EbookLaunch;[72] GetPremades;[73] GoOnWrite;[74] PaperAndSage.[75]

Whoever you use, ideally you will own the copyright on the final cover in exchange for your payment, so that you can do what you want with it (within legal limits). This is always worth clarifying, as some designers will work on the assumption that *they* own the copyright, even after you've paid them to do the work. That may mean you can't make changes to it without returning to them – and paying them again. And you can't have someone else do sequel covers in the same design. Assigning the rights to you doesn't stop the cover designer from including the book cover in their portfolio, with your permission.

Regardless of whatever agreement you make about who *owns* the copyright, remember to credit the designer on the copyright page. Something like "Cover design by Drew Pics". Most cover designers will have a preferred wording, and probably ask for a link to their website after their name. That's standard practice, and worth doing as part of good etiquette. Likewise, if they don't want a link, then respect their wishes. Some designers also try and put their details onto the back cover, but really the copyright page is the correct place, since that's why it exists. Avoid clutter on the cover, especially with advertising for the designer which has no relevance to the readers.

Top Tip: Source Files

If you hire someone to design your cover then always ask about source files at the start. These are the basic cover files, with image and text layers separate, for whatever software was used to design the cover.

This can be a lifesaver if your original cover designer stops doing design work ... dies ... disappears ... loses their backups ... gets abducted by aliens ... or simply stops replying. At least you would still be able to hire someone else to make minor alterations such as a change in the tagline or blurb, or the addition of an award badge or high-profile quote. Likewise, if a new artist has to take over and do sequels in the same style, it is much easier for them to create further designs that fit thematically if they have access to the original cover, so they can exactly match fonts, layout and colour schemes, keeping branding consistent. The source file can even be useful as a basis for creating promotional images for the book.

Some cover designers will flatly refuse, citing licensing issues, or because they want to be paid for future changes. The latter is more often the true reason, since the cover is likely to be a composite of stock images; as long as the image layer is "flattened", they are not passing on the separate images they have licensed, but a new creation. Likewise they can provide links to the fonts so they can be downloaded or purchased – a requirement if the text is editable. By editable I mean the text can be changed, rather than fixed so that it becomes an image, when it is called *rasterised*.

Some cover designers might provide the files but charge for them. Others might provide them for free, as a part of the cover design service. Personally, if a cover artist wants to charge an extortionate fee for these source files, or claims it is all too complicated, I go elsewhere.

Whenever I have designed covers for anyone, I always give them that two-layer source file for free, and details of the fonts and source images so they can license copies for themselves. That's all perfectly legal. In fact, the original image and font creators may end up being paid twice, which is a bonus for them.

Creating Your Own Book Covers

This only applies if you're an independent author. It can be tempting to want to make your own covers to save on money, but bear in mind a cover can make or break a book. It isn't easy to create a professional cover that matches what readers of that genre expect. It's not even worth considering unless you have one or more of the following.

- Some artistic talent or background.

- Experience with digital graphics software and technical considerations such as file formats.

- Design knowledge. Composition, fonts, typography, and use of colour, are all key things – and difficult to get right.

- An understanding of the legal and copyright issues involved, so that you make sure you only use images you have licensed, created, or are authorised to use.

- The ability to spare time from writing in order to create an amazing cover, or learn the skills you lack.

There are books, courses and videos dedicated to the topic of good visual design, that will explain concepts such as rules of thirds, contrast, light and shade, hot and cold colour schemes, leading the eye, use of space and so on. They will give a far better grounding in design topics than I could. Likewise I'm not going to teach you how to use graphics software, and the principles of masks, layer hierarchies, filters, and overlay modes. Again, it's a massive topic, and much of how you'll do things will depend on the software you use. For example, many professional designers use Adobe Photoshop, whereas I find it clunky and overpriced. I much prefer the free and cross-platform software Gimp,[76] which makes it easy to edit images and composite them together. Luckily, many concepts from one piece of software (such as explanations of colour spaces, or brushes, or layer modes) are transferable to other software with a bit of experience and experimentation. And if that's too much, some people praise Canva[77] as a solution.

Where To Get Content

These are a few starting points, and not necessarily recommendations. Some are free, some require payment and licensing. Although this chapter is about cover design, many of these sites are useful for other types of author-related creative content, such as blog posts, or social media posts and banners. They are also fun sites to explore when looking for inspiration.

Fonts:

- Google Fonts[78] (free)
- DaFont[79] (many free)
- Fontspace[80] (free)
- Font Squirrel[81] (free) (which includes a handy font identifier)[82]
- Font Bundles[83] (paid)

Stock photos:

- Pixabay[84] (free)
- Gratisography[85] (free)
- Unsplash[86] (free)
- Pexels[87] (free)
- New Old Stock[88] (free) – vintage photos from archives
- Deposit Photos[89] (paid)
- Dreamstime[90] (paid)
- Shutterstock[91] (paid) – not great for occasional users,

since they delete unused credits after a while

Also consider taking your own photos, which is easy and much lower risk, depending on the subject. I often base my covers on computer graphics I create myself: 3D renders of characters and scenes, so that no one else has exactly the same base images.

Clip art:

- Openclipart[92] (free)

For all types of content in one place (fonts, graphic overlays, images etc):

- Creative Market[93] (paid)

- Design Bundles[94] (paid)

- The Hungry Jpeg[95] (paid)

- Creative Fabrica[96] (paid)

- If you want to re-use things then Creative Commons is one option. The Creative Commons search[97] lets you search for different types of media.

Licensing

Always check permissions! Many of the sites I have linked to offer content that is free as in "no money" and also free as in "no restrictions" (or fewer restrictions) on use. Although the quality of images may not be as consistently high as those on professional stock sites, I have often been impressed with the free ones available.

Not every image on the sites is available for every use, though. Here we get into the issue of **licences** – the rules governing what the photographer or creator allows you to do with their work. Always look at the small print and check in case the images are free for personal use (e.g. decorating a blog post), but not for commercial uses (such as a book cover). Most sites will make the licensing information and permissions clear. Do read this, and abide by it – it's not worth breaking the law for the sake of a minute checking what you can do with an image. If in doubt, go elsewhere. And be aware that even on the same site, different items might have different restrictions. I usually make a screenshot of the licence and save it in a subfolder along with the web address, for future protection.

Sites may well have their own licences, but many use Creative Commons,[98] which has a variety of licences with different meanings. There's also public domain and royalty-free works. Even Creative Commons includes a public domain licence where the creator surrenders all rights in the work, so you can use it for any (legal) purpose.

However, all sites, free or paid, come with some risk. One image-related scam is to use a fake account to seed photos on stock photo sites. Then, when the photos are used in good faith, the scammer can send threatening letters claiming extortionate fees to avoid legal action. Even if you buy the photo from a stock site it doesn't mean you are safe – for example the basic Shutterstock licence only agrees to cover you up to $10,000,[99] which could be a lot less than the courts might make you pay – and that $10,000 figure was the same when I last checked in 2016, whereas the costs of everything have gone up massively since then. Current copyright law means that even when you are sensible, you can still get caught out by copyright trolls.

Drinky's Digressions: Stock Repetition

One of the dangers of using stock photos is that they can be sold multiple times. If it is a good image, chances are that someone else will have used it. Stock photo sites keep selling the same photo without telling you how many times it has already been sold, so they make this problem much more common than authors would like.

As a result, spotting book covers that used the same base images, even though they might be treated differently, has become a kind of hobby for some people. Here are some examples from IndieBookLauncher[100] and blackplume.[101]

I first noticed this after reading *Dark Echo* by F.G. Cottam, then spotting two other books using the same core image. The three were published by Hodder, Penguin, and Harper, respectively. This is obviously an issue for all publishers, including big trade publishers. It's also why good cover designers always make an effort to check if stock imagery has already been used much (e.g. by doing reverse image searches).

The authors probably had no say in the covers, since it is a rarity in trade publishing for the author to be involved with those decisions. The cover is created by a design team based on genre expectations, trying to make the book look like others that have sold well. And so we see a dark echo of covers past.

Top Tip: Keep Covers Updated

If your book cover ever changes at a later date – which is common when refreshing an author's backlist – it may need updating in many places where the cover is shown. If you're trade published then your publisher will deal with most of that, but not all – for example, you may have to update the cover on your website and places like Goodreads or BookBub. If you are an independent author you will also need to update the cover with your distributors (print, ebook and audio, as appropriate).

I list some places where you might need to update the cover in the next chapter's tips, "Keep Blurbs Updated".

Metadata

Chapter 7

Because of my librarian past, the word metadata means a lot to me. Basically it is *data used to describe things*, in order to make it easier to find the relevant item later. A common example is emails, which include metadata about who sent them, and the time of sending.

As I explained in Chapter 1, metadata in our context is bibliographic information (words and numbers) regarding your book. A book's title, author, and date of publication are examples of book metadata. The back of the title page in a printed book is basically just a long list of bibliographic metadata.

Some of it enables readers to find you and your work: for example, when they type keywords into a search engine, including those for online bookshops. Other parts enable bookshops and online stores to correctly categorise your book.

Sometimes a book's title is ambiguous and gives little away. But the metadata – book description, genre/category, and keywords – would clarify the book's contents in great detail. When someone searches for the kind of book they are interested in, the search engine will look at all this metadata and find things that seem relevant. So metadata is important for making a book *discoverable*. To readers. Ideally, the *right* readers, your target audience.

So, at some point in the publication process, someone needs to make decisions on this kind of metadata, since it ties in to distribution and marketing.

Keeping Track Of It

You should record your book's metadata, whether you are traditionally published or an independent author. It's useful for marketing, interviews, administration, and many other purposes where you want to quickly check an ISBN, blurb, or publication date. And that becomes even more vital once you've written a number of books.

There are decisions to make.

- Firstly, what software will you use? A basic word-processed document is fine, with headings for each data type. Or, if you prefer spreadsheets, use one of those to store all the information. They can tabulate word-based data as well as numerical data. You could even use a database, if you are familiar with those.

- Secondly, will you store the metadata for all your books in one document, or in separate ones, with one document per book (or series)? The former system makes it easier to compare data between books, but the second can be less cluttered. If you use spreadsheets then all the data for every book could go in a single sheet, with each book on a separate row, and columns for each type of metadata. Or each book could go on a separate sheet within the document.

- Finally, what metadata will you record? I'm going to cover the main options in this chapter.

As with all these things, it's up to you what system fits best with the way you work and think, and exactly what you record. I'm just here to provide options.

Now let's take a dive into the world of book metadata you might record in your document.

Primary Metadata Types

Title

The title of the book is a key element to tie other data to. Its subtitle is another part of the metadata.

Format

Ebook, audiobook, printed book. If printed then there are other things to record. Is it a paperback or hardback? What is the trim size? What is the paper type? I often just record the colour e.g. cream or white, but you could include details of paper quality and weight. It is also useful to record the cover finish: matt or gloss.

Series

If relevant, record what number the book is in that series, e.g. Lost Solace Book 5.

Keywords

A list of **keywords** (sometimes called **tags**) related to the title. They can reinforce the genre or niche the book fits into. Usually a comma or semicolon is used to separate keywords.

Keywords can be single words, or they can be phrases. This is important, because the key phrase "sugar daddy" means something totally different to the separate keywords "sugar" and "daddy". Further, putting them together as a phrase means a search engine can use synonyms – "Oh, the customers searched for books about sugar daddies, I'll also display books that include rich older men having affairs with younger women".

How many keywords do you need? The list won't be endless: choose the seven best. This forces you to focus on the key fingerprint elements, rather than spamming with every possible keyword. As every writer should know, targeted and specific is more powerful than word soup.

I put mine in priority order, separated by semicolons. E.g. for Lost Solace the current keywords are:

tough female protagonist; space opera; artificial intelligence; first contact; aliens; suspense; spaceships

The keywords chosen may be refined and change over time.

Keywords are used in setting up a title for distribution, as it helps to guide vendors as to what genre or subject categories the book will go in. As such, they are more than just a piece of metadata: they can be the foundation for your marketing ideas, imagery, advertising campaigns that target keywords, and design choices. Some people use them as the foundation of their blurbs, making sure the keywords are sprinkled throughout as a way of reinforcing them. I'll talk more about blurbs soon.

Top Tip: Keyword Considerations

I focus on these categorisations when generating my first list of keywords.

- Describing the main character: divorced dad, superspy, strong female lead, geeky character, military protagonist, plucky young heroine, underdog hero.
- The places where the story is set: Wales, islands, rural,

Manchester, urban.

- The time period: far future, prehistoric, Renaissance, Victorian, contemporary.

- The mood or tone: horror, feel-good, funny, romantic, nostalgic, mourning, suspenseful, dark, life-affirming, practical, wholesome, creepy, dystopian.

- Themes and major topics: revenge, coming of age, xenophobia, first love, survival, families, love, music, physics, relationships, big decisions.

- The subgenre: folk horror, alien invasion, first contact, urban legends, space opera, military sci-fi, short stories, evil scientists, deep sea horror.

- Or even just describe other things that play an important part in the book: monsters, art, supernatural, scary stories, artificial intelligence, aliens, spaceships, chess, kidnap, robots.

It helps to think like a reader. What might they want to feel, or search for? Test those keywords in Amazon's book search, or a search engine, or other book sites, and see if they bring up books like yours. The suggested terms offered by the site can be useful additions or refinements, based on what other people have searched for.

Some final do's and don'ts:

- Keywords and key phrases should be *specific*. Don't use vague ones like "fiction".

- If you've used keywords in your title or subtitle you don't need to repeat them in the keywords fields.

- Don't refer to other authors (or their books or series) in your keywords – that can get you in trouble for being misleading.

- Don't bother with variant spellings or phrasings. If you have artificial intelligence as a key phrase, don't waste others on AI, A.I., and artificial intelligences – just stick to one version.

Subject Categories

Categorisation systems exist to tell book sellers, librarians and distributors what categories (and subcategories) a book belongs to, based on content and subject matter. A category is the same as the genre (fiction) or topic (non-fiction).

If you are an independent author you'll have to specify categories during the distribution phase of publishing. They can significantly enhance your title's visibility and discoverability, since it determines where a book is placed (physical shelves in a library or bookshop; subject categories for online stores). You want people who go looking for books in that category to find your wonderful tome easily.

BISAC (Book Industry Standards and Communications) is perhaps the most-used of the subject heading systems. You can browse the full list of categories[102] – there are more than 4,500 of them, comprehensively covering a vast range of subjects. Or, specifically for fiction.[103]

I always record the top three BISAC categories. Here's an example of what they look like. First is the nine character BISAC codes, then the category and subcategories it relates to:

FIC027020 FICTION / Romance / Contemporary

FIC028000 FICTION / Dystopian

FIC028030 FICTION / Science Fiction / Space Opera

As with keywords, it is best to be as specific as possible. There are broad headings such as "fiction" that can be used, but they are not as good as drilling down the hierarchy. So, if a book is space opera, it is better to use

FICTION / Science Fiction / Space Opera

than just

FICTION / Science Fiction

Choosing the correct categories enables you to target specific niche markets effectively.

There are other subject schemes. For example, IngramSpark allows additional Thema subjects. Thema is similar to BISAC in that it divides topics up and assigns codes, but it uses a three letter system (rather than nine characters). We've already seen how space opera looks as a BISAC category, but in Thema it would be:

FLS – Science fiction: Space opera

You can browse all the Thema subjects, too.[104]

Whatever schemes and categories you use, record them all in your metadata.

Blurb

As I explained in Chapter 1, I use **blurb** to mean the brief **book description** that goes on the back of a paperback book, or as an ebook description in an online store.

It's handy to keep a record of that book description in your metadata document, formatted exactly as it should be, including any use of bold or italics.

Top Tip: Writing A Compelling Blurb

A blurb aims to sell the emotion and story, to make it irresistible to the kind of reader who loves that genre. A good blurb tells us a number of things, as concisely as possible.

- The main character(s). A named person helps the reader to care. Generally only focus on the primary character (or two characters in some books, such as a romance).

- What do they want, and what is stopping them getting it? What difficult choice do they face, and what is at stake if they fail? This is what makes the reader want to know more, as a teaser for the storyline. There must be conflict to create tension.

- The setting (place, time period). This helps to attract the right reader and put off people who won't enjoy it – fans of eighteenth century historical novels are different from fans of future dystopias.

- Clues to the type of book it is (genre, mood, tone). These are further attempts to define the experience being offered, to attract the right audience, and put off the wrong ones (see Ranganathan digression in Chapter 3).

Give readers a sense of what they can expect from the book, capturing its tone and spirit. As such, I recommend writing it in the same voice and style in which the book is written. Funny, angry, bemused, acidic. The blurb's voice should match the book's, or the voice of the main character. If the book's narrator is witty and sarcastic, the blurb should be witty and sarcastic. Is the book an ominous and richly worded gothic mystery? Again, the blurb should capture that voice. A blurb that captures the speech patterns, life and flavour of a character can be particularly striking.

A blurb done in this way is a good illustration of *showing*, not *telling*. An example might be a book with a comical protagonist who is a cheesy and crap superhero vigilante. A blurb based only on *telling* might have the flat and generic:

"Underpant Man must find the villain and clear his name. Follow his exciting and wacky adventures in this humorous novel."

But it could be much better to *show* the book's tone in the blurb:

"Holy Justice! Underpant Man is going to track down his nemesis if it's the last thing he does (it may well be), and then it will be Kapow! time for sure."

I should add that writing a blurb in character is a lot more fun to do, as well.

Most blurbs are written in the third person, present tense: "John Bigwhack is a golfer with a dark secret". It's a direct way of communicating the key information. However, like any rule, it can be broken if the end result works. So, for one of my books that is written in first person with a strong voice, I decided to write the blurb that way as well, to better indicate the tone of the book:

> If you're reading this: HELP! I've been kidnapped.
>
> Me and my big sister stayed together after our parents died. We weren't bothering anybody. But some mean government agents came anyway, and split us up.

Now I'm a prisoner on this space ship. The agents won't even say where we're going.

I hate them.

And things have started to get a bit weird. Null-space is supposed to be empty, but when I look out of the skywindows I can see … something. Out there. And I think it wants to get in here. With us.

My name is Clarissa. I am ten years old.

And they will all be sorry when my big sister comes to rescue me.

My thoughts above all apply to fiction, but non-fiction needs a blurb as well. Although the process is different, we still need to indicate what the book is about, and tempt the (right) person to read on. In this case you may be identifying a problem the reader (rather than protagonist) faces, and how the book will help to solve it. It is fine to use bullet points in a non-fiction blurb, describing elements of what the book will offer the reader. You could end with a picture of what the reader's life will be like after reading the book and implementing the book's suggestions.

Some additional tips for all blurbs:

- Use paragraphs. Space is your friend and helps to break the blurb into bite-size pieces. A single block of text can be off-putting.

- Likewise, use short, punchy sentences (or even sentence fragments).

- Keep it short. Treat it like poetry, where every word earns its place. I've seen authors recommend 200-250 words. I favour the shorter end of the spectrum: 140 words maximum, ideally aiming at below 100. We're not telling a story, just providing a teaser of the core conflict, to help the reader decide if the book is for them or not.

- Blurbs often open with a hook in bold, a sort of killer headline to grab attention. Something engaging, clever, or fresh. Sometimes the cover tagline is repeated at the start of the blurb as the hook if it is a good one (and if it's not a good one, why not?)

- If you include a comp at the end, that may also be in bold. What's a comp? I'll discuss that soon.

- Avoid cliches like the plague. [sic]

- Look at the blurbs of successful books in your genre – found on your bookshelves, or in bookshops and libraries – to see what good blurbs look like. Which ones make you want to read the book, and why?

- If the book wins a major award or is nominated, consider putting that in the blurb.

- Feel free to seek feedback on your blurbs, especially from fans of your work.

Top Tip: Keep Blurbs Updated

If the blurb ever changes at a later date – more likely for independent authors, who can improve things iteratively – then consider updating it wherever it appears. For a minor change of two words I would upload the new blurb metadata to a distributor, but I wouldn't update the paperback cover; whereas for a complete rewrite I would do both.

Here are some possible places where the blurb appears.

- Back of the paperback cover.

- Distributors and places where it is sold such as Draft2Digital, Gumroad, IngramSpark, Audible/ACX.

- Book details on sites like Goodreads, Amazon Author Central, BookBub Partners, and Books2Read.

- Your website, on pages about that book.

- Any book back matter which includes the blurb, for example an "also by" or "read next" page in another title.

Note that if ever the book cover gets updated, you'll need to update it at places similar to those in the list above.

One Liners / Ad Copy

The blurb looks good on the back of a book, but even if you've created a concise and compelling one of under a hundred and forty words, it is still far too long for most advertising purposes. So it is handy to keep much shorter descriptions of the book, in various lengths and styles, from a few words up to one liners, and then versions of two to three sentences. These are useful for different purposes, such as adverts or social media posts. I even pull them from reviews occasionally, if someone summarises the book really well. Here are a few short description examples from Lost Solace:

- A desperate woman. A broken AI. A mysterious spaceship. Lost Solace.

- Space … the fearful frontier.

- What do you get if you cross Aliens, Event Horizon, and Pandorum? Lost Solace.

- A female-centred science fiction space adventure, with lots of action, creepy mystery, and satisfying emotional depth.

They can be longer than that, but as with taglines, it is good to be as concise as possible.

Comps

Comps, or **comparable works**, are other books, series or authors that might be useful comparisons for your work. They are particularly valuable for targeted advertising and general marketing.

If you query agents or publishers, they will be interested in what comps you think exist for your book: ideally recent titles (the last few years), and ones that are at least fairly well known or sold well. This is because they want to assess the potential audience for the work.

One method I use to find them is to browse "also boughts" for my books: when vendor sites provide recommendations of similar authors based on what previous customers purchased. For example, on Amazon you can navigate to an author's page and look for the "Customers Also Bought Items By" section in the sidebar. This is most useful for published authors (we can look at our own pages and books), but it can also be a way for new writers to broaden their list of possible comp authors to investigate.

Other comps come from reviews, where people will compare my book to some other title or author they've read. That's only useful to already-published authors, but is one good reason to look at your reviews (I'll provide other motivations later).

Drinky's Digressions: When Comps Turn Bad

Comps are useful data for authors to record in their private metadata, but we sometimes see comparisons more overtly, such as in the blurb or tagline of a book. They often take the format "If you like Hunger Games then you will love this!", "For fans of Harry Potter!" or "Welcome to the new Stephen King!" It's a tactic used by big trade publishers, and independent authors. The underlying thought is that it's a valuable marketing tool to help readers work out if a book might be for them.

The problem with that kind of comp, whether applied to books, computer games, or films, is that they're often misleading, apart from the most superficial similarity. For example, perhaps the thing I liked about the original doesn't apply at all to the copy. Maybe I loved the original for the quality of the writing, not the dystopian plot; maybe I loved one of the characters and what they said, not the suspense element; and another book for the clever plotting, not the setting. It's why recommendation engines fail so often.

Readers can be put off by comparing a book to other (more famous) works or authors if it looks like a lazy or desperate marketing gimmick. "Do they need someone else's fame and prestige to glorify their own work? Why can't it hold itself up?" There's also the danger of looking derivative. If a reader wants fresh experiences, they may not want to read a book that could be a poor imitation of somebody else's.

In particular, naming other authors as comps might be seen as bad etiquette, irking the named author and possibly leading to vendors penalising your book. I remember the first time I found a book referring to me as a comp: their blurb ended with "Perfect for fans of Jonathan Maberry, Stephen Leather, Larry Correia, Karl Drinkwater, Guy N. Smith, and F. Paul Wilson." Quite a hodgepodge of authors there, who actually don't have much in common. It didn't annoy me, but it did make me question how many readers might end up confused about whether the book was of interest to them or not.

For all those reasons I think the best blurbs skip comps altogether and sell a book on its own merits. Always go back to the core elements: what is the gist of the story, what is its genre and style, what makes it worth reading?

If you do decide to use comps, then skim reviews for your book, and see what fans said in their own comparisons. That is likely to be more accurate than fantasising that your book is the next Hunger Games/Handmaid's Tale/Dune. Likewise, be specific about the *way* your book is a comp, what aspect it captures. That's less likely to lead to disappointment when the readers interpret the comp in a way you didn't intend (and remember that disappointment leads to bad reviews).

An even better approach is – instead of comparing your work to other specific books, authors or series – to compare according to *tropes*. That sidesteps all the negatives discussed above, whilst keeping the positives. So that might mean "Ideal for fans of claustrophobic, dark and dangerous subterranean tales!" rather than "For fans of Metro 2033!"; ditto "Full of uncanny alien weirdness!" rather than "Just like VanderMeer's Annihilation!" Tropes say more about the *feel* of the book, and its concepts, and both are things readers search for. It's why many authors incorporate keywords into the blurb.

If you do use comps in a blurb then don't put them at the start, where they are most likely to cause irritation. By putting them at the end instead, they act more as an easily-skipped final tempter if the reader was wavering.

Editorial Reviews

Editorial reviews are truncated quotes from glowing reviews used as a form of endorsement. In most cases, these will only begin to appear *after* publication.

Editorial reviews are not the same as generic consumer reviews from sites that sell books such as Amazon and Kobo, or reader sites like Goodreads. Customer reviews are just seen as quick opinions from a reader, and intended to help other readers decide whether to purchase the book or not. Sometimes they are little more than a rating. They are important in that they are visible to purchasers on the site where the book is for sale, and can be the final piece of data that makes them click "buy" (or not).

Editorial reviews are more substantial. They are influential and critical reviews from named websites, magazines, newspapers, or respected authors, and may have elements of critique, and an understanding of context. They are seen as more prestigious and reliable, and a good one is worth shouting about.

Even if the whole review is good I try to select just the most representative part that makes a key point. It should illustrate some element of why you are a captivating writer, your authorial fingerprint, the aspects which makes your work and voice unique. So, instead of endless quotes saying "Great writer!" and "I loves me his books, Momma!", you want the quotes that highlight how you create believable characters, or compelling plots, or have a wonderful writing style. As an example, this quote is one of my editorial reviews:

> "Drinkwater is a dab hand at creating an air of dread."—**Altered Instinct**

It defines something about both me and the book at the same time, and gives useful information to a prospective purchaser.

I also select quotes to illustrate different features of the work, rather than all repeating each other. I limit each to one or two sentences only, and make the source bold, preceded by an unspaced em-dash—for attribution. I also use a soft return for the source, so it is directly below the quote, as shown in the example above.

So we're cutting them as short as possible, but there's no need to include ellipses to show omission. Just don't misrepresent anything. If the review said "This book is great if you like badly written prose and want to send yourself to sleep!" don't truncate it to "This book is great!".

Editorial reviews serve a few purposes. Firstly, if you are going to run any advertising, this kind of quote can be the main focus of an advert along with the book cover. Job done! Secondly, you can use editorial reviews with some distributors such as IngramSpark, so that they appear as a section on many sales sites. And since these review extracts are testimonials, you can use particularly good ones, or those from prestigious sources, in any other place where you want to show endorsements: for example, on the cover of the printed book, inside front matter, and on your website. Just don't go overboard with it.

Up to seven short quotes is a good goal to aim for. Don't overdo it. There may be a limit for review quote metadata – if you stick to 1000 characters maximum (total, including spaces) that will work for sources such as Amazon Author Central, and IngramSpark. You can easily check the character total by pasting the quotes into a word processor.

You can (and should) update editorial reviews as the book gets more widely known and appreciated, and more important ones come in. And in your master list of quotes always include notes about (or a link to) the source, so you can prove the quote is genuine.

I'll talk more about reviews in Chapter 9: Marketing.

ISBNs & Publication History

Record the ISBN assigned to each format, such as ebook, paperback, hardback, audiobook, or large print. Obviously not all books get released in all formats. Also list the year and date of publication. I use the international standard format yyyy-mm e.g. 2023-05 for May 2023.

ISBNs applied to a book can never be reassigned to another book, or even to a later edition (which will need a new ISBN). As such, the ISBN and book title are the only two metadata types that never change. Everything else such as keywords, blurbs, editorial reviews and so on, can be modified and updated at will without needing a new ISBN. Metadata is a work in progress.

Other Common Metadata Categories

Here are some other headings you might want to include in a metadata document, depending on your circumstances, publishing method, and how you organise things.

Author

"Surely that's the same every time?" you ask. Well, for me it is. For you, it may be. But if you use multiple pen names for different genres, you could record which pen name goes with each book. I feel a digression coming on ...

Drinky's Digressions: Pen Names

A **pen name** is when a book is published under a pseudonym, rather than the author's real name. Here are some reasons why people might adopt this approach.

1. **Privacy.** Some authors need to keep their true identity private. They may not want people from their past to be able to find them. They may have faced persecution issues. They might even have a professional career in a non-writing sphere and not want colleagues and clients to find their fiction during Internet searches.

2. **Issues with the author's name.** Perhaps it is hard to pronounce or spell, or resembles the name of another author, or is a common name that doesn't stand out. Maybe it sounds inappropriate: perhaps you write unicorn romance but your birth name is Samson Grimdark. You want something more evocative of the books you write. Maybe your name sounds stupid and makes people laugh at you, e.g. Karl Drinkwater. All good reasons to consider a pen name that works better. This heading also covers people choosing a name of the opposite sex if it is traditionally a genre dominated by male or female writers.

3. **Branding.** We often associate an author with a single type of book. William Gibson with cyberpunk and sci-fi. Jane Austen with witty romantic comedies. Clive

Barker with dark fantasy. This makes it easier for fans of the genres: they can pick a book by that author and already know it is within the area of their interests. But if you write in multiple genres then there are risks. For example, my suspense fans might buy one of my contemporary works, only to be disappointed that it isn't horror. (Obviously I hope that wouldn't happen and they'd love all my writing, but people are strange.) Likewise advertising algorithms such as also-boughts can become messed up. By using different pen names for other genres it prevents each "brand" from being diluted. It's why some of Stephen King's thrillers were originally published under the pen name Richard Bachman, or J.K. Rowling's mysteries appeared under the pseudonym Robert Galbraith, so as not to mix the works up with her Harry Potter series. The downside is that if someone wants to read all an author's works, pen names may hide a substantial chunk of their output. Sometimes the change isn't to hide the original author, just to separate them (which means all the work is still discoverable), as when Iain Banks wrote mainstream fiction under his own name but science fiction as Iain M. Banks. Of course, sometimes the author is known for writing a variety of books, and their flexibility is part of the attraction. In which case they might do as I do, and publish all the books under a single name. As a summary, you could say that separate pen names strengthen each *genre* brand, but putting all books under one name strengthens the *author* brand. I'll look at brands in Chapter 9: Marketing.

Pen names can offer advantages, but they come at a cost: each one appears to the world like a separate author, so not only requires restarting awareness raising and marketing for every new name, but it increases the workload in terms of multiple websites, newsletters and social media accounts.

If you use pen names and want to publish your books independently, there is no need for separate accounts with each distributor. You have a single account, in your real name. When you upload a new title to Draft2Digital or IngramSpark, there is a field where you enter the author. So if you have multiple pen names, you just choose the correct one in that field. Job done. This is because most distributors will treat you as a *publisher* rather than an *individual author*.

If you do write in multiple genres under a single name, it is even more important to make sure each book's genre signalling is spot on: cover, title, tagline, blurb, and metadata.

Other Contributors

Co-authors, illustrators, editors, translators.

Publisher

If you are trade published or hybrid, you may work with many publishers during your career. The publisher for a title may even change over time, especially with new editions. This metadata field is a way of keeping track of which publisher published which titles and formats. And since large publishers have imprints for different genres (which are almost like sub-publishers) you could also record the imprint where applicable.

Even if you are an independent author you may create different imprints, so could list the one which you used to publish each title. Or you could use this field for the printer/distributor you used for that edition, such as Draft2Digital, IngramSpark, BookVault etc. We'll learn more about those options in the next chapter.

ASIN

ASIN stands for **Amazon Standard Identification Number**. This is a stock code assigned by Amazon, and everything they sell has its own ASIN. Books get them regardless of whether or not they also have an ISBN.

The ASIN can be useful if you add your book to Goodreads, or need to contact Amazon.

When a book is released exclusively to Amazon, the author might not bother with an ISBN at all and just use the ASIN. That is why most records of books published and sold are highly inaccurate, because they often focus only on books with ISBNs. (Another reason is that sales through some retailers, or books sold directly by authors to readers, are not included in statistics.)

Tagline

As mentioned in the last chapter, a tagline is a concise and intriguing phrase that hints at some story elements: a few words that help clarify the content and entice the reader.

Illustrations

If your book is illustrated, you could record the number and type of images. Line drawings, charts, photographs? Colour, greyscale, true monochrome?

Table of Contents

Useful if you write short story collections or poetry, and want to easily keep track of which stories and poems have been included in which collections.

Audience Type

Adult, children, professional, young adult etc.

Language

Once your books are available in translation this becomes a key piece of metadata.

Type Of Book

Novel, novella, short stories, compilation, non-fiction.

Data About Length

Word count for an ebook, page count for a printed book. For audiobooks I record the duration in the format hh:mm:ss, e.g. 06:18:32 (six hours, eighteen minutes, and thirty-two seconds).

Price

I record the price for each format in both UK and US currencies. You may record it in others.

Status

You could list if a book is available, cancelled, withdrawn, or on pre-order.

Dedication

If you use these, it could be useful to see at a glance who has already had books dedicated to them, and what you said.

Awards

You could include any contests or prizes that the book has won (and when).

Useful Web Addresses

I record Goodreads pages and Universal Book Links (UBLs – discussed in Chapter 9). You could note others, such as the book's page on your website, or links to the book on various vendor sites such as Kobo, Barnes & Noble, Amazon etc. These can be useful to refer to when promoting your book.

Genre

If you write in only one genre this may not be necessary, but if you write in more than one it can be useful to record the book's genre(s). If you use the spreadsheet system you can sort books by whichever column you want: so sorting by genre (for example) will group all the books from each genre together.

Many authors gradually shift genre as their career advances, or they experiment with others out of interest. One of my friends began by writing formula romance but shifted into literary fiction, and has a sideline in erotica under a pen name.

Drinky's Digressions: Genres

Genres are simplified category labels that attempt to describe content. See here[105] for examples from the BISAC subject categories mentioned earlier. The essence of a genre is about *repeating something* but also *changing something*.

Here are two statements:

- **Genres are useful.** Genres tell bookshops which shelf to put a book on. Genres may help readers to find books that they like.

- **Genres are not useful.** Genres can be problematic when books, authors, and reader interests don't fit neatly into the widely-used categories – and that's more common than you'd think. Also, authors can get pigeonholed within genres. It's why some authors use pen names when they write in a different genre (see digression on Pen Names, earlier).

I have no problem with a writer who only enjoys writing in one genre doing just that. At the same time, it shouldn't be a shackle. Most writers want to tell stories, and that might mean writing things that fit into different genres (or none at all). The walls should be broken down. No one would complain if a sculptor known for human effigies switched to sculpting dogs.

I think about this a lot because I write in multiple genres. I find it fascinating when people categorise my books in ways that I hadn't thought of. For example, one review that began with "Cold Fusion 2000 is a novel of incredible genius" (I love that quote), then categorised the book as "romance". I'd never thought of it that way. The mention of romance is spot on, in that it has romantic love as one of the strands, but it probably breaks some of the expected rules relating to "romance" as a genre (e.g. needing a clear happy-ever-after).

It's the old issue of how to pigeon-hole books to aid discovery, without pigeon-holing books in ways that reduce diversity and experimentation.

See, genres aren't always as clear-cut as people like to imply, and some books fall on fuzzy lines between multiple genres. I've always thought the best books cross boundaries. Jane Eyre mixing romance with gothic horror, for example. But it's still useful to at least be able to attempt a broad summary. Adding additional terms can help to pinpoint content more specifically. So *Lost Solace* might be "feminist action sci-fi" or "horror space opera".

A good example of where things get muddy is with *women's fiction*. That is a common label applied to books, as if it is clear and unambiguous – but it's not. The "women" bit refers to the target audience, not the author's sex – but why shouldn't men read good books in this genre too? The terminology of "women's fiction" implies a smaller audience than really exists, and may put off some readers. And just because someone is a woman, doesn't mean they don't read more clearly-defined genres such as crime, dystopian fiction, or erotica. Since women's fiction isn't read exclusively by women, the term tells us little except perhaps the prejudices of the publishers and booksellers. So how should we classify these books?

Calling them *commercial fiction* sidesteps the silly "these are books for only one sex" categorisation, though commercial fiction is a large umbrella that probably covers most of what gets published in various genres – crime, horror, thrillers and so on. It's *all* commercial because it is all popular, or at least the publishers intend it to sell well and count as mass-market fiction. And isn't it silly to categorise books by their estimated sales potential? How does that help readers? Two random commercial fiction titles will have nothing in common in terms of stories, settings or characters.

Some authors prefer the term *contemporary fiction*. Unfortunately it doesn't mean a lot except "fiction written fairly recently that doesn't fit into any other neat category". As such, all sorts of disparate books are also contemporary fiction, and liking one contemporary fiction title is again no guarantee that you'll like the next, because they have so little in common. The contemporary fiction categorisation also confuses things in other ways – what if the book is set in the past? It is contemporary in terms of when it is written (for now ...), but not when it is set.

There's also *literary fiction*, though the term can be a bit of a poisoned chalice, connected with books that win prizes and get applauded by critics but which make many normal readers fall asleep. Obviously that isn't true of all literary fiction, but it is the reputation it has (along with being "difficult" or "requiring work") among many readers. It can also appear elitist in other ways, implying books without the "literary fiction" tag don't have literary qualities such as clever structure or in-depth character portraits or innovative use of language. And, again, books in this category can be wildly different in terms of settings and quality and readability, so it isn't much help to the bemused reader.

So, are there alternatives to genres? At one point I played around with the idea of getting rid of fiction genres and instead describing all stories via three elements, which could be used for films as well as books:

1. Form (e.g. short story, novel, novella; musical, animation, mockumentary)

2. Subject (e.g. horror, politics, romance)

3. Setting (e.g. fantasy, historical, Scotland)

Something to think about: are there any obvious problems with that system?

The Metadata System I Use

In the past I created a word-processed metadata document for each book and stored it in the same folder as all the other documents relating to that work: draft versions, final version, book cover, research material, marketing images and so on. Within the document I used headings for each of the metadata types, then put the correct content below them.

As the number of books I'd written grew (with a separate folder for each), I found it inconvenient to not have the information in one place. Because it was split between many documents, I couldn't easily compare keywords used in different books, or check what each book's shop price was, or see all publication dates and ISBNs at a glance.

In 2023 I changed how I store metadata, and switched to using a single spreadsheet with each book on its own line. That book title column is "locked" and always visible even as I scroll across the worksheet, so I can always see which book the data on that line relates to.

7.1 Detail from my metadata spreadsheet

The columns are the ones where data can easily fit into a single cell, or where I am most likely to want to compare the metadata with other books, namely:

- Title

- Series (and the book's number in that series)

- Type of book (novel, novella, short stories, compilation, non-fiction)

- Genre

- Keywords

- Comps

- BISAC and Thema categories used

- Goodreads link to the book's page, and Books2Read UBL link

- Ebook section (this section is green, indicating all data relates to ebooks): ISBN, publication date, word count, price

- Print section (in blue): ISBN, print format, publication date, page count, trim size, paper type, price

- Audiobook section (in beige): ISBN, publication date, duration, price.

For anything wordier – namely tagline, blurb, one liners / ad copy, and editorial reviews – I still use a word-processed metadata document in the book's folder on my PC. That kind of information is less likely to need comparing with other books anyway.

Top Tip: Keep Things Organised!

I believe that organising *now* saves a lot of time looking for things *later*.

I apply this principle to how I organise books on my PC.

I won't discuss the folders I use for running my business or for future project ideas. But it is worth describing how I organise the folder called "published works".

Within that I have a folder for every series, each of which includes the number of books in that series. e.g. "Lost Tales Of Solace (6)".

Within a series folder there is a subfolder for each book in that series. So that they appear in the correct order, each folder is named by its number in the series, the year of publication, then the book title. e.g. "4 (2022) Raising Solace".

Within the folder for any book there will be five files. Four will be the latest version of the book in different formats (.docx, .epub, .mobi, and .pdf). The fifth is "metadata.odt", as previously discussed.

There will be a "cover" subfolder for all the cover files. Another called "odds" where I put all sorts of things in another set of subfolders: creation notes, early drafts and backups, editorial feedback, marketing images and so on.

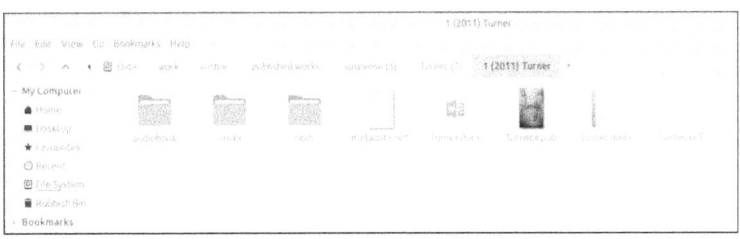

7.2 Detail of the folder for the novel Turner

Where appropriate I may also have subfolders for special versions of the book, such as the audiobook, or translations.

This system keeps everything tidy and makes it easy to find what I want quickly.

Distribution

Chapter 8

This chapter explores topics related to getting books onto shelves (physical or virtual) so that they're available for readers to purchase.

The basic book distribution process is straightforward: a publisher (or independent author, who acts as a publisher of their own work) uploads content to a distributor, along with the relevant metadata and a cover. The distributor sends the information out to vendors (such as Waterstones or Barnes & Noble) and book databases such as Nielsen. Your work is then findable on the seller website by ISBN, title or author.

If a bookshop or library wants copies of your book they will check their suppliers, find all the details, and be able to order a copy.

For ebooks, the content files will also be shared. Vendors can then sell and supply copies, and pay commission back to the distributor, who takes a cut and passes the rest back to the publisher.

With print books there are additional issues with storage and shipping. So when a book is ordered it must be supplied from the vendor's stock, ordered from a warehouse, or even printed to fulfil the order.

The longer the supply chain, the more people take a cut of the profits, and the less there is to pass on to the publisher or author.

Many years ago, widespread distribution of books wasn't possible except through a traditional publisher. That has all changed thanks to technology. Independent authors today can publish books in more than two hundred countries and territories; in digital, audio, and various print formats.

Much of this chapter won't be as relevant to traditionally published authors, since distribution is the job their publishers are best at, and why we licence rights to publishers in the first place. Some of the subtopics I discuss might still be of interest, though.

First, let's explore one of the key concepts used in book distribution chains: ISBNs. I've already discussed them briefly in the Cover Design and Metadata chapters. To recap: most books that get distributed have an ISBN assigned by the publisher. Each format of a book gets its own ISBN. Once assigned, that title and format are permanently linked to the ISBN in the distribution network.

Acquiring ISBNs

Publishers buy blocks of ISBNs from whatever agency is assigned to deal with them by that country's government. For each country there is a single place where a publisher can acquire ISBNs. In some countries ISBNs are free (e.g. France and Canada), in others (such as the UK) you have to pay.

If you are an independent author then you'll probably want to buy a block of ISBNs from your national provider. I say *probably*, because there are pros and cons. On the plus side, the ISBN will be yours. Even if you change distributor, the book can keep the same ISBN, tied to your publishing imprint. Whereas if you use free ISBNs from a distributor (meaning *the distributor* appears as the publisher), and later you change distributor, you'll also need a new ISBN.

In the UK, publishers have to buy ISBNs from Nielsen.[106] As of May 2025 Nielsen charge £93 for a single ISBN. Ouch! Yes, £93 just to record a number in a database. Buy a block of ten and it will cost £174 (so the price goes down to £17.40 per ISBN). Buy a hundred and it costs £387 (£3.87 per ISBN). The final option is buying a thousand for £994 (which is what big publishers do, so they only pay 99 pence per ISBN).

If you are an independent author buying ISBNs then you need to estimate how many you'll need. There's no point buying a thousand if you're only going to publish a few books. But no point buying ten if you'll use them up in a year and then need to buy more at higher prices. This system penalises smaller publishers and independent authors.

Remember that a single book might use a number of ISBNs: one for the ebook, one for the paperback, then a hardback, one for audiobook; maybe more for other print options such as large print, and if there's a second edition that will need new ISBNs for each. As such, for anyone intending to be in this for a long time and release more than a handful of titles, the 100 ISBN block represents the best value.

If you're in the UK and therefore use Nielsen to purchase your ISBNs, it's worth being aware of a few things.

Firstly, Nielsen force you to create an account, even if it's a one-off purchase. That's a pain, but you can close the account afterwards.

Secondly, they maintain Nielsen's Title Editor and try to persuade you to enter details there whenever you assign an ISBN. Don't do it! It doesn't benefit you in any way, but can cause problems, because some sites will then use Nielsen's metadata about the book in preference to metadata from your distributor. So if you change the book's blurb later, for example, and update it with your distributor, many sites will still use the old blurb which they pull from Nielsen. All that you've done is create an additional place where you have to update metadata, for as long as the book is available (so, probably, for the rest of your life). Nielsen are not your distributor, so they don't need your data.

Thirdly, when you first buy ISBNs, Nielsen will try to enter details into their Title Editor without asking permission, causing the problems discussed above. Make sure to instruct them specifically *not* to do that.

Of course, you might wonder why they pressure you to use Nielsen Title Editor? It's because it is tied to data services they sell, such as BookData Online (the pricing of which isn't made public) and "Enhanced Data services" (where publishers have to pay before Nielsen will pass all the metadata on to vendors). Nielsen are a private company profiting from selling access to their large, but incomplete, database which is made up of freely-available metadata.

Pre-orders

The publication date is when the book is available to the public. Copies may be sent to reviewers before that, so they have time to read and review the book ready for its launch.

The metadata and cover is sent to distributors in advance of the publication date. In most cases stores allow customers to pay for copies at that point, even though the customer won't receive what they have paid for until the publication date. This is known as a **pre-order**.

Some pre-orders may be up to twelve months in advance of publication, for books with high demand.

Yes, a pre-order is really just an *order*; the short form for "*or-dering* a book *before* publication". Pre-orders exist for computer games and other consumable media.

Obviously there's a risk in pre-orders for a customer, since they are basing their purchasing choice on the past reputation of the creator. They're buying something without seeing reviews. It might not live up to the expectation. As a consumer I never go for pre-orders, as I've been disappointed in the past. But publishers and authors like pre-orders because it means on publication day all the pre-orders count as sales, boosting the book and pushing it up through the charts. It also acts as a form of publicity in the run-up to launch day, since the book will have already appeared in search results on vendor sites, and people could add it to wishlists.

Pre-orders generally work fine if the book is well in process. The problem is when they are set up too soon, and then the book (or the author) runs into problems. Problems need fixing, which takes time.

Always be generous with time estimations if setting up pre-orders. Normally you can set them up to six months ahead of release, so it is often beneficial to make use of that time. The final interior of the book usually has to be uploaded at least ten days before the release date, and there can be penalties if you fail to do that. Both distributors and customers might get miffed.

Ebook Distribution

As we saw in Chapter 6, ebook covers are simpler to create than printed book covers. Likewise, ebooks are cheaper and easier to publish and distribute than printed books. We'll therefore tackle ebooks first.

Traditional publishers want their authors' books to be available in as many formats and places (both global regions, and individual retailers) as possible, so it is easy for people to buy a copy. This is known as **wide distribution**. Many independent authors want the same thing, but there is a decision to be made here.

Wide Versus Exclusive

Amazon offers authors perks if they enrol their ebooks in KDP Select. To be in KDP Select the author must give Amazon *exclusive* distribution rights for at least ninety days: the opposite of *wide* distribution, where the books are available in every digital store. If the author agrees to exclusivity then their books will be entered into Kindle Unlimited (KU), where Amazon customers who subscribe (for a fee) can read enrolled books for no additional charge. In exchange, Amazon will pay the author a regularly changing figure for the number of pages read by KU subscribers. Amazon also gives access to extra promotional tools. This exclusivity is known as going "all in with Amazon".

Many independent authors go down this route. Some make a lot of money. Other authors prefer wide distribution. Some of *them* make a lot of money, too. So this is a personal choice, and may tie in to how much you like (or dislike) Amazon.

There are downsides to the exclusivity rules from being in KDP Select. For example, while enrolled, you can't sell *or give away* the books anywhere else. It rules out giving copies to reviewers, using them as rewards in crowdfunding, as freebies to fans, or anything else like that.

But there is a bigger issue. For me, the goal is to get books into as many stores as possible so that readers can buy from their preferred place. If a reader avoids Amazon, then any author's books which are exclusive there will not be visible to that reader, and will not be bought. Lost sale. Likewise customers in countries where Amazon doesn't sell have no way of buying your work if you're exclusive to Amazon. Whereas if the ebooks are available on Kobo, Apple, Amazon, Barnes & Noble and so on, then they're available to all your potential readers.

An additional consideration is that, once authors are established in KDP Select, they often find that if they leave then their income drops massively. I suspect it is because they have no audiences on other platforms where their books haven't been available. It takes time, consistency and goodwill to build an audience on each platform, which is a problem for an author who has become dependent on the teat of Amazon.

The choice to go wide is no quick route to riches, but it can be a more sustainable and discoverable approach.

Assuming wide ebook distribution is chosen, what options are there for independent authors?

Going Direct To The Ebook Sellers

You could focus on the main ebook sellers, create accounts with them, then distribute directly to their stores. At present the key vendors would be Amazon, Kobo, Apple, Barnes & Noble, and Google Play.

Benefits of this approach: you often get better royalties by going direct. You may also gain access to extra promotional tools.

Disadvantages of this approach: it is more admin than using an aggregator (which I'll talk about soon), especially if you have a lot of titles. You need to upload the same books and metadata to multiple sites. Any changes need mirroring in all of them. Each will be separate accounts, separate reporting, separate royalty payments. Measuring the impact of a promotion can be more complex. Also, going direct isn't possible in every case: in some countries it might not be an option.

Here are links for going direct with the big five ebook sellers, in alphabetical order.

Amazon KDP[107] Note that if you price the book below $2.99 or above $9.99, Amazon halves the royalties (35% instead of 70%). They also do this for some of the countries they distribute to, where 35% is the maximum royalty they will pay. Additionally, if you are in the 70% royalty option, they charge you for delivery based on the book's file size. Picture-heavy titles such as cookbooks, or anything illustrated, will be particularly hit by this.

Apple Books[108] Unlike Amazon's complicated royalty system, Apple pay a flat 70% royalty. The downside is that you need a Mac computer to upload directly to Apple Books. That's a barrier to Linux or Windows users, and an unnecessary restriction, since the procedures could be fully browser-based and therefore platform-agnostic.

Barnes & Noble Press[109] They pay 70% royalties.

Google Play[110] 70% revenue split, regardless of book price.

Kobo Writing Life[111] They pay 70% royalties for books priced $2.99 and above, and 45% for books priced below $2.99. Kobo provide a number of marketing tools for doing promotions on their platform.

Drinky's Digressions: Amazon Escape

I don't have a KDP or Amazon consumer account any more. I cut Amazon from my life for many reasons. Primarily their algorithms incorrectly created false positives of undefined "suspicious activity" which led to threats to close my account with no right of appeal: none of it was instigated by a human at Amazon, it was all automated. It caused a huge amount of stress and took months before I was able to get someone at Amazon to actually investigate properly, and realise it was an error. I hear about this kind of thing happening to Amazon authors on a regular basis. I suspect the false positive was triggered by a boost in book sales following a big promotion – the ultimate crime of becoming popular – as that was the only thing that occurred around that time, but of course Amazon refused to confirm anything so I am still none the wiser.

I'd had many other issues, such as Amazon failing to update my books and the metadata, Amazon locking me out of my account, Amazon charging customers far more for my paperbacks than the recommended price (sometimes triple the shop price!).

I'm also a fan of Ethical Consumer,[112] and you can probably guess how badly Amazon does with its tax avoidance, awful record on workers' rights, excessive senior pay, privacy violations, animal cruelty, and negative environmental impacts. Amazon has been on their boycott list since 2012.

As such, I am a lot happier now that I no longer have an Amazon account. I do continue to sell books there because I make decisions to benefit my customers (such as letting them buy in the location they want) but I distribute to Amazon via Draft2Digitial, so that I don't have to deal with Amazon directly. Let's discuss how that works.

Using Ebook Aggregators

Another option for independent authors who want to go wide is **ebook aggregators**. Aggregators allow you to upload your ebook to a single place, and they distribute it to multiple retailers, including some that you can't reach any other way such as library providers (OverDrive, Hoopla, Bibliotheca). Although you don't directly and personally put your books on Amazon (for example), the books will be available for sale there, and you'll still get paid royalties on every sale.

Benefits of this approach: it is a lot less admin. You upload books and metadata to a single place. There is only one account, one set of reporting, one set of royalty payments. You only need one book file, not one for each vendor. Cutting out admin can free up time for writing and promotion. The more titles you have, the greater this benefit.

Disadvantages of this approach: you miss out on some royalties as the aggregator will take a cut of your sales in exchange for the work they do: perhaps 10%, so you make 90p in every £1 received from vendors. (The exception was Pronoun, which gave independent authors the full royalties and had many wonderful features; unfortunately Pronoun was bought by the traditional publisher Macmillan in 2016, and they shut it down shortly afterwards. Boo hiss Macmillan.)

Both options – going direct versus using an aggregator – can work out well for an author. It comes down to how much your time is worth in managing multiple accounts and versions, and which things it is easier to pay someone else to do. And that's subjective.

Also note a third option some authors use. They go direct to the main five ebook sellers, but also use one or more aggregators to distribute the ebooks to smaller sites or vendors the author can't distribute to directly, in order to extend the book's reach. This is even more work, but also makes the book widely available without losing out on the better royalty payments of going direct. Note that if taking this approach, the author must disable aggregator distribution to the sites where the author has gone direct – you can't have the same ebook being distributed to the same store twice, and trying to do so could lead to your account being closed. So, for example, if the author distributes directly to Kobo but also uses Draft2Digital (an aggregator I'll discuss below), they must make sure Draft2Digital do not distribute the same title to Kobo. That is done easily enough: you just deselect Kobo from the book's distribution options in the Draft2Digital dashboard.

Here are links for some of the most popular aggregators, in alphabetical order.

Draft2Digital[113] The most popular aggregator, in my opinion. Wide reach, a good dashboard, regular payments to my bank, and good customer service. They offer features such as free book formatting (discussed in Chapter 5) and automated end matter. The latter is useful because if you change an element such as your author bio, then Draft2Digital will not only include the new one in your future books, but it will update all your existing titles too, and send the new versions to distributors for you. Their optional automated end matter includes Further Reading (promoting a single book), an Also By list (which it automatically updates every time you release a new book), and an About the Author page. Draft2Digital take a 10% cut of the retail price (c. 15% of the net profits) in exchange for distributing your book to all the different sales sites. They have distributed well over a million different titles, and paid out more than $250 million to Draft2Digital authors from book sales. There are features I'd love them to implement, such as including metadata fields for subtitles and editorial reviews, or the ability to view royalties and sales by month for the previous twelve months, but overall their service is excellent.

IngramSpark[114] Although mainly known for their print-on-demand service, they also distribute ebooks. However, their service and reach in that area is less developed than other aggregators, and most independent authors don't use IngramSpark to distribute ebooks.

PublishDrive[115] They have a different charging model from other aggregators. Instead of being funded by taking a cut of every sale (a system I am happy with, because it gives aggregators a vested interest in helping you sell more books), PublishDrive use a subscription-based model. You pay a regular fee based on how many books and formats they distribute for you, but then they give the author the full royalties they receive from vendors. Their website is impressive, and they will distribute ebooks, print books, and audiobooks, so really are a one-stop-shop.

However! This is only an option if you sell a *lot* of books. For example, their Standard package is $20.99 a month for them distributing six books. So if your monthly sales don't come to at least $21 every month, you are losing money. Further, they count every *format* of a title as a separate book. So if you have just two titles, and each has ebook, print and audiobook versions, that is your full quota of six books used up on the basic subscription, and as soon as you release another title you'll have to upgrade to the next subscription level ($41.99 a month, allowing up to eighteen "books"). Every time I look at their website I am impressed. Every time I look at their charging system, I know that many authors would be best going elsewhere.

StreetLib[116] An Italian-based aggregator who I hear a lot of good things about.

Drinky's Digressions: Collaborations

I've premised everything on the idea of a single author writing a book. But that's not the only creative option. I've long been interested in creative collaborations between authors, and co-wrote a novella that way. There can be a boost of extra energy from doing this: two people urging each other on during low points, twice as many ideas, half as much work (since tasks and writing get shared).

But collaboration is a huge topic: all the processes of plotting and writing with another person. All the legal issues and contracts. All the decisions regarding royalties, work division, distribution channels, publication, and promotion. Since the process runs across all the stages of book production, from initial idea generation right up to marketing the finished product, a collaboration influences everything.

So I'm not going to talk about the process here, but wanted to point out that it is a possibility – potentially a wonderful one. Draft2Digital have a royalty-share option, so independent authors who co-write and want to publish ebooks and printed books together could do that through Draft2Digital, who would apportion royalties automatically based on the contractual agreement between the authors. For those wanting to sell items direct to readers, Gumroad also has a royalty share option.

Subscriptions

I often phrase things in terms of selling a copy of an ebook, because that's easy to visualise – it's like buying a copy of the physical book. However, I mentioned Kindle Unlimited (KU) above, where people pay for access to a pool of books, rather than for individual copies. In music terms it is like subscribing to Spotify rather than buying the individual mp3s of songs you want.

Monthly reader subscription services are a growing model within ebook (and audiobook) distribution. As well as Amazon's KU there are Everand, Kobo Plus, Storytel, Bookmate and 24symbols. For the price of one book, the reader gets access to a vast library: but as with Spotify, it raises lots of questions about whether creators get fair compensation from these all-you-can-eat word buffets. You will probably also have to deal with restrictive apps and DRM (discussed in Chapter 5's digression on DRM And Piracy).

Ebook Pricing

Many big publishers charge as much for the ebooks as the print books because it means more profits for them (at the readers' expense). It also makes the print book more attractive as a purchasing option, since that's where their mindset lies, and the only part of the distribution chain that they can do better than independent authors.

I've always been of the opinion that ebooks should be far cheaper than print books. There are no printing and physical distribution costs, for a start. Some of that saving should be passed on to the customer, especially as the customer needs devices to read the books and may have to deal with DRM. Why should readers pay as much for an ebook as for a print book, when they can't trade, sell, or loan the former?

There are two things to consider in setting the price for something that has no intrinsic production costs.

Firstly, length. Is it a 20,000 word novella, a 60,000 word novel, or a 200,000 word collection? In general, the longer the book, the more you can charge, assuming the work is highly polished and good quality (as opposed to long just because it hasn't been properly edited). Though it isn't as simple as a price per thousand words, since the acceptable (to book buyers) price range for longer works tends to level out.

Secondly, the market. How much are recent books in your genre? Be as specific as possible, and dive down into the subgenres. A particular audience will have expectations, and it is always best not to stray too far from those.

As a rule of thumb, I usually charge around half the price of a print version for one of my (DRM-free) ebooks. That also gives me flexibility to lower prices for time-limited promotions, which I'll discuss in the next chapter.

Print Distribution

Physical books require printing and distribution. As we'll see soon, there are two different methods of doing this (*offset printing* versus *print-on-demand*). The end goal is getting copies of the physical book to whoever ordered it: a bookshop, library or individual customer.

Printed books generally bring in a lower revenue per copy sold than ebooks, because of the complexity and the need to distribute physical items. But print is important for many of your fans, and some will *only* read books in a printed form.

It you are traditionally published then your publisher will deal with all of this for you, but it is worth knowing about the technologies and processes so you can weigh up whether you are getting a fair deal from your publisher.

Offset Printing

Offset printing (also known as **consignment print runs**) is where a printer sets up an individual title via a complicated series of processes in a modern printing press. This is time consuming to begin with, but once it's done, printing any amount of copies is relatively straightforward. That's why, with offset printing, there is an *economy of scale*, and the bigger the print run, the lower the unit price.

Imagine you only wanted ten copies. The time spent in setting up offset printing might mean it works out costing £20 per copy, and you spend £200 (10 x 20). But if you printed a thousand copies then that initial set up time is less relevant, and the unit price might come down to £5 a copy (though the *total* printing bill will still be higher, in this case £5,000 [1000 x 5]). And so on. The more you print, the lower the price of an individual copy – and so, when it is sold at the recommended retail price (RRP), the greater the profit margin per copy. But that only applies *if you sell every copy*. So this requires assessing demand, and potential sales, correctly.

Once the requested number of copies have been printed, the printer is set up for the next new title and it begins all over again.

Traditional publishers generally use offset printing for a new book release. They will try to estimate likely sales, then add some more to the imaginary number in case demand is greater than expected (which also brings down the unit cost), and they'll print that amount. It's called the **first print run**, or **initial print run**. Then one of two things can happen.

They may sell all those copies. Cue celebration from the publisher and author. And if there is still demand for the book, they will do a second print run (and perhaps wish they'd printed more copies to begin with, since each print run has the initial setup time again that eats into the profitability of every copy). Some books that become big hits may go through a second, third, or even fourth print run.

The other possibility is that demand slows down without all the copies being sold. They may continue to warehouse the books in case demand picks up, but storage is expensive. So the most likely outcome is that many of the unsold copies get pulped, which is obviously a waste of resources, as well as costing money.

Once sales trickle out, many publishers choose to switch from offset printing to the next option, print-on-demand.

Print-On-Demand (POD)

Print-on-demand (**POD**) was made available by technological developments that lowered the cost of printing individual copies. Instead of time-consuming setup, there is just a high quality printing and production flowline that can deal with individual books.

The main advantage is that there are no warehousing costs. When an order for a copy of the book comes in (or for multiple copies), they are printed and shipped out. This also prevents the waste associated with unsold copies that can occur with offset printing.

Another advantage is that, in theory, copies can be printed locally to the place ordering the book, which saves some transport of heavy items. If you think about it, offset printing only works because many copies are printed from a single location. But then those copies need to be transported far and wide to local distribution centres. Whereas POD facilities are smaller, and don't have any complicated setup for each title. So a printer could have one or more POD facilities in each country, and when an order comes in, the book (which exists as a digital file) is printed from the nearest POD location.

So why isn't POD the only method used nowadays? It's down to the economy of scale again. A single copy from offset printing might cost £100 to print. A single copy via POD might cost £10, and always cost that per copy, no matter how many you print. But if you print enough books with offset printing to bring the cost-per-unit down to £4, you can see how much money it can save when a lot of books are going to be sold – such as during the month when it launches.

That's how traditional publishing generally deals with demand for print copies, but if you're an independent author, it's simple: use POD.

Offset printing is riskier, and can lead to forlorn boxes of books sagging in a cobwebbed garage or attic, or the copies eventually being pulped or binned. If a large consignment is printed and the cost per book is £3, that wonderfully low production cost only applies when the last copy is sold. Sell hardly any, and it will turn out you paid hundreds of pounds for every copy sold (and a roomful of unsold ones to dispose of). In short: an independent author only benefits from using offset printing if lots of copies are printed, *and every book is sold*.

In most cases, unless you have a proven sales record, stick to the simplicity and financial safety of POD, even if the profits are lower.

Drinky's Digressions: Rights Reversion In A POD World

For traditionally published authors, their contracts with a publisher will likely include a section on **rights reversion**. This is the conditions whereby the contract ends and all rights revert back to the author so they can seek publication of the title with another publisher, or even publish it themselves. In the past there might have been a condition that if the book ever goes "out of print", then rights revert to the author. In terms of offset printing, that would have meant a decision was made not to do another print run, and existing print copies had been sold or pulped so there were no more available: hence out of print.

That applies to a lesser degree nowadays, since many publishers choose to switch from offset printing to the next option (print-on-demand), once sales slow down. In that case the book will never technically be out of print, since it is always available, so this means of rights reversion may no longer apply. Be aware of this when signing a contract.

Wholesale Discounts

Whether books are created via offset printing, or through POD, no bookshop or wholesaler would sell the books unless they made some money from it. As such, all books are given a **wholesale discount**. The standard wholesale discount is 40%-60% (most likely 55%). So any bookshop or vendor ordering a copy will get it at 55% less than the **recommended retail price (RRP)**; then, when they sell it to a customer for the RRP, they are earning 55% of the cost. So a book with an RRP of £10 would be bought by the bookshop for £4.50, sold to the customer for £10, netting the bookshop £5.50 profit.

At least that's the theory. If you are an independent author and publish print books through IngramSpark (discussed below), the wholesale discount you set isn't the discount a bookshop would receive. That's because the Ingram network (that owns IngramSpark) count themselves as part of the wholesale chain, so actually absorb a chunk of that profit themselves, along with their distribution fee, order handling fee, and the costs of printing and shipping the book. It is standard for every distributor and wholesaler in the chain to get a cut – everyone needs to be paid – but it's something IngramSpark doesn't make explicit. That feels slightly dishonest, as most authors don't realise. If the wholesale discount for a region was set at 30%, I've been told Ingram takes 25% of that 30%, so the shop buying your book only get a 5% discount. That's one of the reasons why some bookshops might not want to stock titles distributed by IngramSpark, and a cause of confusion when the author mistakenly thinks the bookshop receives the full designated wholesale discount.

Author Copies

If you are traditionally published then your contract may well stipulate a certain number of physical author copies. These print books are provided to you free, for your own records or bookshelves.

Independent authors don't get free copies, but print distributors usually have an option for the author to buy as many as they want at base cost (plus shipping). As an example, a paperback on sale for £9.99 might only cost the author £4 per copy from the distributor, meaning they can sell the book directly for less than the full shop price and still make a profit. If you do order author copies it is always best to get a small stack of them at once: if you bought a single copy from IngramSpark, they would add £1.65 as a "handling fee" and £4-£6 for postage, making it cheaper to order that copy in a local bookshop and pay the full price (and then get a slight royalty payment for the sale).

Author copies can be used for signings, or direct-to-customer sales. You can give them to friends and family, or reviewers.

Note that an *author copy* is different from a *proof copy*. The latter is so you can examine every line of the book in case there are any typos or printing errors that need correcting prior to publication. See Chapter 5: Formatting, for a checklist of things to look out for. Proof copies may well be marked as "not for sale".

Printed Book Types

With ebooks, your fans will not choose between formats, only *where* they buy from. But with printed books there may be many different types. This is relevant because some readers prefer one over another, and if a printed book isn't available in that format, they may not buy a copy at all.

Paperbacks are the most common format. Though even here there may be more than one type. For example, a book might have a fancy cover and high quality paper for an initial release when it is most likely to get display space. But after some time, if it still sells but not at a great level, so that it becomes a backlist title, it might get a re-release in a cheaper paperback format. Perhaps a different cover, smaller trim size, lower quality paper, and less space around text (so there are fewer pages and it is cheaper to print).

Hardbacks are seen as a step up in luxury, and also more durable, which is why libraries favour them for in-demand books. As we saw in Chapter 6, the hard cover may be illustrated (called casebound), or it has a removable paper jacket over the top (in which case the cover under the jacket may be more plain, such as cloth).

Large print. We saw that with ebooks the reader can make the font size and spacing larger or smaller, so there is no need for separate large-print ebooks. However, printed copies are not flexible in that way. Some readers require larger text sizes in order to read the books comfortably, which is where large-print editions of a book come in. These will always have more pages, which also pushes them towards being hardbacks: both for the sturdiness of the binding, and because public libraries often have a separate collection of large-print books.

Illustrated books contain images in either black and white, or the more expensive colour option. Sometimes the illustrations are integral to the story, as with children's books. Sometimes they are just ornamental, for example an adult fiction book with full-bleed greyscale background images at the start of a new chapter or part.

Special editions. Sometimes a limited edition is released with a different cover, perhaps a new spacious layout, and other features such as embossing, interior illustrations, maps, bonus materials, or page-marker ribbons. These can also come about as rewards in crowdfunding campaigns, which I'll talk about later.

There are also many paper types on which a book can be printed. Different thicknesses, quality grades, environmental implications, even colour tone. For example, if you look through your printed books you might notice that fiction is often printed on paper with a hint of cream, whereas non-fiction is printed on a starker white. And if there are interior colour images, the paper for those pages is likely to be a higher grade in order to let the brightness of the inks show.

POD Distributors For Independent Authors

There are a number of options here. I won't even pretend to cover them all, especially the smaller print-on-demand distributors based in other countries, but which may still offer an excellent service. All of these would enable customers to buy print copies of your work, and allow bookshops and libraries to order your books if they wanted.

Note that, just because they are *available* for order, does not mean they *will* get stocked in bookshops and libraries. That's where marketing comes in, which I'll cover in the next chapter.

Generally shops won't stock titles by unknown authors, but that is likely to change as you build up your reputation, reviews and presence. There is also the issue of a wholesale discount, and bookshops expecting to be able to do returns. I advise against the latter – not only can that potentially bankrupt an independent author if a bookshop orders hundreds of copies in error and returns them at the author's expense, but there are huge environmental implications, as we'll see at the end of this chapter.

And, finally, what I refer to as POD distributors are technically *wholesale distributors*: they make books available, printing and shipping them when they are ordered, but they don't promote the work. Whereas *full-service distribution* is what trade publishers use, which involves sales reps going to bookshops and trying to tempt the manager into ordering their new titles. That's sometimes tied to payments to the bookshop to promote the titles in front-of-house displays. What, you thought the books face-up on those tables inside stores of a major book chain were placed there because they are the best books? Nope, it's often paid promotion, but not flagged as such.

I'll list the companies in alphabetical order.

Blurb[117] Blurb have a reputation for good quality output, but also for being expensive. Personally, their website put me off as I couldn't find any homepage link to contact them (if customer support was a priority I would have expected that to be easily findable) and some of their pages won't load. Since I care about attention to detail, those kinds of things would give me a cause for concern.

Bookvault[118] Whenever I have contacted Bookvault they've been friendly and helpful. Bookvault offer a good range of printing options, and possibly the lowest printing costs (without sacrificing quality) out of all the services listed here. The only downside is that they are a small company based in the UK, so their international distribution options aren't as all-encompassing as some of the other service providers. Bookvault charges you for book uploads, though lets you make revisions for free; if you are a member of ALLi (the Alliance of Independent Authors)[119] you can get the upload charges waived.

Draft2Digital[120] We saw them as a key distributor in the ebook section, but they also distribute print copies of books, and have tools to help you format them. This has big advantages in terms of managing print and ebook copies (and royalty payments) from the same dashboard. The downside is that – perhaps because their printing is done through a partner company – their royalty rate per print copy sold is low, meaning you have to increase the sale price for a book in order to make any profit. Still, Draft2Digital is one of the better companies to work with, and doing everything through them can make the whole process much more pleasant. Draft2Digital can also generate a paperback cover for you based on the ebook cover, adding your blurb, author bio, and author photo to the back. It won't have unity of fonts, or a wraparound image, but if you have no design skills then it is an easy and free solution for paperback covers.

IngramSpark[121] Possibly the largest and most well-established option, they can certainly distribute your books to all the major stores around the world. IngramSpark let you upload books for free, but charge if you want to make a revision after the first sixty days. The charge is $25 *per file* (cover or interior) changed. Unfortunately, IngramSpark's revision fees actively discourage authors from fixing errors. They also quickly add up if you want to keep your books up to date. For example, if you want to update your author bio or list of titles across five paperbacks and five hardbacks they'll charge you $250. Personally, I've always found IngramSpark's customer support, website, and reporting systems to be frustrating and unfriendly to use.

KDP Print[122] This is Amazon's service to let you distribute print books to its own sites, whilst also offering optional global distribution. Many authors with no objections to Amazon see this as the best way to sell print copies via Amazon's site, since they'll show as "in stock," whereas POD books from anyone else will likely show a worrying out-of-stock message. This is why some authors use both IngramSpark and KDP Print: they upload the print book to KDP Print but disable global distribution, so it only goes to Amazon; they also upload the book to IngramSpark (or another distributor) for global distribution. Yes, that is more work, so it depends on how important Amazon print sales are to you. If you use KDP Print on its own for all your distribution then note that many bookshops will refuse to order Amazon-printed copies due to controversies surrounding Amazon's business practices.

Lulu[123] I used Lulu many years ago, and was generally happy with their service and customer support. They're still going strong, so are worth investigating. Lulu don't charge for uploading books or making revisions, which is a huge positive.

PublishDrive[124] As we saw in the ebooks section, Publishdrive can distribute POD titles too, via their subscription service. In return you get 100% of royalties received. The same downsides apply as with ebooks.

POD Cost Comparison

For my own interest, I did a quick comparison of the pricing of some print-on-demand service providers in April 2025. I entered details using each site's cost calculator. Note that I did not include Blurb as their pricing page[125] is always blank for me, and I couldn't find a full calculator for Publishdrive.

First, the pricing calculators, so you can try them out yourself to get the latest figures:

- Bookvault[126]
- Draft2Digital[127]
- IngramSpark[128]
- KDP Print[129]
- Lulu[130]

These were the base printing prices for a 256 page paperback 5.5 x 8.5 title (lower is better).

- Amazon KDP: £3.41
- Bookvault: £3.70
- Draft2Digital: £4.17
- Lulu: £5.90
- IngramSpark: £5.92 (£4.27 + £1.65 "handling fee")

I also calculated the royalties if the book was sold at £12.99. Draft2Digital do not let you change the retailer discount (it is fixed at 55%). Bookvault and Ingramspark let you choose a lower retailer discount, but for this test I selected 55% so the figures are all comparable. Lulu did not let me set a retailer discount price.

Note that at 55% (rather than 35%) you make far less royalties on each sale, though it does make it more profitable for bookshops to stock your work. The first figure below is the calculated royalties for expanded distribution at those settings (higher is better); and the second (in brackets) are the royalties through the company's own bookshop, if they have one.

- Bookvault: £2.15 (£8.18 via their own store)[131]

- Draft2Digital: £1.68 (they don't have their own bookshop)

- IngramSpark: £1.39 (they don't have their own bookshop)

- Lulu: £0.47 (£5.67 via their own store)[132]

- Amazon KDP: unknown, as it does not calculate expanded distribution (£4.38 for sales on Amazon UK)

Drinky's Digressions: 2FA Improperly Implemented

Whether you are an independent author or a trade-published author, you are likely to use a lot of systems, accounts and websites.

In many cases, a username and password is sufficient to access an online resource. It is certainly the simplest system (both for the end user, and the service provider), and one we are all familiar with.

In recent years there has been a move to add extra security, especially for important accounts. The main system adopted is known as **Two-Factor Authentication (2FA)**, **two-tier authentication**, **two-step authentication**, or **Multi-Factor Authentication (MFA)**. I'll use the term 2FA from now on.

The idea is that access requires both something you know (a username and password, for example), plus an additional factor of *something you have access to*. A code can be sent to that second factor, and that code also has to be entered in order to log in to the service. That way, if a rapscallion stole your username and password, they still wouldn't be able to access your account, because they wouldn't receive the passcode sent to your device.

These are some of the options for 2FA.

- **Landline**. This is one of the options the UK government offers for the HMRC site. When doing my tax return I enter my username and password, the landline phone rings, I answer it, and a code is read out by a computer. I type that into the login page, and can then begin the painful bit of paying taxes.

- **Mobile phone**. This can either work as above (automated voice call giving a code) or the code can be sent by text/SMS.

- **Email**. If I log in to Steam from a new computer I get an email with a passcode, and can copy and paste it to log in.

- **App/software**. Some kind of authentication app generating a code which can be entered. Unfortunately, they are often only available on some computers and platforms, not all; they may be created by companies you prefer to avoid (e.g. Apple, Google, Microsoft); and there may be security risks related to installing the software. If there was an open-source authenticator available on every platform (Linux, Windows, OSX, Android etc) and which all sites and services allowed as a security option, then that would be useful, but it isn't the case. Also, most apps are mobile phone based, so are redundant when the phone could do 2FA already via text.

- **Although it isn't technically 2FA**, it has been standard for many services to have additional passcodes. So my bank account didn't just have a username and password, it had a separate PIN number, and I could also be asked to provide answers to questions like a memorable name or date. That system works well as an easy-to-implement second layer of verification.

None of the options are perfect. And none of them work for everyone, all the time. Therefore, effective implementation of 2FA requires offering at least three options to users: landline, mobile phone (call, text or app), and email. I call this "professional 2FA". Professional 2FA adds an extra layer of security, without excluding or upsetting any of your users, or creating exceptional barriers to access (known as **digital exclusion**).

Unfortunately, many companies and IT people interpret 2FA narrowly as *mobile phone-only*, and don't bother to set up any other options. The IT people either can't be bothered offering alternatives, or they are inept. They think everyone is connected, all the time, via mobile signals and fast networks, where nothing breaks or gets lost. I call this "lazy 2FA".

Implementers of lazy 2FA insist everyone owns a personal mobile phone and must share the number and use that device as a second factor, with no other options. But that approach excludes, or creates barriers for, people who fall into one or more of these categories (which apply to *all* people at *some* time, and *some* people *all* the time):

- people who don't own a mobile phone (through choice or other reason);

- people who don't have access to their mobile phone (lost, broken, misplaced, or stolen);

- people living in or visiting an area with no mobile phone signal;

- people who own a mobile phone but only use it for emergencies, or only give the number to friends and family, and don't want to give the number to anyone else (quite rightly!).

Lazy mobile-only 2FA creates digital exclusion and further barriers for vulnerable people, who already face marginalisation and are in most need of access to services.

Here's an example. I have some elderly friends who live in the highlands of Scotland. Not too far from a city, but still remote. There is no mobile phone signal in their house. When some service forces them to use mobile-based 2FA, they don't receive the code. The only way they can log in is to check the phone is charged (since it is mostly turned off in a drawer, and only used if they go into town or travelling), get kitted up, head out, then trudge up a big hill. It could be dark, icy, chucking it down. They might be ill. Tough. It's inconvenient, unpleasant, time consuming, puts them at risk, and (to cap it all) sometimes they get back home and the code has expired, requiring doing the process all over again. The frustrating thing is, if the code had been sent by landline or email, it would have been no problem at all. They have a phone and broadband.

There is another fundamental problem with 2FA. Once an identity is tied to an extra item, everything is relatively hunky dory whilst access is available.

That's not the real world. Phones break. They get lost, or stolen. People replace them or buy new ones. People pass through areas (or live in them) that have no signal. Email goes down, and email addresses change. People move house, landline numbers change. And so on.

Thus we have a rigmarole of having to plan for change. No, you can't just get a new phone number. First you have to contact every company that has the old one and uses it for 2FA (you do have a list of them, don't you?) You have to access your account, change the number to a new one, use the old phone to authenticate, then the new one to do so. Try explaining all that to your gran. Even when things go perfectly it is a lot of hassle and time for multiple accounts; and every year that goes by, this gets even more complicated.

But when your phone breaks or goes missing, you can't do that. If you don't have a list of every 2FA service you use, you can't do that. Suddenly – as with every case above where access to the second factor is impossible – 2FA doesn't work.

Security is always a balance. The more the security, the more hassles for people, and the greater the chance of being locked out. Security stops being the system that keeps unwanted users out: it becomes the system that puts barriers in place of legitimate users.

The Financial Conduct Authority (FCA) give guidance on 2FA to UK organisations. I contacted the FCA and they said: "It is necessary for a firm to provide different methods of authentication, for example, to take into account the fact that not all service users will possess a mobile phone." Lazy 2FA goes against that guidance. Making a mobile phone a requirement (rather than an option) is digital exclusion, and is a serious issue.

In relation to distributors, note that Amazon KDP and IngramSpark have mandatory phone-based two-step verification, which may put some users off. Luckily Bookvault, Draft2Digital, Gumroad and Lulu don't force you to provide a phone number, because they have a good customer focus and don't want to exclude people.

If you want to do a good deed, as well reinforcing good practice, then – whether you own a mobile phone or not – whenever a company demands your number for 2FA, check that they also offer other options to cover everyone: landline and email. You'll be doing a service for everyone whose life doesn't centre around mobile phones.

Top Tip: Check The Sites!

Whether you are trade published or an independent author, always check how your books appear on the main sale sites such as Kobo, Amazon, Waterstones etc. Do it for all formats: print, ebook, audiobook. Make sure that it displays the cover, correctly formatted blurb, correct metadata details, and a clear preview sample if the platform has that feature. Also that it is connected to your author name (which should be a link leading to a list of all your books available on that site); and if the book is in a series, that it is included with the other books. If there is anything awry then follow it up with your publisher or distributor, since those kind of issues could affect sales.

Audiobook Distribution

I've not discussed audiobooks much because I am mainly focussing on books where you read the words on a screen or on paper. Also, audiobooks present a number of challenges.

For a start, it's not enough to write the words: they then need narrating. Even if a professional can narrate nine thousand words an hour, that's almost nine hours for an 80,000 word novel. You can probably triple that for time listening to the recordings, doing fixes, edits, and taking breaks. That doesn't include post-production quality control and preparing the files for upload. These explain why it's more expensive, time consuming and complex to make audiobooks than print and ebooks. It is also harder to make changes later, and there are fewer distribution options.

On the other hand, audiobooks are a growing market and reach a different audience, since some people *only* listen to audiobooks, and others find them convenient on portable devices or in the car.

Some authors see them as an essential format, but for others they are a bonus, to be considered only once a book's worth has been proven so that it is a worthwhile investment.

If you're traditionally published then the publisher has probably made you sign the audiobook rights to them. That doesn't mean they'll definitely produce an audiobook. They may wait and see what sales are like first. Them having the rights excludes you from producing your own audiobooks, even if they never make one. It's one of the reasons why you should always resist the general publisher rights-grab and limit the rights licensed to only the ones that are actually going to be used (by format, region, and language), and for which you'll therefore be paid. See Licensing Rights in Chapter 2 for a recap.

If you are thinking of producing audiobooks of your own titles then there are three main methods.

1. Pay a third party to do it

That way you can get a professional narrator who specialises in this. They will be comfortable with multiple characters, accents, enlivening prose, and voice projection. They'll also do post-production to bring the audio files up to scratch. It may involve an upfront payment, a royalty-share agreement, or a mix of both.

This is the most expensive option, because of the time it takes to narrate the book, plus all the quality checks by multiple parties, and even the back-and-forths during recording: "How do you pronounce this name … and which accent works best for this character?" kind of thing. I'll give some tips on working with narrators soon.

I love the audio versions of my books, and my choice of hiring professionals. Even though I know the stories and dialogue by heart, I still listen to them with pleasure, because the delivery makes a difference. Tom Freeman's clear tones make *Turner* flow, and he brings out the dark humour in Lord John's scenes in a way that lightens the tension. Rosie Alldred's soft voice is perfect for creepiness, like a hushed house where you listen for the threat you know is there, the floorboard that is bound to creak before long, and you lean in to hear every detail even though you know you might regret it when you realise what's coming. Rosie voiced *Harvest Festival* and *They Move Below*. And Marisha Tapera has been praised in *Lost Solace* reviews again and again for the way she brings the tale to life with excitement and humanity. This is why we hire professional voice actors.

2. DIY

In the non-fiction realm, author-narrated books are popular. Readers like to hear an author's voice, with the big caveat: only if they do it well! The author needs to have a good voice, wonderful intonation and pronunciation, and other skills relating to delivery of the material.

Fiction, with its many characters and dialogue, has even more strenuous requirements. If you have a background in acting or performance you might be fine, but if not then a badly recited audiobook of deadened prose could do more harm than not having an audiobook version at all.

Even with a great voice, narration takes time, and needs regular breaks. Software and hardware is required, but even more important is wonderful soundproofing and acoustics. I know authors who have built their own recording rooms at home, though not all of them ever got around to narrating audiobooks once the immensity of the task hit them.

One told me: "I set up the basement booth at a cost of about £300 for everything, including the screws! I have the perfect mic, a soundless fan, and even the software, but I just can't commit. It's a mental thing, but in my mind I just know the time it will take to learn how to narrate clearly (not just read aloud, but no accents either), how to edit and export with maximum quality… well. It's a lot of work."

Others have hired time in a professional recording studio. In both cases this opens up new options, such as adding music or sound effects to the ebooks.

3. Artificial intelligence (AI)

AI is coming along massively. The term as used in the media is a misnomer, as there's not really any intelligence in the software, it just creates the illusion of a reflective mind behind the drawing, conversation or voice.

Nowadays we're used to artificial voices: terrible phone menus of options designed to send you in loops and prevent you reaching another human; "smart" devices that you give commands to, and then they reply in sultry voices as they fulfil your request of listening to Lady In Red yet again; screen readers and software audiobook readers. Likewise, it's now possible to have audiobooks narrated by AI voices. On the plus side, this can be a cheaper option, and may even open the door to different voices for each character: variant sexes, ages, accents, personalities, and tones (though that will increase the workload).

But it's worth being aware of the negatives. Firstly, some audiobook distributors don't accept AI-narrated audiobooks, so your distribution options are reduced. Secondly, they can be controversial, in the sense that the technology threatens to put professional narrators out of business. Finally, there's the quality issue. The AI voice doesn't really understand context. There won't be acting. No increase of speed and volume in fast action scenes as Panthero Maximus leaps from the flying bus; no subtle slow down and whisper during the creepy tense scenes as Simone sneaks past the undead clown. The AI will be confused by punctuation and pronunciations. The result is that some books might be okay, but others could end up with strange elements that immediately give away the fact that it wasn't a human reading the book.

Still, if you want to experiment with this – maybe to sell audiobooks direct to readers through your website, Gumroad, or a Kickstarter (which I'll discuss when I talk about Crowdfunding later), then here are a few options. I haven't used any of them so this isn't a recommendation list. I also won't include pricing or current offerings as it changes all the time in such a fast-moving area – even while writing this book, some of the companies in the first draft had disappeared.

- DeepZen[133]

- Lovo[134]

- MURF.AI[135]

- PlayHT[136]
- ElevenLabs[137]
- Revoicer[138]
- Synthesis[139]

Top Tip: Think In Audio From The Start

Before I move on to listing some of the audiobook distributors, it's worth mentioning another consideration when it comes to audio.

On the printed page we can see the text. The same applies to an ebook. And that aids comprehension. To take one example: thanks to layout and punctuation, it can be clear when speakers switch during dialogue, even if we don't always include dialogue tags. In fact, it's an element of style to avoid ending every line with a repetitive "Jane said … John said". Good writing omits the dialogue tags when the conversation has been established, and instead just inserts a reminder every now and again to make sure the reader hasn't got lost – or an action to confirm whose line it is.

> "Kind of like this." Karl leaned back and stretched his finger joints with a series of firecracker pops. "Oooh, that feels better."

But when we don't have visual clues, only a voice, it can be harder to spot things such as shifts in speaker. A good narrator will probably do different voices as a means of providing context. That helps. But it is certainly a weakness of most AI software that uses a single voice: dialogue that is clear on the page (even without dialogue tags) could be confusing to listen to, making it almost impossible to tell if there was a pause (but it's the same speaker), or if it is another character now talking. Either way, it's why many books need a significant edit to make them audiobook-suitable; and also why some authors write the story as if it was an audiobook from the start.

For these reasons, and more, you shouldn't underestimate the issues involved in producing a quality audiobook. If it is to be narrated, then tweak the text to make things clearer for the audiobook format, to help the listener always know what is going on. This can be time consuming, but it is vitally important because, unlike an ebook where a new version can be uploaded at any time, it is not easy to change audiobooks.

This is one of the many reasons I always advise reading out your work or having it read to you (see the tips in Chapter 4). And, if you do this enough over time, you may even develop a style of writing that works well for both reading and listening.

Audiobook Distributors

Here are some of your main options for distributing audiobooks. They work on the principle of paying you royalties based on "sales", but it isn't always as simple as with print books where someone buys a copy and there is a clear transaction. Audiobook vendors use many different models, for example credit-based subscriptions, cost per checkout, unlimited subscriptions, and revenue pools. As usual, these services are just in alphabetical order.

Audiobook Creative Exchange (ACX)[140] This is Amazon's audiobook portal. ACX only distributes to Amazon, Audible (another Amazon company) and Apple, so is limited in reach. It is also only available to people living in the United States of America, United Kingdom, Canada, or Ireland. With ACX you have to choose between being exclusive to those three outlets in exchange for a higher royalty rate (40%); or being non-exclusive, so that you can distribute audiobooks to other stores, in which case your royalty is lowered to 25%. In the latter case I can't even see the point in using ACX: if you're going to distribute your audiobook wide, you might as well use another platform, and simplify things. For a long time ACX was the major player, but just as there are many concerns about Amazon, there are also a number of negatives about using ACX. For example, unlike other distributors, you cannot choose the audiobook price: ACX decides what it will be. The compensation mechanisms are confusing because Audible frequently discounts books (over which you have no say), and the royalties are on the *final sale price*, not the full listing price. So you are basically paying for Audible to gain more customers. Other issues include ACX charging authors for returns, even when the listener has heard the whole book, and where ACX has encouraged subscribers to "exchange" a book after listening, as if it is a rental service (which benefits

Amazon, not the authors). Also hidden deductions and lack of transparency, plus (sometimes) non-payment. If you want to know more about these issues, have a look at the Audiblegate website.[141]

Audiobooks Unleashed[142] They have an interesting set of options for royalties and production, and they do royalty splits. However, they won't pay money straight in to your bank account as most services do, but instead require you to set up a Wise account (which requires a mobile phone).

Author's Republic[143] They distribute to a network of over fifty retail, library, and streaming channels, and also have a marketplace that can link you up to a suitable narrator. As a wide distributor, you can set your own audiobook prices.

Findaway Voices[144] Findaway Voices will rebrand as InAudio in August 2025. InAudio has wider distribution options than ACX, and also lets you set your own retail price, which has many promotional and discounting possibilities. InAudio similarly lets you find narrators, though I found their charging structure to be opaque, and you need to check the small print carefully. InAudio is owned by Spotify, which has proven controversial: Spotify is popular with music consumers, but there are many stories about how the subscription model leads to low payments for the actual music creators.

Lantern[145] I know little about these.

StreetLib[146] An Italian-based aggregator mentioned in the ebook aggregator section.

Working With Professional Narrators

Royalty options. If the audiobook company you are working with offers the option of royalty share then it is worth considering, especially if you are new to this. It means that for every sale, you and the narrator will share the royalties. It's a risk for the narrator if the book doesn't sell, but it can make an otherwise expensive process affordable for the author. Whereas if the book already has masses of sales, or you are rich, then you are better off paying a narrator up front.

Audition text. With most audiobook sites that connect you to voice artists, it is standard to send them a scene which they narrate as an audition example. Make sure your audition text is from a good part of the book, emotionally charged or with a strong tone. Pick something with both narration, and dialogue between different characters (and perhaps sexes), to see how the narrator handles multiple voices interacting. I was mean in one of my audition texts, since I required the narrator to sing in a child-like voice out of key, but it really helped to find those who could cope with the book's challenges.

Listen carefully to the audition and samples. I have a list of things I look out for: speed of delivery; clear distinction between speakers, dialogue lines, and section breaks; fidelity to the text; and challenges related to that particular story.

Explain any tricky areas. Give as much information about what you're looking for as you can, so you attract the best potential narrators. You need to cover possible voices, pronunciations, and accents. There may be things that require special consideration: for example, one of my stories was told through text messages, so we used a ping sound effect for each new participant.

Audiobook covers. You need the book's cover in a square format, which is an aspect ratio of 1:1 (think of CDs). 3000 x 3000 is the current standard resolution. And no, don't just try and squash your normal book cover. Elements need resizing and moving.

Finding someone. Many sites let you advertise for narrators, but they also let you browse those which are available and listen to their voice samples. Instead of just putting up an audition and hoping for the best, I find it is better to actively seek narrators that fit what you want, and then invite them to audition. Search and apply filters such as sex, accent, and style to match what you need.

Provide additional commercial information about the book. Bear in mind that with royalty shares the narrator wants reassurance that they will make a similar amount to an upfront payment. Sometimes they spend a lot of time on a book and it sells poorly; or they commit to it and find the full work isn't as polished as it should be. If you have good print or ebook sales and ranking data, or have won awards, then let the potential narrators know.

Character dialects in audio books. Select a voice actor who can do the major accents and voices of the book, and check that they can deal well with switching from male to female voices. Of course, there isn't a single "American accent" or "UK accent" or anywhere else. There are regions. If it's important for the character (because their background is specified), make sure it is the right regional accent. If the text says a character has a broad Mancunian accent then it needs to sound like that, not Brummy or cockney or Texan. Accents are too distinctive to mess with, and incorrect matches introduce discordance: imagine a traditional London-based Sherlock Holmes speaking with an Australian accent for no obvious reason. However, the main non-dialogue narrated text can be in any voice, unless it is first-person POV, in which case it needs to be the character's voice.

You are partners. Don't assume that what comes back from the narrator will be perfect, and that once you've found a narrator the job is done. That's not a collaboration. Your narrator wants feedback on whether they're getting it right. They'll have questions about pronunciation and details. Listen to everything they do, and proof it like you would a printed text. Everyone makes mistakes such as a missing sentence, a mispronounced word, an incorrect volume setting. Don't be afraid of pointing it out. In most cases the narrator will only have to re-record a few sentences, then they snip out the section with errors and paste in the new one. Yes, listening to it all and giving feedback takes a long time. Probably a couple of working days in all. But you need to do it. Follow up any issues. A project could take weeks, or it could take twelve months, from start to finish.

Don't expect to get rich. There is a lot of competition in the audiobook market, and a lot of books already available. Audiobooks are not an easy route to cash. But then, neither is writing. Audiobooks can be a useful extra income stream though, and it is enormously satisfying to hear a good production.

Direct Sales

The great thing about royalties is that each sale represents coins tinkling into your tin cup. However, it's never the full amount that the customer pays, because companies along the supply chain all get to take their slice of the pie first. There will be payment providers, bookshops, aggregators, distributors, possibly publishers and agents all taking their cuts. The author clutches what is left, always aware that the government's tax people are rubbing their hands eagerly at the chance to take 20% as income tax, then a second skimming when the author buys anything with what's left, in the form of 20% VAT. It may not be as bad as the original bag of gold only containing lint and dead moths by the time it reaches you, but it can feel that way sometimes.

In short: the more middlemen there are, the smaller the amount the creator gets from each sale. I do recommend the 2019 Spanish film The Platform (El Hoyo)[147] for a visual metaphor illustrating this.

But suppose an independent author sells a £6 copy of the ebook through Gumroad (or an equivalent), *direct to a customer*. Gumroad take a 10% cut, and the payment provider applies a 40p charge too. So the author this time receives £5 per copy sold, which is more than the £4.20 by selling through a site like Amazon; and much more than the £1.50 a traditionally published author makes.

The more direct the relationship between creator and customer, the more money goes to the creator, especially if they are independent. It's why musicians would rather sell an album directly on Bandcamp than receive royalties on an album sold by a big music publisher.

There are two implications.

Firstly, when we make buying decisions as consumers, it's nice to pick the option that gives most money to the creator. It's no different from going into a local artist's studio and buying a painting you love directly from them. It's why I bought qntm's *There Is No Antimemetics Division* from Gumroad[148] rather than Amazon. It's also why I bought Spiral Dance's *The Quickening* album from Bandcamp,[149] and purchased the excellent horror game *Devotion* from developer Red Candle's own software store.[150] In each case I help the creators more, and was able to get DRM-free files as a bonus.

If you publish any books independently then it's worth thinking about options to sell directly to customers. You get more money as a result, but there are other benefits. For example, it's a more personal connection, and you know who bought the copy. You'll have an email address. Whereas if I sell a book through Amazon, only they have that data, and they won't share it with me (though they will look for ways to monetise it, or to persuade the customer to spend money on other authors' books – "Hey, you bought that, maybe you'd like this!"). Having a direct connection with a customer can be invaluable.

It's easy to sell digital books (ebooks and audiobooks) via sites like these:

- Gumroad.[151] Excellent customer support, easy to set up. No upfront costs.

- Payhip.[152] Requires creating a separate account with PayPal or Stripe. No upfront costs.

- Shopify.[153] Monthly subscription, which may be prohibitively expensive for new authors, though it enables sales of physical items too. It is complicated to set up and has poor customer support, though.

You could also sell signed print books or premium editions directly from your website, if you're happy to deal with the complications (and costs) of shipping, payment plug-ins, and invoicing; all of which favour specialist editions where you sell fewer copies but have a higher mark-up. I will discuss websites in the next chapter.

Or you could set up your site to route orders straight to your distributors for fulfilment, which saves admin but is more expensive and complicated to set up in the first place. Bookvault has UK and US printing locations so can fulfil orders for print copies, via a Payhip, Shopify or Woocommerce site. IngramSpark can also ship copies directly to customers (using their nearest print facility), and for an additional charge add an extra page to the copy so you can use that for a personal message and signature, whilst still benefiting from the book being posted by the printer, rather than having to go via you.

Another option is selling print copies in person, for example stalls at events, conventions, and markets. You buy the copies at basic print cost, and sell them at the recommended store price (or a bit below). I have put some tips on doing this in Chapter 9. Fans appreciate signed copies, but if you don't want to go to all that work then some authors offer signed bookplates that can be stuck in the front of a book to turn it into a signed edition – these don't cost much to post to overseas fans, and are far cheaper than posting a paperback.

Not everyone can sell directly. Since traditionally published authors license all distribution to their publisher, they don't have the option of doing this. Also, independent authors who publish exclusively to KDP Select are forbidden from direct sales of the ebooks (or even giving them away).

Crowdfunding

In the past, rich people funded their own projects. Less-rich people sought backing from wealthy investors. But nowadays there are other options, known collectively as **crowdfunding**. Crowdfunding means that instead of one rich investor putting a lot of money into something, we can seek small contributions from lots of people, which adds up to the same total.

You've probably come across friends using crowdfunding platforms such as GoFundMe[154] for everything from charity runs to help with veterinary bills. But for creative projects, such as a new book or a special edition, the big platform with the most backers is Kickstarter.[155] So I'll use that as an example of how it can work.

In essence, a creator presents some idea that needs funding in order to bring it to life. They set it up as a project and indicate how much funding they seek, along with what rewards backers will receive: usually the finished product, or a luxury version.

Rewards are offered in different tiers, each more expensive than the last. For example, the lowest tier might just be someone making a donation because they want to support it; the next tier might provide them with a finished ebook if the project is successful; another tier might include a printed book, and so on.

If someone likes the idea, they pledge money to support the project, at whatever tier they wish. There may be optional add-ons, where they can pay extra for additional rewards. As an example, one of the successful crowdfunding projects I backed was for environmentally friendly, hand-made running shoes. There were add-ons for shoelaces in various colours.

If the backers' pledges total up to the amount being sought before the deadline, then the project is funded. Kickstarter collects the pledged amounts from backers and passes it on to the creator, minus a cut for the platform (5%) and payment provider (3-5% for Stripe).

The project creator works to fulfil the promised goals and then sends out the appropriate rewards to backers. So it is a system to get an upfront payment for something that might not be possible without that backing. If the funding goal isn't reached in time, no money is collected from anyone, or passed on to the creator.

An alternative to Kickstarter is Indiegogo,[156] which has an option to receive funding even if the goal isn't reached.

In case you are sceptical about the idea of crowdfunding, author Brandon Sanderson made the news (and crowdfunding history) when he independently published four books through Kickstarter in March 2022. His goal was $1 million USD, but he made $15 million in the first twenty-four hours alone, then went on to secure a record-breaking $41 million in pledges by the end. In March 2024 he ran a crowdfunding campaign for another book and raised over $20 million. Don't expect to achieve that – he has a massive and supportive community of adoring fans – but it's significant that a publishing project broke the records and achieved more than even hi-tech projects that had been the crowdfunding exemplars up until then.

There may be fewer options for traditionally published authors. It all depends on what rights you've licensed and the contract you've signed. Can you write and sell a spin-off or side stories? Are you allowed to do one-off luxury editions? Can you sell merchandise related to the world and characters you've created? For Brandon Sanderson's first Kickstarter in 2020, for luxury editions of The Way of Kings (which raised $6,788,517) legend has it that he was able to do so because – even though the books were traditionally published – the contract he'd signed allowed him to create and sell special editions himself. Unfortunately, some authors are so overwhelmed with gratitude for being offered a contract with a publisher that they sign away more than they need to, and it is only in later years that they realise their error. Refer back to *Drinky's Digressions: Licensing Rights* in Chapter 2. I've seen organisations produce contracts and say they are "totally standard," and on further investigation with a specialist it's been found to be far from standard, with all sorts of issues where the solicitor's final advice was not to sign it.

But if you're an independent author then you have full control of your creative business, and are welcome to investigate crowdfunding options.

Tips For Crowdfunding Success

Here are a few tips if you want to give crowdfunding a go.

- Read the platform's guides, blog posts and help pages to find out about the features and how they work.

- Do regular progress updates, both during the pledging period and after it is successfully funded. It reassures people that you are at work, and the goals are achievable.

- Consistency helps. Having run successful projects in the past on that platform builds your audience, and increases the chances of people backing your ideas again.

- It is vital to have a good summary of what you want to achieve, well laid out, with images. Make it clear but exciting. It's your chance to create interest and also build trust in you as a creator. (I have seen some awful ones, with vague goals, bad spelling, and unrealistic expectations.)

- I'll mention images again, because they are so important. Good campaign graphics that look professional and enticing, and illustrate what the supporters will get, are vital. A quick look at other crowdfunding projects that are doing well will indicate what you should aim for.

- Don't ask for too much money: just what you need, and a bit more (perhaps 20%) for dealing with unforeseen circumstances. Remember that on Kickstarter you get nothing if the goal isn't met.

- Look at popular and successful projects on the platform, especially any that are in the same category as the project you propose (e.g. publishing). How were they presented? What rewards did they offer? How much did they ask for, and what was the money going to be spent on?

- Think about your rewards. Ebooks and other digital items are easy as there are no shipping costs. But what else is viable? Exclusive bonus content, or recognition of the supporters in the book? Could a fan suggest a name for something in the story? If you might ship physical items such as signed books then look into the prices first, so you don't lose money. International shipping can be the biggest cost, which is why some people only ship items to their own country – but that misses out on backers from around the world. At the same time, it's good to offer premium products for your super-fans who want to support you. So plan out your offering carefully before building the campaign, rather than rushing into it.

- Back other projects. You're asking for money from a community, so it looks good if you have supported that community in turn.

- If you are doing a special book reward of a limited edition that won't go in the shops, then it doesn't need an ISBN.

- If the platform allows it, consider a limited number of "early bird" tiers, where there is a reduced price for the first backers. This creates early action on the campaign which raises its profile. It may also be nice for fans who really want a reward but normally couldn't afford it.

- Stretch goals are where extra rewards are added once certain levels of backing support are reached, beyond the original funding target. The idea is to reward everyone with extra stuff if the project is more successful than envisioned – which may lead to backers sharing and promoting it. You don't need to have stretch goals, and they can add to the complexity of reward fulfilment. Note that Kickstarter doesn't have an inbuilt system for tracking stretch goals – you just list them in the main text. Some authors like to keep them secret and only reveal each one as the goal is reached.

- Be aware that when you post a project on Kickstarter you will receive spam trying to sell you advertising services. Some will arrive through Kickstarter's own email system, others where the spammer has tracked down your email address and reached you that way. No credible company would tout for business in this (potentially illegal) way, so delete all of these emails and report them as the spam they are. I'm just making you aware of one of the downsides to using Kickstarter (another being the PerimeterX security system they add to their site which regularly locks me out of Kickstarter for not being human ...)

- I recommend writing all the initial text for your crowdfunding campaign in a single document, with headings for different sections. The main proposal text, the reward tiers, any add-ons or stretch goals. Get it all polished and perfect. Once that's done, you can create the graphics to go with it. Only at that stage should you upload the text into your crowdfunding platform. It saves a lot of time and also means you have a backup of everything you said.

- My biggest tip is that crowdfunding is ideal for something you'd do anyway. We don't need laboratories for research and development. We don't need gold to fashion into a necklace. The main resources authors need are imagination, enthusiasm, skill and experience. So if I am going to be writing a book anyway, running a Kickstarter for it just means extra funding and interest, almost acting like a form of pre-order. I've done a number of them on this basis over the last few years, offering something my lovely fans want (such as a signed edition, or a personalised ebook, or bonus materials). It may not be a lot of money, but it is additional to what I would have made if I released the book as normal.

Creator Economies

A **creator economy** is where the payment model switches from a focus purely on sales of shop-sold items (such as books), to ways where supporters directly fund the creators they love: artists, authors, musicians, dancers, film makers. Also known as **direct-to-consumer sales and marketing**, creator-run enterprises are a booming business model.

Crowdfunding was one example of a tool supporting the creator economy. Direct sales to fans (especially of premium or exclusive products) is a second example. We looked at both earlier.

A third way in which this can manifest is through platforms where writers get paid for their work via monthly subscriptions, with options to serialise work as paid content – or to make the main content free and receive subscriptions in other ways, such as for behind-the-scenes posts, non-fiction work, livestreams and interaction, or just to show support. This is an area where distribution (this chapter) crosses over with marketing (next chapter), showing that nothing is truly separate, and many topics permeate boundaries. Life is a gradient, not a binary switch.

I've known authors who felt their work wasn't something that had mass appeal, so rather than spend their life fighting an uphill battle trying to get an agent and publisher, or having to deal with the publication business independently, they decided they'd rather make it available to the thousand people who would really love it. Monthly income and direct interactions from (for example) serialisation may end up being worth much more than the sale of a single book to those fans every couple of years. Because it isn't just about making money from words, but about *deepening our connection with readers*. We cut out the middlemen and have a more rewarding (both financial and personal) relationship as a result. At its heart it is about building a community, which is different from just selling a book as a sterile financial transaction.

I first started thinking about all this in 2021 while looking into platforms for a new online presence that allowed greater engagement with my fans. I wanted a site with these features:

- A combined blog and newsletter. It had to be easy for people to sign up without an account so fans could be informed of new releases. I wanted them to receive it as an emailed newsletter, but for it also to be a linkable blog post afterwards, available to the whole world. I wanted full access to subscriber email addresses, so I don't lose my fans if I move platform.

- An optional paid subscriber list, with posts just for them. Ideally they don't need to have accounts to pay or donate, they just do a normal card transaction.

- Ability to sell items: ebooks (and bundles), audiobooks, editing services, maybe print books.

- Ideally money would go straight into my bank account: that saves me bothering with third parties like Stripe, PayPal or Payoneer.

Your requirements and interests may well be different, so your best bet is to explore the sites in this list. Some are newsletter sites with options to include paid subscriptions, some have other features such as the ability to sell ebooks or take donations. I'm just listing them as starters, none are recommendations. The list is in alphabetical order.

- BuyMeACoffee.[157] Subscriptions, donations

- Gumroad.[158] Newsletter/blog, paid subscriptions option, sell digital products.

- Ko-Fi.[159] Subscriptions, donations. Requires PayPal or Stripe.

- Patreon.[160] Paid subscriptions, sell digital products. Requires Payoneer or PayPal in the UK – bank payments are only an option in the US.

- Payhip.[161] Sell digital products.

- Shopify.[162] Newsletter, sell products.

- Steady.[163]

- Substack.[164] Newsletter/blog, paid subscriptions option.

If you do experiment with paid subscriptions, think about what you can offer in exchange. Free copies of new books? Extra personal news and content? Original short stories? Snippets of works-in-progress? It may be a case of finding out what fans would be interested in before going down this route, and if there would be a demand for it.

The Environment

Since we are taking an idea which does no harm to the world, and turning it into a physical thing people can hold and read, there are implications for resources and energy usage. In the last couple of years big publishers have been challenged regarding the huge environmental impacts of their operations, and their decisions on how to manage the business. At a smaller scale, everything we do as individuals has impacts. In a book about publishing, it would be remiss of us to skip over this topic. We have a responsibility to consider it.

Printed Books: Materials Used

The primary material for printed books is *paper*. That crinkly, foldable, bright skin which acts as a contrast to the darkness of the words.

The process of making paper is resource intensive. Trees are cut down. I've heard it said that for every twenty-five books printed, one tree is chopped down.

Then a paper mill will de-bark, pulp and process the wood, chemically clean and bleach it, and finally form the results into sheets of paper for transportation to paper merchants, and then on to printers. Large-scale traditional printers use a lot of resources, create significant waste, and require vast amounts of space.

A lot of books get published globally, often via massive print runs. Forests store up carbon, but deforestation releases it so we end up with more CO^2 in the atmosphere. Distribution of both the raw paper and the finished physical books requires energy for transportation, adding to the overall carbon footprint of the industry.

The ideal form of paper from an environmental perspective is 100% recycled, from *post-consumer waste* (some paper claiming to be recycled is actually "recycled" from virgin paper, a total con). But that type of paper is not popular with publishers, as they want to sell books as a luxury item, rather than an environmentally friendly one. Next best is recycled paper which isn't fully from post-consumer waste. The third choice would be paper with some kind of certification process such as that by the Forestry Stewardship Council (FSC), though Greenpeace have been critical of the FSC standard. I, also, tend to be dubious about these, since it sounds too much like "sustainable palm oils" (when the only truly sustainable option is not to use tropical fats at all).

And that's part of the issue. How can it be sustainable to keep cutting down trees for paper as we buy more and more books? Well, the forestry and publishing industries would say replacement trees are often planted, but there is an element of greenwashing there. Globally we continue to see ancient forests chopped down in favour of monoculture: fast-growing non-native tree plantations. These cause a massive biodiversity loss, use huge amounts of pesticides and water, force indigenous communities from their land, and (because the clear-cutting system is used instead of less profitable coppicing) there is soil erosion and water run-off. Again, a similar picture to what we see with palm oil plantations.

The scale of the problem is huge. According to Wordsrated[165] the US publishing industry alone uses 32 million trees a year, whilst Isonomia[166] says:

"We can therefore estimate that meeting the demand for the 190 million books sold in the UK in 2018 required around 1.9 million trees: a considerable amount of pulp-based fiction, equivalent to almost a year's worth of the last Government's target of planting 11 million new trees in the UK over five years."

That's just two countries. Think of how enormous the global impact is.

Even slight improvements would have huge effects. According to Wordsrated again, "46% of a book's environmental impact is caused by a reduction in biomass and wood harvest" ... "If the publishing industry committed to using around 30% of waste that could be repurposed and sold to consumers, 4.9 million trees could be saved."

In the last few years we have seen price increases for many products. Paper isn't an exception. Book publishers have been hit with higher prices for that base material as demand from society keeps on growing – often for wasteful products such as disposable nappies and junk mail.

But printed books aren't just paper. They are likely to be produced using a number of potentially toxic chemicals such as glues, oils, and sealants, which are used to bind and finish the book. The printing ink used is also a major component, usually made from fossil fuels but sometimes from crushed shellfish or ground-up calf hooves, even though vegetable ink offers a more environmentally friendly and kind option.

In recent years there has been a worrying trend to add foils, glitters, laminates and varnishes to the covers of books, as if they were greeting cards. And as with cards, these books are even more damaging as it makes recycling harder, leading to only low grade recycled output. The only reason for adding these finishes to covers is for the sake of appearance, to make things shinier to tempt people into buying them. Once one publisher started doing it, the others copied them, as it became an arms war where each felt they needed to keep up with the others so their books looked just as good in bookshop displays. The trend then creates consumer expectations, leading to a self-reinforcing process despite the great environmental cost.

It reminds me of computer games when they were sold in shops in the nineties. The game was stored on a small floppy disk or CD-ROM, but some publishers would put them into a huge box so they dominated everything else on the game shelves. Then others would copy the approach so their wares stood out, too. You would take your purchase home, open the huge box, and just find a small game and a lot of hot air. In both cases (books and games) the blame is partly on publishers for their awful waste, and partly on consumers for supporting it.

In an ideal world printed books would be made using only environmentally friendly chemicals, so that they were basically compostable. We could have been doing that for the last hundred years, but, thanks to choices made by publishers and the printing industry, that isn't the case.

This topic has been on the agenda a lot more since the March 2023 London Book Fair featured a sustainability lounge. Following on from that, in April 2023 The Society of Authors launched their Tree to Me campaign,[167] encouraging authors to pressure their publishers to improve the sustainability of books in terms of energy used, companies invested in, and carbon emissions.

Printed Books: Offset Printing And Returns

Earlier in this chapter I discussed how offset printing involves traditional publishers guessing at how many books are needed, then doing bulk print runs of many thousands of copies in advance. There is a tendency to overestimate because the larger the print run, the lower the unit cost. The books then get stacked up in warehouses, or transported by lorry to bookshops (and possibly back again, with environmental costs both ways).

Why would they come back? It's tied to one of the book industry's dirty secrets: returns. You'd expect that, compared to perishable foods, books last forever on a shelf. Unfortunately the reality of economics and the pressure of new releases means books almost have a best-before date, since many copies that bookshops don't sell in the first month will be returned to the publisher for a refund.

And if the books can't be sold, the publisher doesn't want to pay to warehouse the copies indefinitely just because someone's sales predictions didn't match the reality. And so the surplus books get pulped as low-grade paper (though in the past were sometimes dumped in landfill, as famously happened when Atari buried 700,000 unsold video game cartridges and other hardware in a New Mexico site in 1983).

Publishers are tight-lipped about the figures because they don't want readers to know the waste involved, but according to one article[168] 20-25% of traditionally printed books are returned unsold, and author Dean Wesley Smith says the return rate was as high as 50% during the 1990s. So half of the printed books were returned to be destroyed. As one of my friends said when I raised this topic:

> "I worked in the book selling and warehouse management world back in the late 80s/90s – the returns got stocked out 'the back' and you could help yourself to anything you wanted. Sometimes entire stock was ordered incorrectly by the bookstore, returned to wholesale and left collecting dust. They are probably still there! I had so many books – free books! Everyone got books for presents ... but a real pain when you had to move flat."

Orna Ross and Dan Parsons discussed this topic in one of their podcasts.[169] Dan used to work in a bookshop, and was aware of how the books that didn't sell in the first six months were seen as yesterday's news and returned to the publisher to be pulped. Orna's reply was: "The thing a lot of people don't realise about trade publishing is that it's based on 80%, probably more, failing. So, the publishing house will make money because it has lots of authors, and they don't care which one wins, as they know that they will get a winner in that season, and they're happy with that, and all their budgeting and everything is done on the basis that most of the books won't succeed."

Robin Cutler, who used to be Director of IngramSpark, is quoted in *Your Book in Bookstores: ALLi's Guide to Print Book Distribution for Authors* (Debbie P. Young, 2021) as saying that in some situations involving full-service distribution (where reps promote books to bookshops directly, encouraging them to make orders) there is an average *60% return rate.*

According to Wordsrated,[170] even nowadays "Each year consumers waste more than 16,000 truckloads of books which have not been read once. [...] Around 10 million trees are killed for the production of books that eventually end up getting destroyed rather than read."

One fix for this situation of printing masses of books, then shipping them around the world just to be destroyed, is to *stop allowing returns*. Publishers don't want to go down that route because they think they would then have fewer books ordered and sold, and profit comes before preventing waste.

However, if you're an independent author, then your POD distributor may well have a check box where you can choose whether to allow returns or not. As stated earlier in this chapter, I strongly recommend *never* enabling returns. Not only would returns get charged to your account, but there are also the environmental issues mentioned above.

Better for a book to be reduced in price and sold, than wasted. At least that way everyone benefits to a degree: the author still gets paid; the customer gets a bargain; the bookshop clears inventory and has a happy customer who is more likely to return.

Printed Books: Print-On-Demand

"Karl, you're a depressing person. It's made even worse by the way you talk to yourself all the time."

True. So I'd like to offer a bit of hope, thanks to a technological innovation we discussed earlier, that has affected the publishing industry in the last twenty years: print-on-demand (POD).

If offset printing is associated with waste from its large print runs and returns system, then the fix is to avoid as much waste as possible. And you can't get much more efficient than printing on demand. The book exists as digital files until a physical version is ordered, at which point the single copy is printed and delivered, which also cuts out the need for warehouse storage. And because someone requested it, there really is a demand for this copy, unlike the speculative distribution of traditionally printed books.

POD is the system used by just about every independent author, helping them achieve a more sustainable business model than traditional publishing. And since most independent authors sell a lot more ebooks than print books, the physical copy part of their business uses far fewer resources than the mass print runs of traditional publishing.

If POD is so great, why isn't it the only system in use? Because it is more expensive per copy, as we saw earlier. POD can't compete with the economy of scale where offset printing can lead to a cheaper unit cost, even factoring in the waste and warehousing. In capitalist free markets, economics takes precedence over the environment.

Before I say farewell to the environmental impact of printed books, I'd like to end on a positive. Waste and endless consumerism go hand in hand. The urge to buy more, to throw away, to replace rather than repair, to seek only the latest thing because that's what we see in crappy advertising. But it is not an inevitable way of life. Remember: a wonderful book that you cherish for fifty years is not wasteful. A book that is shared with others again and again is not wasteful. A single treasured book has more value than twenty inconsequential and forgettable ones.

So we don't have to feel guilty for owning some books that we adore, where the words are worthy of reading and rereading. Reverence and selectivity *is* sustainable.

Ebooks (And Hardware)

Ebooks have no physical presence, apart from the device they're stored on, and the energy and networks used to transmit them. But that device is the part of the equation that could have the biggest environmental impact.

First, the ebook reader (or whatever gadget is used, such as a smartphone or tablet PC) has to be made. That requires all sorts of non-renewable materials that have to be mined and transported, with all the environmental and human exploitation implications of those activities. According to Popsci[171] a single e-reader uses 33 pounds of minerals and materials (such as copper, lithium, cobalt, and plastic) in its manufacturing process alone. Ethical Consumer has written about conflict minerals in tech goods and home appliances,[172] as well as more generally on environmental issues in the tech industry.[173]

There is a way to mitigate all that massively, though: second-hand e-readers and gadgets. Then you're reducing demand by reusing already-manufactured items. It's a case of changing mindsets, to resist the "replace with new" attitude that is pushed by the harmful consumerist elements of our culture, and the awful companies that benefit from it.

We should also be aware of how many tech companies engineer inbuilt obsolescence. They do this in three ways: mechanically, by making things that aren't robust enough to last; through software updates that prevent older models working; and through social engineering and advertising. They don't want you to be using the same smartphone or tablet PC a decade from now, they want you to buy a new one every few years, because that makes shareholders richer and gives bigger bonuses to senior managers. They must hate me, because I have only ever owned one mobile phone. It's about fourteen years old, the screen only half works and there's no way to update it so that it can run apps, but it still works as an emergency phone, mp3 player and camera, which is all I'll ever need it for.

I encountered this issue again in April 2024. Netflix worked perfectly on an old Kindle Fire tablet. But then Netflix released an update that completely blocked the service from devices like mine, with no way around it. Their tech support told me to buy another device and bin the old one, even though it could technically run the service flawlessly. Amazon also chose to stop its Audible service from working on older Kindle Fires the same year, even though the app only streamed audio and had worked perfectly before. I wrote about inbuilt obsolescence as a result of that.[174]

Which leads on to the issue of end-of-life for devices. They are rarely recycled, certainly not fully. E-waste is a massive global issue, and unlikely to improve any time soon. Ethical Consumer has a good article on "toxic techno trash".[175]

Next, power is needed. Firstly it is required for the infrastructure that supports digital downloads. As we transition to more online services, world data centre storage and transmission networks use massive – and increasing – amounts of electricity. Whether it be streamed films and music, or ebook storage and downloads, the International Energy Agency[176] claims energy demand from data centres and routers "each account for 1-1.5% of global electricity use". In January 2025 we found out that Labour wants to build many more data and AI centres, and construct nuclear power plants just to provide a portion of the massive amounts of power they will require. As an environmentalist, that horrifies me.

Secondly, the e-reader device itself needs power to run. We all know how that works. Electricity bills in particular are a huge part of the modern cost of living, otherwise CEOs of electric companies wouldn't have private jets and islands. I would love a future where microgeneration (such as solar panels) means most electricity is produced locally from renewable sources, with excess sold to the grid at a fair rate. Until then, the other option to improve things is perhaps to switch to a renewable energy provider, and to lobby governments to better support renewable options.

Not all devices use power at the same rate. A lot of that is determined by the screen: an important aspect for both comfort and power consumption, if you are going to read a lot of ebooks. And there are two main options.

One is an **e-ink screen**, sometimes called **electronic paper**. And that's because the text on it does look like words on a printed page. They tend to be greyscale only, and slower to refresh than a colour LCD screen. Another key difference is that e-ink isn't backlit, so – just like a print book – you need a light source such as a lamp or daylight to read.

LCD screens are what we're used to from TVs, smartphones and laptops. (I'm using LCD generically – there are actually many different types and technologies, such as OLED, but the average person wouldn't be able to tell between them just by looking, so LCD is good enough for our purposes.) They are colour, have fast refresh rates, and are backlit – they emit light.

The light element is important for reading ebooks. You want to read e-ink in bed? You need to put the lamp on. Whereas an LCD screen can be used in the dark. But if you are sat in the garden on a sunny day, most LCD screens are rubbish, and you'd be squinting to make out the text, since the backlighting can't compete with the sun. But an e-ink screen would be perfect in those conditions. E-ink is more relaxing for your eyes than bombarding them with light from TV-type screens.

E-ink also uses a lot less power. The technology basically draws the text and then uses hardly any energy to keep it displayed until you turn to a new page. Some e-ink devices could even be turned off and still display the current page. Whereas LCD screens use a lot of energy to display anything as they blast potentially harmful blue light through a screen and update sixty times a second. This is why you may find you have to charge a smartphone or tablet PC every day (even when you've hardly used it), whereas an e-ink ebook reader might go weeks or months between charges, depending on how much it's used.

So there are pros and cons to each device, and much of it comes down to how you will use them.

Suppose you don't care about apps, and mobile games, and watching films on devices. You just want to read books. Well, you'd obviously be best with a specialised e-reader, and probably one that uses e-ink and could last decades.

But what if you want to watch films, play games, use all sorts of apps? You could go down the route of having different devices for different purposes. A Steamdeck for games. An e-reader for ebooks. A large-screen smartphone or tablet for films and comms. You'll get the best performance for each function, but will be spending more money and end up in charging cable hell as each device has to be continually topped up. And, obviously, this will be the most harmful option for the environment. Or just pick the single multifunction device that provides the best compromise for all your needs.

So, Which Is Best For The Environment?

Whether ebooks or printed books are better for the environment purely comes down to how many you read.

Here's another figure related to the environmental impacts of both types of reading. According to Wordsrated: "The lifecycle of a Kindle device produces around 168 kg of CO_2. [...] Purchasing three paper books a month for four years produces around 1,074 kg of CO_2 in comparison."[177]

So in terms of CO_2 alone, buying a Kindle to read only a handful of books would be a huge waste, but using it to read a lot of books over time would work out much kinder on the environment than buying each new book as a paperback.

Popsci quote the director of the Center for Sustainable Systems at the University of Michigan,[178] who summarises this as: "On a mass basis, comparing the production of one kilogram of paper with one kilogram of electronics equipment, the e-reader would have a much greater impact. But the utility of the e-reader for downloading and reading multiple books is where there is the advantage, even when considering the energy requirements during use and storage of data on servers."

With paperbacks, printing and transport means each copy will add the same additional amount to the total environmental costs of your reading. Whereas, once you have an e-reader (with its initial larger environmental cost), each ebook added to it only has a tiny additional resource implication.

So how many books would you need to read to reach the tipping point where an e-reader was the more environmentally friendly option? There's always going to be some ambiguity about that. Wordsrated say: "A consumer could purchase around 22.5 paper books before it would be more environmentally friendly to use a Kindle."

Popsci summarises other research on this topic, which gives various figures: 36 books, 60 books, 100 books. Just so I can give some rough guidance, let's find the mean average of all those numbers. The result is: 55 books.

There we have it. Buying and reading 55 printed books may roughly equal the environmental impact of reading 55 books on an e-reader. So if you are going to read thousands of books, you're better off with an e-reader. If you are only going to buy a few a year, you might as well stick to paperbacks (and give any that you don't want to keep forever on to someone else who will enjoy them).

In terms of passing books on: second-hand books or those borrowed from libraries are the most environmentally friendly and least wasteful options of all. The ethical consideration for me is always this one:

Reduce > Re-use > Recycle.

Second-hand books count as re-use, whilst also reducing the demand for new products, so it is a double win.

The other advantage of second-hand sellers is that you can get books and editions that are no longer in print. Hopefully you have second-hand bookshops, jumble sales, car-boot sales or charity shops near you. If not, here are some options that don't require creating an account, since you can checkout as a guest:

- BetterWorldBooks[179]
- Biblio[180]
- World of Books[181]

Another option is to swap books with friends and turn it into a social activity. And after reading them, you have a shared book in common and can discuss the story and characters, what worked about the book and what didn't, and while away the hours in an evening garden gathering with a bottle of wine.

Drinky's Digressions: Should Authors Be Worried About Second-hand Books?

No.

Some authors will whine that they don't get extra payments from second-hand sales. To them I'd say: when you resell your sofa, your phone, your DVDs or your car, the original manufacturer doesn't get a cut – why should books be any different? And my librarian persona also likes to shout "Reading is good, and culture should be shared!" at the top of its voice. Usually before they cart me away in the little white van.

I encourage people to do what they want with my books. I don't mind if they're given to libraries, charity shops, friends, sold on, composted, or carved into book sculptures in my noble likeness.

In the long run, the more widely your work is spread, the more people will have awareness of you. It's like music or games. When I was a kid people shared these around on cassettes. Some of those games, musicians, bands and developers went on to become my favourites, where I'd buy everything they created – but if I'd never received copies for free off someone else, I'd never have become a fan.

Buying books is a commitment (partly money, partly time, and partly storage space), and only occurs if the reader has enough impetus to make that commitment. And that requires a number of things, one of which is interest in the author, which often comes from having seen their previous work. So don't be worried. The more your name is out there, the more it is shared (for good things), the more chance you have of becoming a name that people will pay for and support.

Marketing

Chapter 9

I consider marketing to be the final stage of book production. Although I've included it after distribution (since in most cases you need the book to be available before you can promote it) note that a key chunk of marketing takes place *before* publication. Teasers, advance review copies, generating buzz, letting fans know what's coming and so on. There are always promotional activities to do, and if it isn't for your next release, then it is for your backlist. For simplicity I have moved everything to do with marketing into a single stage, and therefore a single chapter. This topic will be a big chunk of your life from now on. Yes, I know that's a depressing thought for many of you.

I see marketing as identifying your ideal audience of readers, writing something that will appeal to them, and then working out how to raise awareness of your book with that audience. And doing so in an ethical fashion. So there are elements of gathering information about audiences (input), and then promotion (output), where we try to increase sales by enticing people to buy the book.

Most of this is aimed at making a book *discoverable* to readers looking for a book like yours. Much of the metadata in Chapter 7 was part of that task. And as well as readers, it can be handy to build good relationships through networking: with reviewers, bloggers, reporters, and other authors. The more people who know of your work and are well-disposed towards you, the more exposure you might be able to generate.

Some people try to distinguish between *publicity* and *marketing*. They say the former is time-limited promotions, the latter is longer-term awareness raising. Personally, I find the distinction unhelpful, and many activities blur between them. Whether you call it marketing or publicity, the goal is the same: creating conditions to let the right readers know your books exist.

"Hey, Karl, I *hate* marketing! That's why I want to go with a traditional publisher, so I can just write books!"

Once I've stopped laughing I'll point out that there's no getting away from this for most authors. If you're traditionally published then the publisher will still expect you to be doing most of these things. In fact, in many cases one of the factors in them *deciding* to publish a book is how marketable the author is, and what platform they already have or will be able to build. On the plus side, they'll (hopefully) arrange some of this for you. On the downside, they'll focus mainly on the book launch, and unless the book sells in massive numbers, they'll then just consider it backlist and move on to new books by other authors. To keep the flame alive, you'll still need to do marketing. And no, in most cases the publisher won't be promoting your book on billboards and buses: the reality is that your book will be buried along with others at the back of a bookshop. Publishers tend to only invest in promotion for the books deemed likely to recoup the investment, which is often top-ten books with the £250,000+ advances.

The marketing topic could easily fill ten volumes, so I'm just going to briefly mention a few things that are worth considering. Some of them apply to book launches (especially building buzz, press coverage or book tours), others apply to more general marketing (such as developing your website). The key thing is that everything you do to promote your work should provide something positive: profit (ideally), publicity (conceivably), and pleasure (hopefully, both for you and the recipient).

Marketing isn't just asking people to buy your book. That's ineffective and annoying. Good marketing is about creating, building and strengthening relationships with your readers. They then become supportive friends and fans, and even superfans who will champion your work and be excited about your new books.

Clever marketing is about focussing on your true audience, people who will love the book. It is about being selective. Remember Ranganathan, and "Every reader their book, and every book its reader"? Well, every book has an ideal audience which is smaller than the full reading population (Karl's Law).

Whereas *stupid marketing* is a broad attack on everyone. It is the equivalent of junk mail through the letterbox, a scattergun approach that leads to masses of waste and annoyance from people who have no interest in the product.

This has many important implications for targeting a work. If a book is not selling then it could be the content, blurb or cover at fault. If they are all good then it is a discoverability issue. No one hears of the book so no one sees it and no one buys it. Without sales there are no also-boughts, so all the main discovery mechanisms start to shut down. We have to make sure marketing is in place and working, to get onto the upwards, self-reinforcing opposite spiral: the cycle where you have sales, so reviews and also-boughts, and increased visibility, and it all feeds in to keep growing.

But do note that book sales aren't as important as health, love, and family, so keep working on it, but don't lose sleep or make yourself ill worrying about it.

Lastly, marketing needn't be all-consuming. Many authors break it into small tasks, and try to do one thing a day. And so I will break this chapter up into a Smörgåsbord of savoury topics you can dip into.

Author Platform

No, it isn't the low table I stand on when a big spider runs across the floor.

Your author platform is the totality of your online presence, and the many means by which you interact with your audience. So at the core will probably be your website, your newsletter, and your social media profiles. Each serves different purposes, often for different audiences.

The aim is to have a reasonable spread, so that the majority of people have a fairly easy time finding out about you and your work.

Website

This is the first key element of your author platform. It is a showcase of your work. The corner of the Web that you control.

At its simplest it has a bit about you (often on a page called "About"), and a bit about your books and where to buy them. It will also link to any other places where you have an online presence, such as social media sites, and a means to contact you via email or a form. If you have a newsletter, people should be able to sign up here. That's why your website is the hub of your communications empire, and the key thing you direct fans to.

Don't forget to refresh your website every time you release a new book, adding its details and cover and putting it front and centre so visitors see it. Likewise you'll announce it in your newsletter and on social media (if you use it) – I'll cover those soon.

When you are starting out I recommend a really simple site, which doesn't overwhelm anyone with information or take a lot of clicks to get anywhere. I like designs that are attractive but unfussy, and work equally well whether viewed on a desktop PC browser, or a small-screen mobile device.

Whatever you choose, make sure you back up your content in some way, at the very least copying web page text into documents saved on your PC.

Website Options

Unless otherwise specified, none are recommendations or ones I have used, so buyer beware. They should all offer a choice of themes. Do pay attention to their costs: some are much pricier than others.

Small sites

- Carrd.[182] I host my website on Carrd, which is great for minimalist designs and also cheap, but with good support and an intuitive interface.
- Ucraft.[183]
- Strikingly.[184]
- IM Creator.[185]
- 8b.[186]

More complex hosted sites

- Wordpress.[187] Note that the free plan puts adverts on

your website: as the owner of the site you won't see them if you are logged in, but visitors will (and they'll assume you endorse the adverts being shown).

- Squarespace.[188]

- Pub Site.[189] Aimed at authors.

- Author Websites.[190] A new service by BookBub.

- Shopify.[191] Includes direct selling options, but see the criticisms in the Direct Sales section of Chapter 8.

I would avoid Weebly as they block their sites from some nations, and keep that list secret.[192] That means if you use Weebly as your web host your website won't be visible to fans in some countries. And if you boycott Israel because of its ongoing military occupation of Palestine, apartheid system, land theft, or oppression of Palestinians, then you'll want to avoid Wix as it is an Israeli company.

Custom Domains

A domain name is the text version of a website's address. It usually has what we think of as the "name" part, followed by a top-level suffix such as .com, .edu, .co.uk, or .org.

When you first set up a website the domain name may be that of the website hosting service, plus a personal element tagged on. So if I used Wordpress for my website, I might end up with karldrinkwater.wordpress.com, for example.

A custom domain looks more professional because it is separate from the website host's, something like yourname.org, or john smith.scot, or karldrinkwater.uk.

Whoever you use for your website, you might want to consider your own domain name. Check your website host can work with custom domains first, though I'd be surprised if they didn't, as it is a standard requirement. A good website host will let you easily configure things so that anyone going to that domain address will see your website.

If you have a common name then, when choosing your domain, you could try adding "author" e.g. authorjohnsmith, or sandrajonesauthor.

I'm not going to talk about all the companies who can sell you domains, but it may be that you can already do that through your ISP or website host.

One of the key advantages to owning your own domain is that you can take it with you if you change website platform, such as switching from using Carrd to Wordpress. Then all your links (in books, on business cards, on sites where you've been interviewed) will still work. The web address people visit won't change – they'll just see the new website when they get there.

Some website services will let you buy a domain through them, but it is often not transferrable if you move to another company, missing out on one of the main reasons to pay for a custom domain. It's why it is better to buy your domain from a place that isn't tied to your website host. It's similar to the situation with ISBNs: if I own my own, I can use them with any vendor. However, if I distribute books through IngramSpark and use *their* ISBNs, the book can only ever be distributed via IngramSpark and if I choose a new distributor, I need a new ISBN. Transferrable is always better, for domains and ISBNs.

Note that you can't buy a domain forever – it is a recurring charge, usually every two to three years. The cost and frequency is often determined by the domain suffix, such as .com, .org.uk, .net etc. When choosing domains you should be presented with a number of choices and their different prices.

Own-domain Email

Your domain should come with the facility to set up email addresses. This may be included in the package, or you may need to pay extra to include email facilities. You definitely should. It means you can have an email address composed of something of your choice preceding the @, and then the domain. So if your domain is sallygreen.com then you could have addresses such as info@sallygreen.com, sally@sallygreen.com or whatever. This can be handy for segregating communications. For example, one address used for fans and writing, another used for friends and family. I have one that I register with services when setting up accounts, but don't use for anything personal. I also have one called junkotron@karldrinkwater.uk which I only use for one-off registrations or cases where I don't want to hear back. I never check that account or set it up in software, it's very much my autodestruct email.

Using the same domain name for your website and email looks seventy-four times more professional than using freebies like gmail or yahoo for your email address.

Top Tip: Metadata

We looked at book metadata in Chapter 7, but websites have metadata too. Make sure you enter a good description of your website on whatever platform you host your website on. That is what search engines will use and display when linking to your site in search results.

A particular type of metadata pertaining only to websites is the **favicon**. You know when you go to a website, your browser usually has a small icon for it somewhere in the address bar? It is also used if you save a link to that website. Well, that's called a favicon, and all good websites hosts should prompt you for one. If not, look through the settings. They are small, square images, and adding a favicon makes your website stand out in a list of bookmarks, as well as looking more professional. A good one ties in to your author branding, logos, and colour choices, and is distinctive even at a small size.

Newsletter

I discussed newsletters a bit in the Creator Economies section of Chapter 8. Now I can expand on the marketing options and value they provide, as the second key element of your author platform.

With social media sites you may have followers and fans. Yay! But the site itself owns that data, and monetises it in various ways. If you had a million followers on what-was-Twitter and leave the platform, you don't have direct contact details for those million people (nor permission to contact them – just as important!) ... you have *nothing*. They're not transferrable. It's one of the ways social media sites keep you chained to their systems, since you feel you've put in so much work to create a following that you can't bear to lose it and start all over again.

That's the key advantage of a newsletter. People provide their email addresses and permission to send them emails, so you can inform them when you have a new book out. Instead of the contact details being hidden from you, *you have them*. Even if you change newsletter provider, any decent one lets you export the email addresses and names and take them with you, to import into the new service provider. So, unlike social media where you're squatting in someone else's playhouse and subject to their rules, with your newsletter you actually have a contacts list of interested people that you can build over time.

It's the same reason why I don't use Draft2Digital's "New Release Notifications sign-up" automated end matter. It lets readers enter their email to get told of new releases, but since you won't have access to that subscriber data it is always better to guide readers to your own newsletter instead.

What Newsletter Platform Should You Use?

I listed a number of newsletter options (with or without paid subscription features) when I discussed Creator Economies in Chapter 8. I have used a number of them, but feel that if you are starting out then your best bet is Substack[193] or Gumroad.[194] Both feel writerly and friendly to me, plus they are both free.

If you already have a website that offers a newsletter option (as Shopify does) then you may be better off using that.

Professional marketers may complain that we should be using complex mailing systems with features like onboarding routes, automations, campaigns, A/B split tests, integrations, segmented audiences and so on ... but to me that's overkill if all you do is send simple newsletters. It's why I hated using Mailchimp. But you use the platform that works best for you, and if you want all those tools, have a look at those platforms which charge a monthly fee such as MailerLite or Mailchimp.

Remember that you should be able to export your subscriber list and use it on another platform if you ever change. It's the whole reason for having access to that data.

Newsletter Content

You need to create engaging newsletters for those who subscribe, but the actual content, style and presentation will vary from author to author. The only constant is that it should match the voice you use in your books, or the way you present yourself. If all your books are chatty and light-hearted, then your newsletter should be as well. This ties in to your author brand, which I'll get to soon.

I think the best newsletters have a bit about the person (which creates a connection with them), and a bit about their work. It's a balance. If it's all about their books, it comes across as hard-sell spam. If it's all about the person, it comes across as egotistical and unrelated to their work (which is probably the reason someone signed up to the newsletter in the first place).

I like to include something personal and interesting about my life or where I live, maybe with a photo or two. Fans often tell me that's their favourite part. Then a bit about my current or future books and plans, new book releases, major news, opportunities, requests, and special offers.

As with giving talks, try to keep things brief, and they will be appreciated more.

That ties in to retention. There's nothing gained if you get hundreds of people signing up to your newsletter if hundreds of people unsubscribe again a week later. That means you're either attracting the wrong people, or they don't like your newsletter once they see it. Both are bad. It's why I don't do freebies (called **lead magnets** in marketing articles) in exchange for people signing up to my newsletter – you just get lots of signups where people are only joining for the freebie. They may not even supply an email address they ever check, so it means your **open rate** (a percentage of how many people who received the newsletter actually opened it – not an accurate figure, but vaguely useful for assessing engagement) will always be low. I'd rather have a newsletter that grows in numbers slowly and organically, and represents truly interested fans.

If you keep your emails short and interesting and don't send too many, people will stay subscribed because they like what you offer, and the personal connection to an author as a person. They want to know when you have a new book out. With my newsletter it's even set up so a recipient can click reply and send a message straight back to my inbox.

I recommend subscribing to the newsletters of authors you like, and seeing what they include. Which newsletters do you enjoy receiving, and why? That may guide you as to how to shape your own.

Drinky's Digressions: Good And Bad Links

As we saw in Chapter 5, it is standard to have a newsletter signup link in the back matter of a book. Interested readers have the option to subscribe in order to get notified of new releases, and it is easily ignored if they aren't interested.

But you might hear that doing so can get you and your work permanently banned on Amazon, and as with all rumours, there is an underlying element of truth. The cause is this Amazon rule:[195]

> "Some examples of prohibited external links include: [...] Links to web forms that request customer information (e.g., email address, physical address or similar)"

Which, at a literal level, *would* exclude a newsletter link to a form where someone is required to enter their email address.

But John Doppler, in his ALLi Watchdog role, reassured me in February 2024:

> "The rule is confusing, so I contacted Amazon for clarification. The prohibition is actually on *content* that is hidden behind a paywall, mailing list signup, or other barrier; not on having a link at the back of your book.
>
> Years ago, 'scampreneurs' were placing ebooks on Amazon that would have the first few chapters included, but if you wanted to see the rest of the book, you had to fill out a sign-up form on an external website (or pay an additional fee). This rule was implemented to ban those sorts of schemes. There is no restriction on placing a link to your mailing list signup at the back of your book, as long as content is not dependent on that signup.
>
> However, Amazon's screeners have had a few mis-

fires where they incorrectly assumed that the link to a mailing list was a content offloading scheme, and removed the book from sale until the author set them straight. Those were errors, and were eventually reversed.

The other rules about links to pornography, other retailers, and malware are more straightforward and can be taken at face value."

See also the KDP rules roundup where this is mentioned.[196]

Draft2Digital also confirmed that John is correct: "Links are okay, but setting up paywalls, or requiring mailing list signup to be able to see the content you bought and paid for is where the violation comes in. 'If you liked the first chapter then join my mailing list to receive the rest of the book for free!' Hard to believe people do that, or think it is in any way okay, but they do. They absolutely do."

I'll mention ethics and professionalism later, but in brief: don't abuse or trick your customers. It harms your business, and that of other authors.

Top Tip: Domain And Newsletter Privacy

If you buy a domain, your name and address are often made public by default. This is something determined by the provider you buy the domain from, and is worth checking in advance.

As with newsletters below, the revelation of an address is not a problem for companies with official premises, but if you are a sole trader and it is your home address, you won't want that. So make sure privacy is enabled on your domain. A good domain provider won't charge you for this.

You can check what shows by visiting Whois[197] and entering a domain. So go there and enter karldrinkwater.uk and you will see my domain registration details, but not my address. Whereas a search for amazon.com will bring up a registered address for their legal department. (This is sometimes a handy way to get a company's contact details.)

A similar issue pertains to newsletters.

In this modern world, we're often affected by laws made in other countries. In the UK you don't have to include a physical address in an email newsletter. However, the USA passed a law in 2003 called CAN-SPAM which, bizarrely, makes spam emails more likely. One of the many badly-thought-out elements was the requirement to include a physical address in the footer of your newsletters. And even though I don't live in the US, I'm forced to comply with this because my newsletters might go there. (Note that those sending illegal spam just ignore this or fake an address; like DRM, it doesn't penalise criminals, only normal people.)

Why is a postal address an issue? If you run a small freelance business such as being an author, then your only address is your home address. And, understandably, you don't want to be giving that out to strangers. It's a legitimate safety concern. No one is ever going to write to you when they can just reply to the email; but weirdos certainly might make use of knowing where you live, and it's a key piece of information used in identity theft, so raises all sorts of security issues.

Since in 99.99% of cases no one legitimate will ever use the listed physical location, I have heard of authors who just shorten their address so people can't turn up on their doorstep. A "house name" rather than number, for example. Or they *accidentally* mistype their postcode, or leave in an old address, because … well, mistakes happen. Even fake PO Boxes have been used, since it is hard for anyone to confirm it. Unless you somehow attract the ire of the US Government and they investigate the address in small print at the bottom of your newsletters, no one apart from dodgy weirdos and criminals would ever know. (Note: don't come to me for legal advice, I'm just pointing out how stupid some laws are.)

The CAN-SPAM act does allow the use of PO box addresses and their like, but that's a poor option for a few reasons. Firstly, it's a paid service, so if you aren't making much money from writing it can knock you into the red. It's certainly not cheap. Secondly these aren't fully anonymous – to set them up you have to provide your real postal address, and there are systems in place to get that real address associated with a PO box. Thirdly, for many of these services you have to provide all sorts of identity information, maybe even uploading scans of your passport or driving licence – which is a massive ID theft security issue. As soon as that scan is out there you have no control over where it ends up. Companies get hacked, employees steal data, companies go bankrupt and get sold, and policies change. The drive to confirm identities often leads to serious issues that *increase* the risk of identity theft. One private PO box rental service required all your phone numbers, your date of birth, and a copy of your passport, driving licence or birth certificates: a data grab which seriously opens you up to the risk of identity theft.

For all these reasons a decent newsletter service would offer their own address as the sender for any sole traders such as authors. It's why I'm not a fan of big sites like Mailchimp, which really don't have a mindset for dealing with home-working authors, and who aim their services more at big corporate bodies. So this is something to be aware of when setting up a newsletter. I love the approach Gumroad and Substack take: they put their own physical address on as the sender, and sidestep all the problems, whilst still complying with the law.

Social Media

Social media is the third element of your author platform. It is a way to engage with your readership, to attract and hold their interest. It helps if you enjoy being there so that the joy comes across in your posts, rather than appearing like a desultory grump. You are building relationships, and as such, interaction is more important than follower numbers. Quality, not quantity.

Don't forget that social media, while it is a tool for interacting with fans, can also be a *support mechanism* for authors. There are many author communities that share useful information, and where you can ask questions and get advice. Sometimes it's not about audiences, but about you, and your needs.

Which Sites Should I Use?

No reader uses every social networking site. Most people have accounts on one or two. As such, whichever one you're on, you'll be able to reach a large number of people – but not everyone. If I'm on Facebook, I'll never reach the people who only use Instagram, and vice versa.

You, too, don't have time to be on every site. As such, you must be selective. Pick the social media sites that have the biggest fan base for the kind of thing you write, or the sites you're more familiar with, or even just feel most comfortable on. For example, if you love being on camera, then picking Youtube or a social media site that works well with video would be key. If you like having live interactions with fans, you'd look for the social media network with more of those features. If you prefer to post photos, then again, some sites are better suited for that than others. But since it takes time to post, to create engaging content, and to interact with people, it's better to use one to three sites well than ten sites badly.

If you do use multiple platforms, then there are ways to be efficient with your time. You could draft your posts in a word processor, then copy-paste the same content into each social media platform, tweaking as necessary. Upload any images you've already prepared to go with the post, so the same content goes to multiple places. If you blog, then a similar thing can be done, so that every time you write a new blog post or create your next newsletter, you'll link to it from each of your social media profiles. There are even tools that allow you to post content to multiple social networks in one go, scheduling and preparing posts in advance.

Social media platforms are big, with a broad audience, many of whom have zero interest in your books. As such, it's also better to identify appropriate subcommunities within the social media site, such as those interested in reading books, which are obviously more relevant to you. So if I write romance books I will be thinking about communities of romance readers on the site I choose.

So which will you choose? Facebook? Bluesky? Youtube? Pinterest? Instagram? LinkedIn? TikTok? The thing that used to be called Twitter? Discord? Mastodon? There's a list of some of the biggies on Wikipedia.[198]

There are even sites which aren't pure social media platforms, but which include many of the functions of them, and which can create communities of supporters. Kickstarter, for example. Or subscription sites like Patreon and Substack. Sometimes it is worth thinking in broader terms.

And there are sites that are tailor-made for fans of books:

- Goodreads[199] (owned by Amazon)
- BookBub[200]

- StoryGraph[201]

- LibraryThing[202]

All are places where people rate, review and recommend books to each other. You might find yourself more at home in those smaller, but more focussed, communities.

Make The Most Of Your Choice

Wherever you appear, take time to learn the basics of that platform, the tools it offers, and become familiar with community expectations. If they have space for a bio, include a compelling one. Can you add links to your website and other places? Look at platform features such as live streaming video, or opportunities for interaction events such as author Q&As with fans. If it's not so good for live stuff then prerecorded author chats and book trailers might work better.

Social media is often visual. Does your chosen site allow header images? If so, create a good one of the right resolution. On Facebook and Twitter I'd make a header image promoting my current book, and update it when I had a new release. Find out the best resolutions for images, so that if you include one with words, it won't get cropped in ways that hide key parts of the text. See the section on *Where To Get Content* in Chapter 6, which has links to some sources you can also use for social media posts. Bookmark those that are useful to you.

Examine any statistics the platform provides you with, as they may help you to understand the demographics of your readership, which has multiple knock-on effects for targeting your marketing. I remember poring over Facebook and Goodreads statistics which showed that 74% of my readers at the time were women aged 35-54. Your website may also provide some statistics, including the countries of visitors. This can all be useful, especially when assessing the impact of any advertising, where you would expect a corresponding increase in site visitors.

What Kind Of Content Should You Post?

It partly depends on your author brand (which I'll discuss soon), voice, genre, and audience. But it is always worth making things personal so you aren't just some stranger they don't know trying to sell them something.

It's good to create a mixture of post types – text, shares (when you share someone else's post to your own timeline), video, photos, personal posts, links to information and articles, quotes from your books or reviews, and interesting images. The best idea is to follow other authors who write in your genre, and see what they do. Ideally popular authors, so you can understand part of *why* they might be popular.

I keep a folder on my PC's desktop, which contains little notes, images and photos, ideas and musings, and interesting links to share, so I dip in there for social media and newsletter content whenever I need inspiration.

Reach

A key concept to understand is **reach**. This refers to how many of your followers will see something you post. When you first start out you might assume that if you have a hundred followers, and post an item about your new book, all one hundred will see it. Nope! On most platforms like Facebook, they'll only show the post to a small number of your followers. Why? Because they expect you to pay to "boost" the post and show it to more people. And to make that option more attractive, they restrict the reach. So maybe Facebook will only show your post to a tenth of the followers.

Yes, that's a bit depressing. It's one of the reasons I closed my Twitter (as was) and Facebook author accounts. I'd been running them for over a decade, and had thousands of followers in total. Years ago, if I posted something, a large number of people would see it. But, over time, Twitter and Facebook restricted the reach of posts if I didn't pay to boost them. By the end, it was showing my posts to fewer than 1% of my followers. So I said "What's the point?" and closed the accounts, along with Instagram. I wrote about my own disillusionment with those sites here[203] and here.[204]

It's like the point I made earlier, that if you have the email addresses of fans then you have a direct connection, but on social media sites it is the company that owns the data, and usually monetises it in various ways. Restricted reach is one of them.

It's a reason to consider sites that have no advertising, and therefore don't build in paid restrictions. For example, Bluesky[205] (which also doesn't suffer from the political censorship of Twitter and Facebook).

Drinky's Digressions: Clean Links

In recent years there has been an explosion in the amount of data collected about us without our permission, much of it driven by the desire to make money from ramming advertising down our throats (and some of it in order to manipulate us, as with Facebook's Cambridge Analytica political machinations). Websites can find out a lot about where you are, and what technology you use just by clicking a link – see this site for a demonstration.[206]

Cookies are one type of tracker. Small files that websites save onto your PC. Sometimes they can be useful, such as the ones which save you from logging in every time. But mostly they are a form of tracking and spying.

You know how every website says you are giving them permission to save cookies "to enhance your experience," even though you are only reading a few paragraphs? "Enhance your experience" is a euphemism for "so we can profile you and make money from compiling and sharing that data with loads of dodgy companies". As one example, I dug down to the "Privacy Policy" (such an unintentionally ironic name) of a site I visit often, and found that by default they share my data with 660 advertising companies. Six hundred and sixty! Just from one website visit. And it states they can "Match and combine data from other data sources," "Identify devices," and "Link different devices," and share that information with those companies: with no way to opt out.

The default position taken by 99% of websites is that you have "opted in" to tracking unless you explicitly state otherwise – which is not in the least bit practical. I visit hundreds of sites a day, and using the web would be impossible if I had to find the settings and opt out of the forced spying on every site. Worse, it would usually only apply to a single browser on a single system, because – in order to opt out – they save another cookie to your computer! So you have to do it all over again, thousands of times, if you switch browser, or change PC, or use a different gadget, or clear your cache, or reinstall your operating system ... blatantly it is impossible to opt out. And that doesn't even take account of all the other tracking whenever you log into a site.

Sometimes tracking takes place via the construction of the web address (also called a **URL – uniform resource locator**), which has elements added to record where you came from and what you did, which are then stored by the website and connected to your account or PC.

A particular issue for authors and reviewers is Amazon, one of the companies making heavy use of automated data gathering and algorithms based on software-run assumptions. Assumptions which are often wrong (as I mentioned in Chapter 8, the Amazon Escape section, where I fell foul of automated red herrings), and can cause all sorts of problems.

Why is this relevant here? Because it's common to share links on social media. We share links to good reviews, to our books for sale on websites, to our profiles, to interviews. We may share the links in other places too, such as via our website, or newsletters, or emails. So it is important to understand links, especially any which point to Amazon.

When sharing Amazon links to products, including your own books, you must use "clean" links. These are basically a copied URL with tracking information removed. It's easiest to explain this with an example.

If I search Amazon for my wonderful book Lost Solace, then copy the URL from the browser bar (e.g. to send it to someone else), I get something like this:

> https://www.amazon.com/Lost-Solace-Karl-Drinkwater-ebook/dp/B0787HLF4X/ref=sr_1_1?crid=372BH8R33H7M3&dib=eyJ2IjoiMSJ9.6jA-P9ih5YSkQM_nWhb0LEY2ax2yMVg0d1THl9HxfsdsLXs9FafiUci327QOUOEYHamTh4qB-RpKjlPu6ruwuXTe_PCs5aEwmcXCld72IzOs2BR0sKYy_NcBdLp-Vu0FOkwkigLooXA_NNb1xnfwtMbWZjZPGGCKTDNmIx4J9MIg1YCIRoygpJfaVXpRTTYmXRmmS0JCz6TtXsyAGXby3dcPPH10hU2ufrRvB6Sq9-0.ZGxj--oE_EK-l7mZu5dt80d7kEa0li8nZpEX6rh81Gw&dib_tag=se&keywords=lost+solace&qid=1708350241&s=b

ooks&sprefix=lost+solace%2Cstripbooks-intl-ship%2C497&sr=1-1

The format is as follows.

- **https://www.amazon.com/** The base URL

- **/Lost-Solace-Karl-Drinkwater-ebook/** Additional book data is included, though it is unnecessary and can be deleted entirely – the URL will still work.

- **/dp/** Just means "detail page".

- **/B0787HLF4X /** The ASIN, Amazon's internal code for the book. It's like an ISBN, as discussed in Chapter 7.

- The rest of the URL is additional unnecessary gunk, including the keywords I typed in to find the book. Some sections such as **qid=1708350241** are purely tracking data. qid marks a unique "query ID" in a database, and acts as a timestamp.

That tracking data is the bit that connects the search to a database entry, which will also probably include the date and time of the visit, the country, the account doing the search (if logged into Amazon), the email addresses and physical addresses stored on the account, computer identification information, and connections to cookies saved on the PC – Amazon ones, maybe others too, such as Facebook. So all sorts of stuff is tracked, and because it is then stored in an Amazon database, you can't see it or remove it. Amazon is secretive about how all this works.

The problem is that if you share that long URL (just copying and pasting it) then it includes your tracking information; and if someone else clicks on it, *their data* is connected to that ID as well.

This can lead to all sorts of issues. Suppose lots of people click on that link (for example, if it had been included in a review on a website), and they go on to buy the book and maybe review it – Amazon may then flag it up as "suspicious," linking the accounts and thinking they might be connected, such as accounts from a review manipulation farm, or friends and family reviewing books for an author. All of those can lead to the reviews being removed, and sometimes also reviewing privileges, with no comeback or warning.

As I explained earlier, Amazon's algorithms are automated and often faulty, as my own examples showed. And there's no way to question Amazon's data, or find out what evidence they are basing their incorrect assumptions on. And all that can potentially stem from just clicking on an Amazon link that had tracking codes in.

Therefore, if sharing Amazon links anywhere (blogs, emails, social media) the only safe option is to strip out the tracking data to create a **clean link**. Basically, everything after the ASIN needs to be deleted, so you end up with this:

> https://www.amazon.com/Lost-Solace-Karl-Drinkwater-ebook/dp/B0787HLF4X/

That's a clean and safe link.

As I mentioned earlier, the book title can also safely be removed if it is present, so you just have the Amazon site and book's ASIN:

> https://www.amazon.com/dp/B0787HLF4X/

That goes to the same location as the longer link above it, but is much tidier, and also 100% safe to share. I always recommend sharing Amazon links in this truncated format.

Author Brand

Your author brand is all the "you" that you present to the world of readers. It's about making sure each of the things we produce, or which are connected to us as an author, have a distinctive fingerprint connecting them. It includes the design decisions which make something recognisably yours.

Ideally it threads itself through all of your marketing. So, for example, the genre, type of writing and subject matter might lead to a set of font, layout and imagery choices. Stephen King's book covers and brand look different to Barbara Cartland's. As a result their name appears in a particular way on their books, in a certain font, maybe with a logo or graphic elements. That name design could also be the header for their website, perhaps with a quote or author tagline. That would also appear in their social media headers, and at the top of their newsletter. Email signatures (and the links they point to) are also extensions of the author brand. Colour schemes can also be part of it. So, for example, the colour scheme on their best-selling book may also be the scheme of their website and social media channels. It's about consistency.

Author Bios

The section about you as an author is often referred to as your **author bio** (biographical details about the author). As with writing blurbs, there's a skill to making them interesting and concise. In fact, the author bio pretty much *is* a blurb: but for a person, rather than a book.

That description of yourself is also part of your author brand. It makes you and your work sound interesting to the right readers. There are a number of elements it might include.

- The kind of thing you write, what qualities make it distinctive, what genre(s) you work in.

- Personal stuff: hobbies, inspiration, places. (Don't just put that you like reading books and watching TV: it's not a dating profile.)

- Do you have a background that ties in to your writing and adds credibility? Maybe you used to be a detective and now write crime fiction. This is especially important for non-fiction, since it is a chance to explain what makes you an authority on the topic.

- Awards or other accolades. Have you won prizes or been on a major award shortlist? Was one of your books a bestseller? (Be specific, since "bestseller" is a term that is so overused it puts many people off, on the assumption that even my shopping list could be a bestseller nowadays. If you sold ten books then one may be *your* best seller, but that doesn't make it a *best-selling book*.)

- Consider writing it in your voice, the way you write books, so it gives a flavour of your individual style and tone.

- Possibly include links to your website and social media profiles. Whatever is most important to you.

When developing your bio you could read those of authors you admire. Find them on their website, or book sales site, or Goodreads, or even from any print books you have. See which bios you like, what details strike you, how long they are and what style they are written in, then try to create something similar but in your own voice.

It is useful to create versions of different lengths. So there's the long one, but then a shorter version, and maybe one or two more, with the shortest suitable for things like social media bios where you may only be allowed a certain number of characters. This way you always have one for different purposes and word counts, from the web page (longest) to the bio in a book (shorter), to the one that will fit on a business card.

Here's an example of my old medium-length bio (81 words):

> Karl Drinkwater writes dystopian space opera, dark suspense and diverse social fiction. If you want compelling stories and characters worth caring about, then you're in the right place. Welcome!
>
> Karl lives in Scotland and owns two kilts. He has degrees in librarianship, literature and classics, but also studied astronomy and philosophy. Dolly the cat helps him finish books by sleeping on his lap so he can't leave the desk. When he isn't writing he loves music, nature, games and vegan cake.

And then the super-short version (18 words):

> Author of dystopian space opera, dark suspense and diverse social fiction. Compelling stories and characters worth caring about.

It is also useful to think about your **USP** (**Unique Selling Point**) when writing an author bio: what do you offer that other authors might not? Perhaps you're the master of school-based horror and teen dialects, or you combine recipes with holiday mysteries, or you mix surrealism with Afrofuturism. It's worth thinking about what you do well, and what might help an audience for that kind of thing find you and your work more easily. Define your author fingerprint.

Your author photo is a key part of your author brand, and should match it. If you write grimdark fantasy or misery lit, then a colour photo of you smiling and waving a pink sparkle wand might cause dissonance. A writer of animal stories might have a photo of them stroking a dog, whereas a thriller author could have a picture of them jumping out of an aeroplane (hopefully with a parachute). Make sure the photo looks professional, and says something about you.

We discussed pen names in the previous chapter. If you have multiple pen names, then you need multiple author brands, one for each genre. It's more work, but it can pay dividends in terms of establishing yourself within each niche as a recognisable entity for readers who love those types of books.

Top Tip: Keep Bios Updated

Your author bio will change over time. Sometimes you'll rewrite it to freshen things up, but you may also create new versions as your career progresses and you win awards or publish more books.

Likewise, make sure your author photo is updated every few years. It can be misleading to stick to the one from your university graduation thirty years ago just because you like it.

As with blurbs, if the author bio or your photo ever changes at a later date, then update it wherever it appears so the author brand is consistent.

If you have different lengths of bio, you could create a list of places, along with which length is used there (full, medium or short) and whether it includes a photo. Here are some possible places, but your list would be different:

- Distributors and sites where your books are sold such as Draft2Digital, Gumroad, IngramSpark, InAudio or wherever.

- Profile pages about you, such as Books2Read, Goodreads, Amazon Author Central, BookBub Partners, Kickstarter, Substack, and profiles on other sites.

- Social media profiles: Facebook, Bluesky, Instagram, TikTok, Discord etc.

- Your website About page.

- In the back matter of your books.

Drinky's Digressions: Naming Consistency

Which is correct?

- K.D. Wordman?

- K. D. Wordman?

- KD Wordman?

- K D Wordman?

It's a tricky one because style guides differ on this.

- According to *Hart's Rules* (Chapter Six: Names) it would be K. D. Wordman with a space. BUT! They admit spaces and points are not always used, and they also make a mistake: they use J. K. Rowling as an example, when it is really J.K. Rowling with no space between the initials (see her website and social media accounts: it's something Wikipedia gets wrong too, listing the incorrect punctuation for over a decade).

- According to newspaper styles such as *Guardian Style* (p160) it would be KD Wordman. Personally, I think that looks weird outside of newspapers.

It's an issue because, to a search engine, they may look like four different names.

For an author choosing how they wish to appear, and using multiple initials for their forenames, my advice is to be absolutely precise about the punctuation you choose and use it consistently everywhere. Ditto with hyphens, middle initials, apostrophes or spaces. Either pick a style guide and stick to it, or look at what other authors who write in your genre do, especially well-known ones.

I once helped a new author who had made the mistake of not thinking about this, and I found she had used different variants of her name. (I'm changing it for reasons of privacy.)

On her website and book covers she was G.T. Bambridge (no space). But on many other sites she had entered her name in the format G. T. Bambridge (space between initials), or even used both forms on different parts of the bio. We chatted about punctuation rules and she settled on one and used it consistently in all places after that, to prevent confusion.

Reviews

These are important. Let us examine the reasons why.

Reviews As Publicity

Authors have many concerns beyond good characterisation, exciting plots, broken pencils, and avoiding being distracted by pictures of cats on the Internet. Reviews, for example.

Reviews are important. They count as social proof – evidence that your book is being read, and liked, which gives confidence to potential purchasers. I covered editorial reviews in Chapter 7: Metadata. But the value of reviews is greater than handy evidence of literary worth.

I wrote about the long tail in Chapter 3 with regards to sales, and that's why reviews at any point are useful. I regularly get reviews for my books years later, and it is incredibly valuable as reviews have a *long-term* impact on sales, and *sales affect your visibility*. You have to sell a lot of books to increase your Amazon ranking before Amazon starts including your book in "customers also bought …" messages, for example.

Note that there isn't cosmic justice recognising effort or quality, in any field. Sometimes the most amazing things go undiscovered by most of the people that would love them, while derivative and valueless things are widely lauded.

Lack of reviews, or only having bad reviews, can kill a book. Lots of good reviews (and a high average rating) can boost it. If a percentage of purchasers review a book, then the more books you sell, the more reviews you are likely to get.

And so we have this infinite loop of sales > reviews > sales > reviews. The loop can also be negative: the more something falls under the radar, the less it is purchased, enjoyed, discussed, and therefore the less it sells. Lack of sales > lack of reviews > lack of sales. Without luck or a big budget, no matter what the quality, the item may not be able to reach above the slush.

This is all about scale, and each review is the small push that, when added up, could get the ball rolling so that momentum then deals with itself and something of value manages to get past the things of little value.

Reviews have to be true opinions. Otherwise they are valueless as a guide. I say that as an author, but also as a reader who wants to find excellent books for my limited time on this planet. If a book has all positive reviews, or all negative, I am always surprised, and mildly suspicious. No book is for everyone, so I expect a mix of responses. If I am interested in buying a book I look at the positive and negative reviews, see what they flag up, then go further with a look inside.

An author is not an emotionless AI, but a human being. (Well, maybe I am an AI, and programmed not to be able to perceive my nature. I have no way of knowing.) As such, some people find it difficult to read negative reviews. Fine. The reviews are really there for other readers. For my own books I always welcome genuine negative and middling reviews, just as I do the positives. I want to attract readers, but the right ones. Sales to the wrong reader are pointless to all concerned. It all goes back to the Library Laws of Ranganathan I keep repeating: "Every reader their book, and every book its reader." Matching those is the key, whether as a librarian, a reviewer, an author, or a book buyer.

And a final point. I mentioned how reviews help sales in the long-term, but I am not saying customer reviews are *only* important because they help us sell books. There are many other reasons to love reviews, such as:

- A direct form of reader feedback that shows where the writing and story are doing well, and where they could be improved.

- Reviews help people find your work, but also help to deter people who wouldn't enjoy it (life's too short to read books that don't suit you).

- An extrinsic reward in the form of recognition for the years you have put in to enhancing your authorial skills and writing the novel.

Reviews As Data

Some authors never read their reviews. In that case they're missing out on potentially useful feedback, as seen in the first bullet point above. How can you know whether you're connecting with your target audience unless you read what they say? How can you identify parts of the book people love and which you might want to repeat, versus elements people hated and which need improving in your future work? How can you hone your craft and targeting if you don't know what a broad range of people think about your writing?

Reviews lead to useful comparisons that can feed back into your marketing: "This book reminded me of [insert title or author] because [insert reason]." Additionally, a review might contain a brilliant summary that actually works as a tagline or enhancement to the blurb.

Since reviews can also be an indicator of popularity, it's worth monitoring them. I used to keep a spreadsheet where I tracked how many reviews my books had on Amazon and Goodreads every few months. That's perhaps going too far, and I stopped once the reviews reached the hundreds.

The professional middleground is to treat them as useful data, then move on. And, over time as you see more and more reviews of your books, you do tend to adopt a more balanced view of whatever people say about your work. Study the critiques, ignore the arseholes. We don't have to assume every review is right, but we do need to gauge overall opinion.

Pay most attention to the 3, 4, and 5 star reviews. 1 and 2 star reviewers are probably not your audience, so don't tweak things for their preferences or you might lose what your fans like.

How To Get Reviews

Some reviews will come naturally, as a result of sales; though the proportion of reviews to sales is disappointingly low. A big-name author may have a thousand times more reviews than a debut author, but they are also selling a thousand times more books.

So what is that proportion? We can add up sales over a year, and also new reviews over a year (on sites like Goodreads, Amazon, and review blogs). It's not exact, but usually works out at about five reviews for every thousand sales. So 0.5% of readers leave a review, one in two hundred. Many of those two hundred might have loved the book – maybe all of them did! – but only one of them tells anyone else about it with a review. Yes, that's sometimes depressing, especially because of a quirk of human nature whereby, if someone has a mild dislike for something, they often rush to leave a one-star review; but if they love it, they are less likely to do anything. We complain about poor companies and service, but rarely praise the other end of the spectrum. As such, it skews things towards negativity.

So, a brilliant book, but which isn't getting much attention, may start off with a few hundred sales. In that case it may not even get a single review. So it looks unloved. Potential readers ask: why is no one reviewing it? They move on to the mass-market title with a hundred reviews, because that's obviously better, right? The cycle continues.

So work has to be done, rather than leaving it to chance.

You can seek out reviewers and influencers who might like your work. Check their website to see if they're currently open to submissions. Then send them a polite email, making sure to follow any guidelines they have listed. Something along the lines of:

> Dear xxx,
>
> I'm contacting you to see if you might be interested in reviewing my latest book, [title].
>
> *[Talk about what makes it interesting, and include the cover image.]*
>
> *[You could include useful information e.g. publication date, publisher, book length in pages or words, back cover blurb etc.]*
>
> *[Include something about yourself, such as a short version of your author bio. If you follow their blog or*

have interacted them, mention it! Also why it might be of interest to their readership.]

[Make sure you include any relevant links: to the book on Goodreads or Amazon, your website, social media links etc.]

[Maybe discuss whether you are offering only the ebook, or if you would be able to send a print copy; though this may be something already covered in their guidelines.]

Many thanks for your time and consideration, *[which is also how you traditionally end a letter to an agent or publisher!]*

If you're stuck with where to begin then try a directory such as Reedsy's Best Book Review Blogs,[207] which can be sorted by genre. Though, if you write in a genre you love, then hopefully you already read and follow and interact with book lovers from within that category, who can be good starting points.

It might be worth considering a blog tour as a way of getting people to review your work. Those are like a virtual book tour of book-related websites, that may well include reviews, guest posts and interviews as a kind of celebration. I'll discuss blog tours a bit more below.

It's fine to have a short **Call To Action (CTA)** in the back matter of your books, asking readers who enjoyed the work to consider leaving a brief review on Goodreads or their online bookseller of choice. Or just a thanks to those who have done so. Though you may have other CTAs such as asking them to buy the next book in a series, or sign up for a newsletter, or follow you on social media, or ... and too many of these means they *all* get ignored.

Likewise you can ask your newsletter subscribers to consider leaving an honest review. Or ask in social media. But don't do it often or it becomes a nag and you will look desperate. Even if you *are* desperate, you don't want the world to know. Something short, along the lines of:

> "If you enjoyed [book] then please review it on Goodreads or Amazon. Even a few words can encourage someone else to buy, so is important to the livelihood of authors. Thank you!"

You can reassure them that it only needs to be a rating and a sentence or two about what they enjoyed – no need to break down the structure, plot, characterisation, imagery, and style (unless they're the kind of reader who likes to talk about those things!)

Always include shortcut links to make it easier for fans to leave reviews.

Don't pay for reviews, or offer any other compensation for reviewing the book (apart from the book itself – see below). It's unnecessary, unethical, and could get you into trouble. The last thing you want is for Amazon to decide some reviewers are breaking their terms by being offered compensation, then look at the books being reviewed, and decide they were paid reviews and penalties need to be applied: whether it be removing a huge number of reviews, or even removing the books from sale. Yes, it has happened.

Also, don't ask friends and family to leave reviews. Only unbiased, genuine reviews have value. Further, reviews that look like you *might* have asked friends or family to say positive things to boost sales (even if you haven't done that) can breach guidelines, and look tacky to some readers. The *perception* of bias can be as harmful as true bias. Likewise don't do amateur things like "review swaps" with other authors, where you leave positive reviews for each other's books. Again, you'll get into hot water.

Giving away a copy of the book being reviewed is fine, though, and doesn't count as compensation or break any rules. And if you're asking someone to review your book, that's expected. They're doing you a favour. At least meet them halfway. An **ARC – Advance Review Copy** – is a standard part of the business, where early reviewers receive an ARC of the book prior to the official publication date, so they can read it in advance and have a review ready when the book launches. Traditional publishers have done this for decades.

Some independent authors develop **ARC teams** (or **Reader Teams**) for this same purpose. Though do be aware of ethics: if, for example, a trade publisher only grants the free book to reviewers who write positive reviews of their work, and stops giving them to any reviewers who didn't leave a gushing review of the previous work, then that is an attempt to manipulate the reviewers. Publishers are only rewarding people who leave positive reviews. That treads a fine ethical line as to how unbiased the ARC reviews are. (We get a similar issue with sponsored posts and videos by media influencers; they are given money and items as long as they keep saying good things about the company, which throws balance out of the window.)

There are paid review services which claim to help you get legitimate reviews, such as Booksirens,[208] Booksprout,[209] StoryOrigin[210] or HiddenGems.[211]

Their model is that you pay the service, and it matches your book up to reviewers who have expressed an interest in that genre. The reviewer themselves receives no payment (so it breaks no guidelines) apart from the copy of the book; also the reviews are not necessarily positive as they are meant to be unbiased. But do be aware that there are also many scam artists in this area, promising only positive reviews – which, if true, would get you banned from Amazon quickly for dodgy dealings.

Top Tip: Sending Books To A Reviewer

Ebooks can be emailed, but if you ever send print books out for review there are a few options.

You could send them straight from your home. That's ideal if you are signing them. If you are trade published you might get free copies (and the publisher will hopefully be sending copies out for review without you needing to do anything). If independent, you may keep stock at home, which you buy at almost print cost.

But posting books can be time consuming and costly, especially to other countries. I often send books straight from a distributor – for example, if you use IngramSpark or BookVault, you can choose the print location when ordering a copy, so if I send a book to the US or UK I get it printed and shipped from the relevant country. This is cheaper and more efficient. But one thing I'd avoid is sending books to a reviewer via Amazon. Amazon algorithms may join your account and the reviewer's account (via their address) and see it as a "connection" which can lead to subsequent reviews being deleted.

What To Do With Reviews

Well, you could show gratitude to the reviewers. I never cease to be thankful that people liked my words enough to write words of their own. It seems like an act of respect for me to share some of those reviews more widely. I do eventually read all reviews of my work, even the weird ones from people who are furiously angry about everything, or who seem to be writing a review for a different item.

So share the reviews on social media (if you use it) or in your newsletter. It not only indicates qualities of the book which might tempt fans to buy, but also says thanks to the reviewer and amplifies their voice, showing how much they mean to you. Just quote a few words and link to the original source (customer review, blog post or Goodreads). Another option is to use them as the basis for social media promo graphics, e.g. an image with the book cover on one side, short quote and source on the other.

As discussed earlier, if you share links to reviews, always make it a clean URL first. Most websites add extra data to the web address for tracking purposes. For example, we saw how Amazon does this on book pages, and reviews are no different. So if people click on a link to an Amazon review for your book, which has tracking data associating them to you, and then they leave a review, the automated algorithms might think you are "connected" and remove the reviews or mistakenly threaten you with account closure for review manipulation. Both for your benefit, and for good practice, only ever share short, clean URLs.

As an example, this is what appears in the address bar for one of my reviews on Amazon:

>https://www.amazon.com/gp/customer-reviews/R11PNVQBCPNAAV/ref=cm_cr_dp_d_rvw_ttl?ie=UTF8&ASIN=1911278142

If I wanted to share a link to that review I would delete all the extraneous information from the end, and just share this:

https://www.amazon.com/gp/customer-reviews/
R11PNVQBCPNAAV/

Editorial reviews (discussed in Chapter 7) can also be shared. Obviously they should go on your website. They can also be included in book metadata, but note that many vendors (e.g. Amazon) reject books that include editorial reviews in the book description (blurb) field. They make an exception for trade publishers, who seem to include them in book descriptions with impunity, but that is forbidden to independent authors – it's one of Amazon's many double standards, since Amazon actively looks for, flags, and blocks anyone including reviews in their book descriptions. The KDP guidelines say: "We cannot accept any of the following information in the description: Reviews, quotes, or testimonials".[212]

Some distributors for independent authors, such as IngramSpark, get around this by having separate metadata fields for editorial reviews (IngramSpark calls them "Review Quotes"), though that option isn't available with all distributors. For example, Draft2Digital doesn't have an editorial reviews metadata field, so the only option to get them on to Amazon is to use Amazon's Author Central (or Awful Central, as I refer to it), and you can't have editorial reviews at all on other ebook stores Draft2Digital distribute to.

The alternative is to include them as the first page of the book, so readers skimming the print book or free sample of the ebook will see them.

Note that I've been mainly talking about reviews of an individual book. Sometimes elements can be extracted which relate more to the author and their style. These can be used generically as part of the author brand and promotion of the author's body of work as a whole; that's why you'll often see "Praise for [author name]" sections in books or on the author's website. It's also possible to have a "Praise for [series]" and include review quotes relating to more than one book in the series.

Blog Tours

I mentioned blog tours earlier. They're a useful technique for launching (or relaunching) a book, and getting reviews.

Blog tours work best for standalone books or the first in a series: since later books in a series probably require knowledge of what has gone before, they tend not to be so tempting to book bloggers who have never read your work.

Why do them? Blog tours are not about selling books and don't directly drive sales. The primary value is the social proof. They furnish things that authors can link to in social media as mini promotions, and often the quotes prove great candidates for editorial reviews, since a named blog looks better than generic Goodreads/Amazon customer reviews. The tours also help create connections between authors and book lovers. The social proof and buzz hopefully give the books a better platform for future sales, which is the only way any author should ever approach them.

How? You could organise one yourself. It requires making contact with book bloggers who seem like a good fit in terms of the kinds of books they like, and find out if they want to take part. You have to set up a schedule and create promotional banners with the dates and web addresses of all the stops on the blog tour. You need to send copies of the book to the hosts (usually ebooks, but some bloggers request print) and any promotional materials they require such as an author bio, purchase and social media links, blog tour summary images, book blurbs and covers. You will liaise with the hosts regularly in the run-up to their stop on the blog tour, and during the event. You may need to submit extra material for guest posts, such as character profiles, background, or book excerpts, or take part in interviews. Much of the work has to be scheduled a significant time in advance (at least a month), especially if the book bloggers are expected to review the book.

There's a lot of work involved, which is why many authors prefer to pay someone else to run it for them. Tour organisers also have the advantage of existing relationships with lots of book bloggers who can make up the stops on the blog tour. Some blog tour service providers specialise in certain genres.

Here's a list of some blog tour organisers, in case you want to look at the services they offer and pricing. These aren't recommendations, just examples, in alphabetical order.

- Bewitching Book Tours[213]
- Rachel's Random Resources[214]

- Random Things Tours[215]
- R&R Book Tours[216]
- Xpresso Book Tours[217]
- Zooloo's Book Tours[218]

Before and during. Make sure you promote the blog tour in your newsletter and any social media sites you use. Link to the hosts of each blog. Promote every stop of the tour on your social media outlets, remembering to tag the book blogger in question. The blogger will do the same and, if you're lucky, all the book blogger's friends will share the posts too.

After each stop on the tour make sure you thank the hosts. The author-blogger relationship is one of working together. Interact with the hosts and any fans or readers who show up. Also thank the tour organiser if you use one.

Finally, save links to any reviews, share the good ones, and save any fees paid as expenses for your author business.

Top Tip: Review Wording

According to some rules, a reviewer should cite if they received a free copy of the book for review purposes. As such, some reviewers might add a line at the end of the review, such as "I received a copy of the book in exchange for a review."

No!

Amazon guidelines have altered over time, but when I checked May 2025, it said:[219]

> "Compensated reviews. Reviews should reflect your honest opinion. We don't allow reviews that are created, edited, or removed in exchange for compensation. Compensation includes cash, discounts, free products, gift cards, and refunds. [...] Exceptions: [...] It's OK to review a free or discounted book (advanced reader copy) that you received from an author or publisher. However, they can't require a review in exchange or try to influence the review."

Note that last sentence. So saying in the review that they received a book "in exchange for a review" (even though it was unbiased) can lead to automated checks flagging it and getting the review removed; or worse, such as threatening to close accounts. It is better to avoid that potentially misleading text entirely.

I always recommend reviewers add a note such as "I received a free review copy from the publisher," "I received an ARC," or "I received a free copy of this book with no obligation to review." Those wordings are all fine, it is just the "exchange for" phrase that can be a problem and imply rule-breaking compensation.

Drinky's Digressions: The Evil Power Of The Troll

Earlier I suggested one in two hundred readers leave reviews. If the reviews were always genuine, then at least there would be good reviews for a good book. But that isn't always the case, because of potentially unethical things going on, and some of the negative sides of human nature, combined with the possibility of being anonymous.

I know an author who released a large novel, and planned to do his publicity later on. And yet, *on the day of release* it gained a number of one-star reviews on Amazon (each review being only a few words that didn't make sense, as if plucked randomly from a dictionary). Well, it was unlikely that people had bought his book on release day, read the whole thing in one night, hated it, then left a garbled review. It's fairly safe to rule that out, especially because other authors reported seeing this same pattern. Oh, and these were not Verified Reviews – which means the reviewer did not buy the book on the platform they are reviewing on. (Not bought it at all, according to the evidence.)

So where do the one-star reviews come from?

One possibility is related to the propensity for trolling. People who enjoy being able to aggravate, annoy, and cause disruption, just for the sake of making themselves feel better. So people who may enjoy the ease with which they can leave one-star ratings anonymously, and see how it affects a product's rating.

When a book is first released, the trolls can have a much bigger impact. For a book with a hundred positive reviews gathered over a long time, the one-star rating won't have any impact, since it will hardly affect the overall score. But a book that has yet to gain a review? It has a huge impact, as the book is immediately summarised as "average rating: one star". And a one-star average screams at potential buyers "Run away, do not buy, this book is a travesty!". To counteract the low average might take a stack of glowing reviews, so that if there are ten of them then the one star has little effect any more – but to get ten glowing reviews might require two thousand sales, and you're not going to get the two thousand sales if the only thing people see when they view the book is a one-star summary. It makes it many times less likely to get a sale, meaning it is also unlikely to get real reviews. As a result, the book is almost dead in the water, no matter how wonderful it is. And if the troll slaps multiple reviews from different fake accounts, they can surely kill it. "Ha ha, silly author wasting years and their savings on this book, pouring their heart into it, when a handful of fake accounts can mean it will never sell, or at least sell far more poorly, and set back the impact of future books too, maybe even end their career because of the failure of that book!" A few minutes of spite can do that. So there is a huge amount of power in the troll's hands, to affect others, and to ruin dreams.

In some cases, I think there is an element of that. It's not even personal. Trolls just pick on new releases with no reviews. You look at their account activity, and it is often bare of anything like a real human, just mostly strings of negative comments. Oh, and if you report it to Amazon, hoping they might look into it, they won't. "The user's review is their protected opinion," Amazon say, even if the text makes it clear they are reviewing the wrong item, e.g. a review for a hair dryer wrongly copied to a book, or if they are reviewing something like Amazon's delivery service: "the book did not arrive" or "one star because it was left in the rain," rather than the item.

Goodreads (owned by Amazon) suffers a lot of this too, and won't delete things which are probably fake, either, such as accounts which only post one-star ratings, with no comment or review. I did my own investigative work in 2017 and reported some obviously fake accounts which broke their Terms of Use (fake names and photos – some even had the copyright notice on from the source where they'd been copied!). The accounts are still there in 2025. Goodreads don't care much about enforcing their own rules.

Mmm, profiles that seem anonymous and with little humanity? That points to the other possible reason.

Money skews most human endeavours, and for many people it comes before ethics, kindness, or respect. One of the issues in the business of selling *anything* is fake reviews. If reviews help sell (or prevent from selling), then they also affect profit. If they make money, then they have a value attached. If something has a value attached, it can be sold. And hence the proliferation of review-selling services. Same as you can pay for fake "followers" on social media, and of equally little value and quality.

A company is paid in exchange for a number of fake positive reviews on your product. How do they do it? At the biggest scale the companies have whole warehouses of mobile devices and computers, all with their own accounts on many services. If someone pays for positive reviews on a product, each device and account will leave one. No real person is behind any of them. Amazon tried to cut back on it by saying accounts need to have spent money, but that is little disincentive – the criminals make so much from selling reviews that some can be funnelled into purchases, often for more devices to expand the number of reviews that can be left, and in turn the amount that can be charged for the service.

However, there is a wrinkle in this. If the criminals only leave the good reviews they have been paid for, they can easily be detected by algorithms. "Let's scan for accounts that leave a massive number of positive reviews, and analyse if the reviews look real, if a person could really read that many books/eat that many pots of jam/use fifty different brands of chainsaw". Once tracked down, it's often easy to see it doesn't look like real human behaviour or a real profile, the words and purchasing choices are too suspicious. This can lead on to looking at other positive reviews on that product, to see if it is part of mass review manipulation. But that requires time and staffing, so companies like Amazon do the barest checks unless it is affecting their overall profit. An easy way for the criminals to confuse the algorithm is to leave a *mix* of ratings, some positive, some negative. Then it looks – to an algorithm examining patterns – more like a human account with a range of interests and values.

So, in order to keep selling positive reviews to clients, these companies mix it up with negative reviews for non-clients. Often there is no vindictiveness, they just randomly select a number of products and their software leaves negative reviews there. The result is that they don't get spotted by checks for fake reviews. They can keep making money from their shady (but profitable) score manipulation business. But that does mean huge numbers of negative reviews being left on other products.

Perhaps this is the reason we see the one-star reviews so often, with no text, and a very basic account. It's not persecution, not trolling for kicks, just a side effect of a drive for profit that is part of the consumerist world that most of our culture conforms to.

That's of little consolation to the aforementioned person with hardly any reviews, where the fake negatives have a disproportionate effect that wouldn't even be noticed by a bestseller. For those with a new product or book, yet to find its tribe and gain its footing, it can be a major setback on sales, or stop them from ever beginning.

That's why real reviews are so important: not just helping a book reach those who might like it, but also to counteract false scores and reviews. It's why we should be grateful to the readers who do leave a genuine review on Goodreads or Amazon or wherever they bought the book.

Universal Book Links (UBLs)

Regardless of whether you're traditionally published or an independent author, your books will be on sale in various formats (paperback, hardback, ebook and audio) and in thousands of stores (both physical and online).

Not only that, but sites like Amazon and Apple have multiple *regions*, such as UK, USA and Canada, with the prices appearing in the local currency and customers expected to order from their regional site. This is known as geolocation, but automatic redirection is imperfect.

If a reader asks where to buy your books, a comprehensive list would be hundreds of links, which is impractical and would send any fan running away! Or you could ask what country the fan resides in, what format they prefer, what stores they use and so on – which can be time consuming for both of you.

A better way to deal with it is a page on your website that links to all the major stores selling your books. Then you have a single URL you can share. Some authors prefer a separate web page for each book, and will add buy icons for the major sites. Both options can be clunky to maintain and use.

That's where **universal linkers**, also known as **universal book links (UBL**s) come in. It is a single link for a book, that goes to a page where the reader can choose from a list of websites selling it (such as Kobo, Amazon or Waterstones). They can also choose their region where appropriate, or a good booklinker will work that out automatically based on the IP address of the visitor's computer and take them to the correct regional site.

UBLs require some time to set up, but they save time in making it easy to provide purchasing options to people, and simplify the process of maintaining those links. If you have a page about the book on your site, you can have a single "Buy now!" button which points to the UBL for that title. Easy peasy.

Except the ideal doesn't quite match the reality. After doing my research I couldn't find a UBL service (free or paid) that deals with geolocation, multiple book formats, and all the sales sites that you might want to link to.

The nearest fit, and the most popular site, is Books2Read.[220] It is maintained by Draft2Digital, and if you publish through them Books2Read can automate some of the tasks and populate the links for you. However, Books2Read is free to all authors, regardless of how your books are published. You need either a Draft2Digital or Books2Read account in order to access all the features, such as setting a custom URL for each book.

With Books2Read each title has its own Book Tab that you can share a link to. Books2Read also lets you create an Author Page which lists all your books, so if you want to share a single link that offers every purchasing option for every book (rather than the purchasing options for just one book), you can do it easily. Another nice feature is the inclusion of ebooks, print books and audiobooks.

MARKETING

9.1 Detail from a Books2Read page, with links to sites that sell the book

Books2Read has some clunky issues in working with the site, but I won't go into those now as I think it is still the best free option, and I'd like to work with Draft2Digital to improve the service for authors.

I haven't used any of the following alternative options extensively, but know they are popular with some authors.

- **BookLinker**.[221] Free. Only works with Amazon and Apple, even though it misleadingly promotes itself as "One book link, every store". Run by Genius Link. I couldn't get it to work, for the reasons given in my digression below.

- **1link**.[222] A paid service if you have more than one book. Doesn't include all social link options, and doesn't seem to send people to the correct region on geolocated sites like Amazon.

- **Linktree.**[223] Paid. Doesn't include many book vendors as link options.

- **Genius Link.**[224] Advanced tools. A paid service. Also doesn't include many book vendors as link options.

In Chapter 8 I talked about the difference between exclusive and wide distribution. The relevant point here is that if you only distribute your books through Amazon, there are far fewer links to your work (since the books are only available on a single site), so you probably don't need UBLs. Your "Buy now!" buttons will just point to the appropriate Amazon page.

Drinky's Digressions: Adblockers

BookLinker didn't work for me in August 2022 as it rejected Apple and Amazon links as invalid. After investigation we discovered it was because I had an adblocker in Firefox which protected me from the tracker they used – and there is no way I will ever go to a website without an adblocker active! Booklinker told me they hoped to fix it soon but still hadn't fixed this as I go to press in 2025.

In terms of tracking and annoying ads, which I covered earlier, I highly recommend installing the free plug-ins uBlock Origin[225] (which removes ads from most websites and makes the web feel usable again; I can't browse without it) and Privacy Badger[226] (which helps prevent a bit of the tracking). They're probably in your browser's plugin store, too. I also disable third party cookies in my browser (in Firefox this is done by choosing the "Strict" option in the Privacy section of the settings) – no good website will be affected by you choosing this option.

Paid Advertising

Otherwise known as the money pit. It could be adverts in consumer or trade magazines, but nowadays is more likely to be advert bidding systems on sites like Amazon, Google, Facebook and BookBub.

This is where you bid against other advertisers to show your advert to a target audience. The more you offer as a bid, the more likely your advert is to be shown. This is why companies with big pockets can make paid advertising too expensive to be worth it for the likes of new indie authors.

Some advertising campaigns are set up to pay for each time someone clicks on the advert – **CPC (Cost Per Click)** basis. Others are set up where you try and reach as many people as possible, and pay per thousand people the advert is shown to. Each showing is called an **impression** – so a thousand views = a thousand impressions. This system is known as **CPM (Cost Per Mille)**. Both methods have advantages and disadvantages.

With bid-type promotions, if you're advertising to popular keyword targets and genres, the bid price can be prohibitively expensive. Sometimes to the point where you make a loss even if most people who click on your advert actually buy your book. As an example, suppose you are paying 15p every time someone clicks on the advert. And only one in twenty people go on to buy the book. That has cost you £3 for every sale. You might not even make that much profit in royalties. And the set budgets can be swallowed up very quickly.

You must target the adverts specifically. Detective fiction is more specific than crime fiction, since the latter includes police procedurals and heist capers, which detective fiction fans may not enjoy. Why be specific? The **click-through-rate (CTR)** is the proportion of people who click on the advert after being shown it. You want this metric to be as high as possible, ideally 5% or above. The broader your targeting, and therefore bigger the target audience, the lower the CTR will probably be. You'll be paying to show the advert to people who aren't interested. So it is better to be specific and focussed on the smaller (but more relevant) audience who are most likely to love your work.

This is where knowledge of comps (see my discussion in Chapter 7) can be useful, along with good keywords which may target other books, series or authors. Also include your own name as a keyword. Not only does this help link your name to the other authors and works, but it makes sure the advert is shown to people who like your work.

For any marketing tools with a cost, such as paid advertising, it is handy to keep track of your **Return on Investment (ROI)**, or at least **profit versus loss** (royalties from extra sales attributed to the promotion, versus the cost of the promotion). You want a positive ROI – so you are making more from the adverts than you are paying. Whereas a negative ROI means you are losing money. Note that generating a positive ROI is easier said than done, and people do whole courses on using paid advertising, and spend considerable sums to tweak adverts, and even then not everyone ends up with a positive ROI.

Let's pause a moment and try to sum this up with another example.

If 5% of people who see an advert click on it (a 5% click-through-rate), that's one in twenty people. Of those, not all of them who clicked on the advert will go on to buy the book. Maybe you are lucky and one in ten will. So 0.5% of the people seeing the advert will buy the book. Perhaps it is an ebook selling at $8, and you'll get 70% royalties. So you get $5.60 per sale. If your cost per click is $0.20 and only 0.5% will buy the book, that means you have to show the advert 200 times for a sale. 200 x $0.20 = $40. So you would lose $34.40 for every sale. It's why you have to do these sums, and in this case you would need to have a lower cost per click, or a huge increase in the likelihood of people buying the book, in order to make a profit. The alchemy of making paid advertising work (without just throwing endless money at it) can be a difficult balance where the only guaranteed winners are the advertising platforms selling the ads – they get paid regardless of whether it works or not. All you can do is study, refine, and make sure the basics are in place: a wonderful book blurb and cover, with lots of positive reviews, and a great advert carefully targeted at the perfect audience.

Paid advertising can also work better when there's a hook, such as a book being up for a major award, or a limited-time price reduction. In the latter case it works in terms of tempting people to click on it, but not necessarily in terms of profitability. That's because if it is a price-reduced book then *income per sale will be reduced*, and it is much harder to make the advert have a positive ROI unless the book is the first in a series with good sell-through.

Two quick tips if you go down this route:

- Ad text for biddable adverts such as Facebook often needs to be short. *Really* short. For example 150 characters for Amazon ads. Often shorter for BookBub. As short as the tagline and book image, or a review quote extract from a reputable source, or one of your "one liners," as discussed in Chapter 7: Metadata.

- When creating an advert, make sure you either set an end date for the advertising campaign, or a maximum budget. If you forget that, then the advertising platform will keep racking up the bill, which could soon bankrupt a new author.

I don't really use paid advertising, which is almost certainly one of the things that means my work isn't as well known as it could be. Whereas there are top-level authors of such renown that, for them, paid advertising would always work out positively. Money makes money. But for many other authors it requires a lot of study, experimentation and constant refinement to make it work.

I respect those with the time and patience to master advertising. And there's no shortage of information out there: books, articles, Facebook groups, whole websites dedicated to how to make paid advertising work. They are on the cutting edge and will provide much more useful information than I could.

For me, I rely more on word of mouth, and hope my fans love my work so much they tell other people about it, or buy copies as gifts for friends, or write reviews on Goodreads or Amazon or blogs. This is known as **organic growth**. I have issues with our consumerist culture and how advertising is almost inescapable, so don't want to hand money to an industry which I feel is responsible for privacy invasion and treating people as data points. But I'm certainly not a normal person. Let's move on before I begin writing my utopian manifesto.

For you? Maybe paid advertising is the thing. Every book and situation is different. If advertising produces measurable results for you, I am happy that you benefit from it. The biggest danger is that few services and advertisers guarantee that £x spent on advertising will lead to more money coming back into your pocket, with a refund if it doesn't. Unlike the advertising industry, almost every other service we use states what you will get back for your money, so you can weigh up whether it offers good value. Unless there is some minimum guarantee of results, beware of how much money you spend for perhaps no benefit at all.

Drinky's Digressions: Read-through

Read-through (or **sell-through**) is defined as the percentage of a book's readers who go on to read (or buy) the next book in a series. So if sales of book one are always double book two, that would mean only half of people reading book one go on to continue with the series: a fifty per cent drop in read-through.

You want the read-through to be as high as possible: that indicates that the readers are gripped and just have to know what happens next. If the read-through from one book is low (e.g. less than 25%) then it could indicate a major problem that puts three quarters of the readers off from wanting to know what happens in the next book. This is why it is worth monitoring sales figures for all the books in a series, not just the first two: it can identify weak points.

I monitor this with my Lost Solace series. Sales figures for each book are almost equal, so it means nearly everyone who reads book one goes on to read the others. Possibly a 90% read-through. That's what we want to aim for if we write series. (Most of my other books are standalones, so don't get to benefit from the read-through effect.)

This ties in to the discussions of paid advertising in the previous section. A lot of adverts do not generate enough sales to pay for the cost of advertising, which is why many authors don't use paid adverts for a standalone book. Instead they use them for the first book in a *series*. Yes, they lose money on each sale of that book, but the hope is that the series has good read-through and the buyer will enjoy the book enough to buy books two, three, and onwards. Suddenly the advertising *is* profitable. This is one of the reasons why authors choose to write in series: it opens up promotional opportunities that you don't get with standalone books. Obviously big names like Stephen King can write standalone books and they'll sell like hot cakes, but most of us aren't in those exalted realms.

Promotional Graphics Using 3D Mock-ups

A book cover is more than a wrapping: it's a key element in promotion of the book. A flat image of the book cover is useful, but sometimes a **3D mock-up** is better. Also known as a **mock-up image** or **3D render**, it is a graphic where you can see the book's cover as an ebook on an e-reader or a phone, or perhaps a printed book which could be lying down, stood up, or in a pile.

The mock-up will have a transparent background so it can be easily combined with other images, and used in many ways to create promotional images. The backgrounds might be scenes, elements from the book cover or related themes, textured backgrounds, even the wraparound print cover without any text. As an example, perhaps a book about a holiday romance might have a sunny beach image in the background.

9.2 A basic 3D mock-up of a paperback book

That's why 3D mock-ups have many marketing uses, from sale pages to adverts, banners, social media headers and posts, or your website.

9.3 A 3D ebook mock-up used in a promotional image

As well as the 3D mock-up and background, a third element will be text. It could just be the author and title, in which case it is useful to have them extracted from the book cover as transparent-background png files, so they can be resized and moved around on different backgrounds. But the text could also be:

- brief extracts from reviews;

- a short quote from the book: a snappy and illustrative sentence, or something a character says;

- a one-sentence summary or tagline (see One Liners in Chapter 7: Metadata);

- a link to your primary retailer (using a URL shortening service if necessary) or a UBL to provide readers with all the options;

- some claim to fame (did it sell a million copies?);

- a call to action such as "read today", "coming soon", "available now", "order now", "only 99p today", "on sale now!" etc.;

- where to go for further information, such as the author's website or social media accounts.

As with all good graphic design, the images should be harmonious, text clear and readable. Keep a look out for examples that you think work well, since they can provide you with new ideas for your own promotional images.

Creating The Base Mock-up

It's easiest to create 3D mock-ups at the same time as creating the book cover. If you hire a cover designer or your publisher arranges it, ask for the 3D mock-ups to use in book promotion and social media. If you design covers yourself, then generate your own: an option also available to you even if you are trade published, as long as you are provided with an image file for the book cover.

For my own books I tend to use templates in graphics software and manipulate the cover images that way. However, if you prefer to take the easy route then DIY Book Design[227] is a good option. It's a site run by Derek Murphy, who once designed one of my book covers. DIY Book Design mock-ups are free, and it's a painless process.

Turning Them Into Promotional Graphics

One option is to do them yourself with graphics software. GIMP[228] is free, cross-platform, and offline (so you won't lose work if there are connection issues). I use this for pretty much everything graphics-related, and find it to be far better for my needs than something like Adobe Photoshop.

Other graphics options include Photopea[229] which is a free, online tool. It's handy if you need to quickly edit an image, perhaps while not on your own PC. It's similar to Photoshop and will work with the same files.

Other authors prefer to use Canva.[230] You can do some things for free, but other features are restricted to those with a paid subscription.

If you'd rather take the easy route, then BookBrush[231] is a popular commercial option. Try it out for free to see if it will be useful. It can create full images of the cover and text against a background, and would deal with all your marketing needs.

Lastly, there are other ways to create promotional graphics featuring your book.

Placeit[232] is a paid service, and has a 3D mock-up category specifically for books, focussed on making the book covers look like part of a photograph.

PhotoFunia[233] lets you create a fun image of your book cover on a poster, or book title against some appropriate background.

Price Promotions

If you are traditionally published then you'll have no say in pricing, or special offers. Move on to the next section and hope your publisher makes use of this for you.

However, if you're an independent author, control of price is one of your main tools. And it's free!

A **price promotion** is when the price of a book is temporarily lowered. If sales of a book flag, try a price promotion where the price is lowered for a set period of time, perhaps coinciding with an event. For example, romance books often get promoted around Valentine's Day, and horror books at Samhain. If you write in a series you can lower the price of the first book in the hope of high read-through.

Note that I am talking about ebooks. Since print books have fixed costs, there's often no way to do a discount on those without losing money.

Promo Sites

If you do a price promotion then you need to let people know about it. Obviously there are your usual methods such as social media and your newsletter, both of which I discussed as key parts of your author platform. But there is another option.

Promo sites exist to connect readers to book bargains. Readers sign up to the site for free, and on the better quality sites are able to specify their preferences in terms of genre and online stores. Authors and publishers inform the promo site of any upcoming price reductions, which the promo site then includes in its newsletter to signed-up readers.

So promo sites are like mailing lists that exist solely to inform readers of discounts. If you have a price promotion, then including it in one of the promo site mailouts can improve its visibility.

However, inclusion isn't free. As well as promo sites often using affiliate links to generate income, authors pay the promo site to be included in the newsletter. This often shocks new authors:

"What, I am making my book available for free or at a discounted price, and I have to *pay* to tell people about it?"

The theory is that it leads to new readers, sales and reviews. And if the book is in a series, you should get read-through to later titles. The goal is that so many people hear about the reduction and are tempted by the book that your sales lead to increased royalties that hopefully pay for the promo, and even give you a bit extra, along with new fans.

This system depends on the promo services having not just "a huge list of people!" but that the list is properly curated: current email addresses, of people who actually buy books. Also that your promo details go to fans of that genre, but not to people who have no interest. So a big part of it is dependent on the service having a high-quality segmented list. Another key element is that they are selective in the books they promote. If they include anything and everything then it may be more democratic, but many subscribers will soon unsubscribe again when they are swamped with low quality books.

Promo sites love to market themselves as powerful tools for authors. That depends on many factors, some out of their control, but the promise is always that using them is in some way worthwhile. One would also expect that the price they charge for the service is realistically proportionate to the results you'd hope to see, assuming all the basics are in place. Even better if they have some kind of policy for dealing with situations where the price-to-impact ratio proves to be vastly disproportionate, at the author's expense. For many new authors money may be tight, and losses on marketing can have a big impact on their livelihood.

There are lots of promo sites. I have probably tried all the well-known ones, and many lesser known. And in general I have found them to be pretty useless. Worse, some services that had shiny websites proved to be all sheen and no substance. One of the promo services I tried sent out broken links on the day of the promotion, and ignored all my attempts to contact them once I'd paid. Another monitored promos on their rival sites, gathered the contact details of the authors using them, then spammed the authors offering discounts for their own service. Tacky.

BookBub

The exception to the rule is BookBub, the empress of promo sites. Whenever I had one of their coveted Featured Deals, I made back the cost of the promo and more, along with a huge influx of new fans. Yes, they were massively expensive, but they worked. I could have thrown the same amount of money at every non-BookBub service and just been better off burning it. I suspect BookBub's selectivity is what sets them apart from everything else, in that their list is both huge and full of ravenous readers, who only receive the kind of content they signed up for. However, BookBub is in high demand, and increasing interest from traditional publishers leads to heavy competition for relatively few daily Featured Deal slots. If you'd like to know more:

- BookBub Partners,[234] where you can apply for a Featured Deal (you have to create an account, unfortunately)

- Pricing[235]

- The BookBub site for readers,[236] listing new deals

Promo Stacking

Some authors take it further by using multiple promotion sites in a process known as **promo stacking**. The idea behind this is that you advertise the promotion on multiple different sites, one after the other, ideally with each boosting the next. Imagine a boulder rolling downhill and gathering momentum. Each promo site reaches different audiences with the aim of spreading out the sales so that it leads the book to move up through the rankings, rather than spiking for a day and then fading back to baseline sales.

Stacked promos require more work to set up, and cost more, but it is supposed to lead to better results than individual promos (which will almost always be a loss).

Promo stacking works best for established authors with substantial backlists; though those authors probably do well with a variety of promotional tools anyway, as they have momentum behind them (fans, social proof, and spare income to invest in marketing). The effect may not be so pronounced on authors that aren't as well known. Another downside is that, if the promos are too close together, it can be hard to identify which sites were having the impact on sales and worth using again in the future, versus which were duds. And if too far apart, the stacking principle loses momentum.

Promo stacking has never worked for me, but maybe I'm an exception. I wrote a short piece for the ALLi website (published in July 2023) about some promo stacking tests I did, and fellow authors confirmed my experiences weren't outliers. Many authors had found these promo sites (whether singly or stacked) to be a loss, even on well-reviewed books with lots of positive ratings. That's why it is so useful for authors to share our experiences in every area of publishing and marketing, to separate the glossy promises from the reality, and to identify services which may be overpriced for what you get, especially without any minimum impact guarantees. There are definite dangers in terms of how things are presented to new authors who are often desperate to sell books or reach audiences.

Here are some of the sites in case you do want to try advertising a price promotion through any of them. They're in alphabetical order, and although I've used all of these, none of them are recommendations, as they all had disappointing elements and cost far more than I gained in sales. None of them offer guarantees of effectiveness or have a publicised refund policy as far as I am aware, though in some cases where it doesn't work out they may agree to run a second promotion for free, or to give a full or partial refund. That's the exception though, not the norm, and I recommend checking their policy before giving them any money.

- Bargain Booksy[237]

- Book Barbarian.[238] Sci-fi and fantasy books only (they have partner sites, one for romance,[239] one for mysteries and thrillers.[240]

- Booksends[241]

- ENT (Ereader News Today)[242]

- eReaderIQ[243]

- Robin Reads[244]

I excluded any that require creating accounts (with themselves or PayPal), or ones where I've been disappointed with the results and service.

Top Tips: Making The Most Of A Price Promotion

- If the book is part of a series that has to be read in order, you should only ever promote the first book (or a collected edition). However, when promoting the first book, it is worth reducing the prices of the subsequent books in a staggered effect, to encourage multiple purchases and read-through. As an example, a five-book series might have each ebook costing $6.99. So, for a staggered promo, the first book (that is being promoted) might be on sale at $0.99; book two at $1.99; book three at $2.99, and so on.

- If the book is part of a series that can be read in any order because each book is a standalone story (just featuring the same setting or main character) then they are all suitable for one of these promotions. It is recommended to vary the books promoted.

- If using a promo site then subscribe to the service *as a reader* before your promo date arrives. Then you can see what the readers will see, and make sure your book appears as promised, with no mistakes.

- Even better: subscribe to the service *before paying anything*. Then you can check out the quality of its newsletters, how well laid out they are, and whether the links all work. You can see whether they segment lists by genre and vendor. You can also examine the quality of the books they promote: are they titles that you would be proud to see your book alongside? These are all indications of how much care and attention they pay to their newsletters, and how selective they are in promoting books. I've seen some awful promotional site emails with broken links, bad layout, and amateur design, which would certainly put me off giving the company any money.

- In the days leading up to the promo create a checklist, including items such as the following:

- a) Set the book's pricing to match the offer price. Since it can take a few days for the price change to go through, do it ahead of the promo date.

- b) Promote the offer on whatever author platform channels you have available: social media, newsletter and so on. Ask people to spread the word about the promotion. You could consider pinning that post on social media, or making a banner image for it.

- c) Double check that the price is correct on the day before the promo; if not, follow it up as a matter of urgency.

- After the promotion, record the results: sales figures, profit, screenshots of any impressive rankings, especially if your book made the top ten in a vendor chart – that's a whole other thing to celebrate on social media, blog posts and newsletters. Likewise if it achieves bestseller status anywhere.

- Remember to save a record of the fee paid: it's a business expense.

Drinky's Digressions: Pretty Pricing

You know how things are often priced at £2.99 rather than £2.84, or the tidier £3? It's called **pretty pricing** (or **odd pricing**). Most retailers and manufacturers do it. I read once that 90% of prices in retail end with either 9 or 5.

I think originally it came from manufacturers and psychologists assuming that we're all idiots, and if we see something for £2.99 it will seem a lot cheaper than £3 so we'll buy it. Hence more complicated sums and much more requirement for shops to have lots of change ever since. I've always said advertising and marketing departments are almost as evil as bribed politicians.

Anyway, if you are an independent author and pricing things yourself, especially when considering price promotions, it is something to be aware of. Particularly in our globally connected world of sales.

It becomes a particular consideration with items sold in more than one currency. For example, if an author is setting the prices for an ebook or print book, there is normally one main currency: often US dollars, or the currency for the country the distributor is based in. Then the price may be converted to other currencies based on the current conversion rate. So a book might be £2.99 in GBP, but $6.14 in NZD and $4.96 in CAD. Most distributors let you manually alter the price for different regions, so it is fairly standard for people to round prices up to the nearest .99 (or occasionally, to round it down). So the author might choose to alter the prices to $5.99 in NZD and $4.99 in CAD, adopting pretty pricing.

A variant of that is to round up or down to the nearest .50 or .99. That involves less extreme price hikes, especially in low-value items. Changing £209 to £209.99 is an increase of only 0.33%, whereas changing £1.01 to £1.99 is an increase of almost 100%. Having a .50 option at halfway (so £1.50) means it is only a 50% price hike.

Or you could round up or down to the nearest *whole unit* or 0.50. So instead of £1.99 or £1.49 you have £2 or £1.50.

It can be a lot of work to manipulate and tidy prices in this way across all regions. Also note that currency conversion rates change daily, so they quickly go out of date. It's why I'd always be tempted to leave odd prices. I find something charming about £1.33, $2.81 and so on. It makes things stand out for me. But I have always been weird.

There is even an argument to keep it simple and have prices as whole numbers, that it may contribute to a feeling of luxury due to prices ending with .99 reminding us of budget deals.

There may be no definites, but if you are an independent author it's worth spending time thinking about how you will price your books, and noting what other people do.

Press Releases And Sell Sheets

The local press is always looking for news, and being able to include a piece about the achievements of someone who lives in the area means a good opportunity to get word out and generate interest. Hence letting them know about you and your book via a **press release**.

Writing a press release is a useful skill to develop. And you have to angle it to play up the local interest, or something noteworthy. Is the book set locally? Have you recently won an award? Is there some other news item it can be linked to?

The best press releases are concise, informative, and have an engaging headline. Include a brief bit about you, and any important links, such as to your website or further information. Also, write a few quotes as if they'd interviewed you. They print press releases as you write them, so it's fine to add things such as:

> Karl said, "I love Scotland and many locations are ideal backdrops for my zombie flesh-eating alien chainsaw horror books."

Also make sure press releases are sent to the correct journalist. Keep a document that has all the basic information about the local press such as papers and radio – names, contacts, web addresses, emails, phone numbers – to save time whenever you have a new book launch.

Of course, you can go much further. I called this section press releases but it includes any form of media coverage you can get, from radio to magazines.

Sell sheets are different from press releases. Sell sheets include all the basic information and key selling points of a book. If the book is not yet available then the sell sheet would be referred to as an **advance information sheet**.

Not only can you include a sell sheet with press releases so that the journalist has all the information at their fingertips, but it can be used for other purposes, such as sent to local libraries as purchase requests, included in ARCs sent to reviewers (so they have all the correct details), printed out as takeaways for use on stalls, or given to bookshops in case they want to consider stocking your books. They are often A4, single sided, sometimes in colour.

It should include some or all of the following, depending on purpose:

- the book's author and title;
- the book's cover art;
- the book blurb;
- the genre it falls into;
- ISBN and format (paperback, hardback, ebook, audiobook);
- an indication of length e.g. printed page count, or even just stating if it is a novel, novella, or short story collection;
- price;
- publication date;
- maybe a bit about the author (especially if it has local relevance) – optional author photo;
- a sample of quotes from editorial reviews or press coverage;

- the publisher / imprint;

- ordering details (e.g. the standard distributors such as Gardners, Bertrams, Askews etc);

- possibly contact details so they can get in touch.

The most attractive sell sheets will be designed to echo the style and colours of the book cover. They should be easy to read, whilst conveying all the key information in a nicely organised way.

9.4 An example sell sheet for one of author Sally Hanan's books

Live Readings And Performances

I'm interested in how different types of artist communicate with their audiences, and how fans support them. With authors, the main form is for fans to buy – and read – their books. This is certainly the main financial transaction. So the principle relationship is written words on a page, transmitted after the event "cold" (even though they may have been written in heat).

With musicians it is similar when you buy their music in physical form, such as a CD or LP. The finished product, set in plastic with fiery lithography, then cooled as the heat fades to leave the impression of the sounds and words, unchanging and final. And it is good. But the extra option of seeing an artist perform *live*, in the fire of passion, is actually a major income source for many singer-songwriters and bands. You get the immediacy, the warm malleability of a live performance, an extra level of closeness as the sound vibrations reach your ears unmediated – a valuable form of contact with an artist.

Many fans appreciate the personal. They want to know the author as a human being. That's where opportunities for something more direct can be popular. Readings and other events are about putting ourselves (and our work) out there, and being approachable. When people like you, they're more likely to buy your books.

And then there's the impact of spoken words. As an act of communication it can transfer emotion. I believe the ears are less of a censor than the eyes, so the words go straight into your brain. You will read the page-printed words "I love you and I hate you" in one way, but different speakers will perform that phrase *fifty* different ways. Angry, soft, shouted, sneering, plaintive, emotionless. I studied Classics at university, translating poems that were never meant to be read on a page, that would have been exciting oral performances spanning several evenings of entertainment (thanks, Homer et al) because *performance* is the key word.

In a performance you can't skip ahead. The story will unveil itself at its own pace. And the story has more chance to surprise or shock you. I once wrote a nasty character piece: a dramatic monologue about a vile man describing his wife's death. I read it out to a group of fellow writers, and afterwards the room was silent. The anger I felt while reading aloud communicated itself only too well. One of the authors later wrote about it on his blog:

> "Another interesting thing was that Karl read a powerful, challenging story. Karl's story was an assault on the psyche of everyone in the room. It was vile, repugnant, out of control, despicable – and deliberately so. At the end of the story, the response was not an intellectual one of 'I like what you did with X, but not so keen on Y,' rather it was a coming to terms with the emotions we were each feeling, and why we were so appalled, and what it meant for the person in the story. It was an important lesson."

Written words do not assault the mind as spoken words do, because we can shut our eyes and take the power away from the words on the page; but we can not block out another person, cannot close our ears, so easily. If the story is an accusation then we can't help but identify with the accused. It's the identification with another being that powers most fiction. And, so help us, this world needs a lot more empathy.

Various Tips For Public Appearances

When you have the courage to stand up and share your words with conviction it creates moments in the lives of each observer that wouldn't have existed otherwise.

- Look out for opportunities. Perhaps hold a book launch in your local bookshop. Or there might be some kind of spoken word or open mic event in a venue near you that you can take part in. Maybe a local radio station wants to interview you. They can be an opportunity to either read a few passages from your latest work, or even to try out new material, new styles, new voices, and see what the reaction is.

- Content. Have faith in your words, but also make a good selection in what you'll read. The best bit on the page may not be the best bit to read out. You want something that allows variety. Also that feels self-contained, even if it is a fragment. Good material is your starting point.

- And don't select too much. Things run over. You may be performer number twenty. A bit of context and a fun five minutes is better than sending people to sleep with twenty minutes of monologue. Aim for impact, and leave people wanting more.

- Eye contact is engagement. Memorising the work helps you achieve this, freeing you from the tyranny of staring at a notebook instead of the audience. Sure, have a prompt, but don't let it become a barrier. You want the opposite: to bring the listeners *into* your world.

- Spoken voice allows us to bring in the four elements of interest: variety in rhythm, in speed (including use of pauses), in volume, and in pitch. Some of us make use of one or two, but manipulating all four is tricky. With these you can elevate your delivery to the next level, even if not all the audience can pinpoint how you did it. Flat and regular speech quickly becomes monotonous and kills the greatest poem, whereas speaking too quickly can also lose people. The speed and other elements should support the words and emotions in order to make them come alive.

Think of it not as a reading but a *performance*. As if the words are so lively they have to pour out. You are allowed to move! To use gestures and facial expressions! Obviously only where appropriate, and you must be true to yourself and what you project. The readings that stick in my mind are the ones with vitality. Here is part of my diary entry for Sunday the 12th March 2023:

> "Last night was the Loud Poets poetry slam. Spoke to lots of people. Amazing poetry and performances. Everyone did brilliantly, so many styles and topics. I was particularly proud of the five people I know from WRITE who took part. As ever, I am in awe of their talent and confidence. On top of that, I'd never seen Joelle Taylor perform, but when she did her extended poem, it wasn't just words, it WAS a performance, scary and funny and entertaining and thought-provoking. When Joelle got angry, I actually felt like she was shouting at me, and going to punch me! Awesome projection and a powerhouse performance ending with 'Men are just broken things breaking things'. The way she used words and pauses made language fresh and surprising, as poetry should. I'm so mightily impressed. The third round, where poetry had to be done to live music, was such fun. There's nothing quite like the energy of live events."

You can see Joelle's performance here.[245] Also Chelsie Nash's:[246] she had scary-eyed stares, clawed hands, and barely-contained nuclear fission. Performance should flow from you, so it is not false acting, more a hyperreality that's unique and appropriate.

If I did Chelsie's poem and tried to emulate her, it would appear false. I need to be me, but with the dial turned up.

When you have the courage to stand up and share your words with conviction it creates moments in the lives of each observer that wouldn't have existed otherwise.

Bookstore Launches

If you do have a launch or in-store event in a venue like a bookshop, don't expect the bookshop to do all the work. It's *your* party, so invest in it. A good display, drinks, enough stock to sell.

Although the bookshop will advertise the event, the public won't necessarily turn up in large numbers, so make sure you publicise it widely and invite as many people as possible. Bring your own audience of friends and fans. It will impress the bookshop and act as support for you.

Encourage attendees to buy any books they want from the shop that evening (not just yours!). You and the bookshop are allies, and everything you can do to help them thrive is a boost to your relationship.

Hopefully it will be a well-attended and popular event that creates buzz in the bookshop, and it will be the start of a positive connection that will lead to your books being stocked there in future.

Point people to the bookshop in your social media posts or from your website, and include the ISBNs to help people order directly from their local store. It will always be appreciated.

Consider doing a joint event with another author if there's a match in style, content or genre. Double the fun, and sharing audiences with each other is a win-win situation.

Tips For If You Get Nervous

"Karl, you make it seem easy, but I doubt I could even read my material confidently, let alone blow anyone's socks off."

In that case we take a step back. Speaking in public events is a skill, and with time you get better at it.

Before I became an author I was a librarian, and in that career I would happily give lively presentations to a hundred students, with good audience participation, laughter, and interest even when the topic might be as dry as bibliographic databases.

But it wasn't always like that. The first time I stood up in a lecture theatre to introduce myself briefly at a departmental introduction, I almost froze up, rushed my words, didn't make eye contact, and my voice went up two octaves in pitch. I couldn't wait to get off the stage. Such a contrast to a few years later. I wasn't a natural: I just paid attention, learnt techniques, and got better at it. Then, in time, enjoyed it.

Being an author was my second career, and when I started to give readings and talks at arts centres and book festivals about my fiction, I did get nervous again, since it felt much more like I myself was being judged. My creative competency was bared, leaving no protection for the ego. What would friends, colleagues and family think of my work? It was so much more personal.

I remember one reading, at a book launch in Wales, where I was incredibly anxious, even though I told myself that we should always try to conquer our fears. When I got to the venue (a bookshop) it was full to capacity, with a number of people I knew in the audience. I felt even more tense because I had chosen to read out a seduction scene (since I never make things too easy for myself – a top tip is to select sections that you feel comfortable reading!). Extra embarrassment might have come from the fact that it was a story about an English department university academic seducing a student, and there were some English department university academics (and students) in the room. However, the talk went well and people said nice things afterwards.

Those kind of events got easier over time. And they will for you, too. So if you do get nervous, here are a few tips:

- Rehearse. Practise reading the material aloud at home. Once it gets familiar you'll flow better, and no longer need to look at your notes. That boosts your confidence and makes the delivery more natural. Tell yourself it is okay to miss bits out, or add new material in the moment if it feels appropriate.

- Breathe. Deep, slow, calming breaths before you go on,

and keep your breathing regular throughout. This tells your body that it isn't entering a dangerous situation where it needs to go into panic mode; instead, this is a nice situation, and it is safe to relax.

- Smile. Smile when you go on stage. Smile when you make a joke. Smile when someone asks a question. Smile even when you're doing the deep breathing before your talk. Smiling also tells your body that everything is fine. It shows the audience that you are confident and engaged. It ripples through everything. I remember when I made phone calls I would smile as I spoke, and it somehow comes through in your voice even when people can't see your face. Smiling tricks your brain into thinking it is having fun.

- Make eye contact with the audience. Not scary stares, just occasional connections. It makes a difference to the audience, but also helps you, in terms of engaging with your listeners.

- Your attitude to things can change the outcome. If you enter a room with the assumption that everyone in there is an enemy out to get you, looking for the slightest mistake on which they'll pounce, then it will come across in your delivery. People won't feel any warmth. They'll switch off or get angry. A self-fulfilling prophecy comes true. On the other hand, if you adopt the view that all the people in the room are your friends (you just haven't got to know them all yet), with shared interests, and they're here to support you – then it changes the dynamic, and you interact with them as friends, and they are more likely to reciprocate.

- If people tell you to imagine the audience is naked, ignore them. It's not a good tip. It's kind of creepy at best, and at worst might lead you to interact with people in weird ways, or you might get the giggles, or any other strange thing. You don't need gimmicks: just treat people as friendly equals and you'll be fine. That's a useful life tip even outside of presentations.

- Sometimes it's not a reading, but a talk on a subject. Many of the same tips apply. It always helps to be passionate about your subject. After all, if it bores you, what will it do to the audience? Whereas if you're enthusiastic, that will be communicated, like the good kind of infection.

- You can talk about your own experiences – good and bad. Anecdotes, with a bit of honesty and humour, entertain the audience and help you relax.

Top Tip: Introduce Yourself Locally

Once you've had a bit of success with your writing it can be worth introducing yourself to local book-related places. That's especially true if you're the kind of soul who likes to do marketing in person, and enjoys giving talks and readings.

I do *not* mean turn up at a bookshop unexpectedly, wave your book around and demand to see the manager to tell them how great you are. You'll look unprofessional and give a bad first impression (and make them scared of meeting authors in the future). People have jobs to do, and they're probably busy. It is much better to give them the option of meeting you or not; provide some background; and meet up (if they invite you) at a mutually convenient time.

So send them an email or letter. Make sure you find out their name, role, and the correct contact details first.

Who might you make contact with? Here are some possibilities:

- The manager of your local bookshop.

- The reader development librarian at your local library.

- The staff at any relevant local arts and community organisations, if those organisations put on events and workshops. Things like arts centres, creative community organisations, cultural centres. Obviously only ones that include literary arts in their programme. There's no point promoting yourself to the local ceramic crafts centre – unless you write books that have some relevance to their work. Be prepared for a variety of role titles, from Artistic Director to Literature Lead, from Head of Communications & Engagement to Events Guru.

In the initial communication you want to come across as professional and respectful of their time. No twenty-page screeds with quotes from every review, please. Briefly explain who you are, that you're a local author, and give any relevant background. Do you frequent the library/bookshop/centre? If so, tell them what they mean to you!

It's fine to mention the kind of books you write, and any successes you've had. You can devote a separate paragraph to that.

Explain why you are contacting them: to introduce yourself, make connections, to see if they'd like to meet up so you could talk about your work and how it might tie in to their priorities and future goals or events. Obviously the possibilities will vary for the different types of organisation: for a bookshop you might offer to be involved with any author reading programmes they do, whereas for a library you might be able to contribute to reading groups, or special events for World Book Day.

What we're aiming at with these communications is for the person we contact to be aware of us, and if they have a list of local authors they can approach when they are putting on events, then ideally you want to be on that.

Make sure you include some links to your website, lists of books or whatever – ways where they can find out more about you, and decide if you're the kind of author they'd like to work with. It's why it is so important to have an author platform, as discussed earlier. You can include your writing CV if you have one, which lists articles written, books published, teaching done, and notable writing achievements.

As an aside, a great-looking writing CV has many uses, including when you apply for grants or awards. It's also a handy reference for you, summarising all that you have done, and when, so that you can immediately refer to it to find the year you judged a certain writing competition, or when you taught on a course. My master CV is many pages long, but I truncate it to two A4 sides before sending it out; just to show the most recent events, or those most relevant to the reason I am sending it.

If they do agree to meet up to find out more and discuss possibilities, well done! You obviously made the right impression, to the right person.

When I go to one of these I always see them as a friendly chat. First of all let them talk about their role and the kind of events they do, and any plans for the future. You can then talk about your work and experiences, the kind of audience which enjoys your books, what you can offer, and any ideas you have. Sometimes plans begin to formulate; other times it is just a connection made, someone who will remember you later when they have an author-related need or are planning the next year's events.

Always take some materials with you. I usually have a mix of the following kinds of things, whatever is most relevant – it's not an attempt to overwhelm them!

- A printout of my writing CV. This is useful to the person you meet in terms of them seeing where you might fit in to their business, but also as an aide memoir for you.

- A list of the books you've written, sorted by series or genre if appropriate. I just print out the list of Other Titles from the back of one of my books.

- A sheet of quotes from reviews, "Praise For Karl Drinkwater" or something like that. Ideally quotes from websites and publications, rather than anonymous Amazon reviewers. See the Editorial Reviews section in Chapter 7, and the reviews section earlier in this chapter.

- Sell Sheets / Advance Information Sheets (as discussed earlier).

- Your books! The best way to win someone over is when they look at your work and can see how nice your books look, with great covers, compelling blurbs, and lovely interior formatting. I usually offer them a copy to keep as a sample. It shows you're confident in the quality of your writing, and also means they'll have a far better idea of your potential audience (and how that could tie in to their events) after at least skimming your work. And if they love your work then you'll be prominent in their mind when they think about future events.

It's useful to prepare for the meeting, but since it is a conversation your main goal is to be friendly and professional. Let them know that if any opportunities to work together occur in the future, you'd look forward to being involved. Over time you will be more familiar with the topics that may come up, such as discussions about author payments.

A key part of being professional is being respectful of someone's time. Don't overstay your welcome, and always thank them for their time in seeing you.

In the past I've found all sorts of opportunities come out of this kind of thing. Sometimes I've been asked to do readings. Sometimes a library has ordered copies of my books for stock. Sometimes I've pitched ideas for projects which eventually came to fruition, e.g. my proposal for the monthly WRITE! sessions I run, which has proven to be one of the most popular events run by the community organisation that hosts it. And other times the person I met recommended me to someone else when an opportunity occurred that required an author. Fingers crossed for you.

Lastly, if ever you move home to live in a different area, repeat this process once you have settled in.

Stalls At Events

If for any reason you end up running a stall at an event – whether it be a book festival, or even a stall at your local market – then it can be a great chance to sell signed books, to meet fans, and to promote your newsletter.

If you do try this, here are some tips.

- Have book stacks, with at least a few face out. If you have series, you'll need more copies of the first in the series than the later books, as some people might just want to try the first book.

- Take bookmarks and business cards or anything else relevant that can go on the stall, especially if it's something that can be taken away if someone doesn't buy a book. They can then think about it later.

- Maybe take a tablet computer with a newsletter sign-up on it, so they can do it at the stall. (And remember to keep the screen clean!)

- Some people print short promotional flyers that can be taken away, with the cover of a book, its blurb, and any relevant details.

- If you're selling stuff for cash, make sure you have change. Price books at round numbers like £10 to make the transactions easier, rather than the traditional (but stupid) £9.99. You can either write the price inside the books, or have a flyer with prices on. Nowadays you may also want a card payment device or app for people who prefer more money to go towards a bank's profits.

- Sometimes it is better to be standing up in order to greet people and seem more approachable, rather than staying sat and hidden behind piles of books.

- Consider a shared stall with another creator. It will mean more interesting content for visitors; someone to chat to during quiet times; and the ability to nip off to the toilet without worrying that a literary thief is going to run away with all your books. (Or stagger off dragging a sack of them, more likely.)

- It's good to have an attractive stand. If you haven't got printed banners then make do with what you do have, such as books, flyers, and posters. Signage is key, and it needs to be large enough, attractive, neat, readable, and colourful. Ideally all at once. You can also use various types of light shelving to raise books up and create verticality to your display.

- Towards the end of the day, feel free to create impromptu special offers if it helps to clear your stock, e.g. extra discounts, or special prices for multi-buys. Fans enjoy bargains, and it feels better going home with empty boxes and full, jingling pockets.

- It's handy to have promotional cards or business cards for any event where there are interactions with other humans, including talks, professional networking, and book signings. Hand them out to adoring fans, interested agents, besuited publishers. Make sure they match your branding and have links to key contact details and addresses, such as your website, social media profiles, and email address. You can get cards printed from online sites or your nearest printshop (it's good to support local businesses). Attractive business cards can double as bookmarks for fans. Look into the paper options, and go for the most environmentally friendly – which means avoiding foils and lamination (as we saw in the previous chapter's section on the environment and book printing).

- Since writers are self-employed and have to do a self-assessment tax return, bear in mind that the cost of promotional cards, stall rental or display equipment are legitimate expenses to include.

Compilations

Once an author has a few books available, a new option appears: compilations. Although this is particularly relevant to making a compilation edition of books in a series, it can also apply to themed books (e.g. a horror collection, even if each of the horror books is a standalone title) or a compilation of work by more than one author working together (e.g. three authors each supplying a book to a steamy romance compilation).

Note that this is a topic that crosses over marketing, formatting, and distribution, and could fit into any of those chapters. In the end I put it here as a promotional technique, but be aware of the breadth of the subject.

Why do this? Well, the books are already written, so for a bit of formatting, a new cover and an ISBN or two there can be a new release, offering great value to readers and acting as a new title with the current year as its publication date. This is often done with long series, where the cost of buying all the books separately can be prohibitive, meaning sales of later books in the series tail off. By creating a collection of some of the earlier books at a lower price than buying them individually, it can tempt readers to purchase the collection, and also lead them to later books in the series. As such, release of an ebook collection is often used as a promotional tool for a book series, and a great marketing opportunity for older books, to refresh a backlist. Also, compilations often appeal to a different binge-reading demographic (sometimes referred to by authors as "whale readers") from those who prefer single titles. So compilations can be like free money.

Print Versus Electronic. If you put together a boxed set of printed books then the cost of production increases, whether they are true collections of books in a boxed case, or reformatted as multiple works in a single volume. As the number of pages increases, the cost increases, and there is no easy way around that. However, ebooks generally have no distribution cost, and an ebook of a hundred pages costs the same to distribute as a thousand pages. That's why ebook compilations win out. Since ebooks can be larger, and they are easier to format, a popular option with independent authors is to group separate books together into a single volume.

Terminology. Compilations are sometimes referred to as "box sets" but that term is incorrect in most cases. A box set is a collection of physical books, each separate, but bought together in an attractive case which holds the printed books. The term is inappropriate for ebook compilations, which have no box. It also doesn't apply to a printed book where the separate titles are bound into a single volume (again, no box). As such, it's usually best to avoid the term "box set" entirely, and stick to calling it a compilation, collection, collected edition, or omnibus edition.

Formatting multi-book collections. Whatever tool you use (as discussed in Chapter Five) you need to put all of the books into a single document. This may involve deleting replicated front matter and back matter, so that there is only one copyright page at the start of the book, for example. And, since there will be so much more text than a normal book (and you may be presenting this as a bargain edition), it is worth considering whether the back matter from each title is still needed or if it can be cut e.g. things like discussion questions or notes.

I recommend you make a title page for each book to separate them within the body of the compilation. See the discussion of part titles in Chapter Five. For clarity they might have the work's title preceded by BOOK # e.g. BOOK 1: TURNER, and then when that finishes and the next begins, BOOK 2: HARVEST FESTIVAL. These title pages introducing the start of the next book can be made fancier, for example having the titles appear as they do on the covers, or even including the original book cover on the page.

Pricing. Compilations usually offer a bargain, and should be cheaper than buying the individual books. This bargain element is why the print version might have smaller text and lose some of the bonus content, in order to cut pages and reduce printing costs for the publisher.

However, there is an issue with ebook pricing. As noted earlier, Amazon reduces your royalty rate to 35% (from 70%) if you price a book higher than $9.99. You make more from a book at $9 (9 x 0.70 = $6.30) than you would selling it at the higher price of $12 (12 x 0.35 = $4.20)! So there is a tension, as the more books included in the compilation, the higher the price should be (but still less than buying the ebooks individually); but then you will be penalised by Amazon with half royalties. That's why some authors don't publish compilations to Amazon, only to ebook vendors that don't punish them for charging more than $9.99. Or even sell the compilation editions directly from the author's website, or a Kickstarter, again avoiding the Amazon price-manipulation penalty.

The other option is breaking the books down into sets, with each compilation including books that would add up to something like $12.99, and then selling the compilation edition at $9.99.

Describing the compilation. The title, cover image, and description should all make it clear that the reader is purchasing multiple books in a collected edition. For example, the description might include each component book's title and brief blurb.

One easy naming option for a complete series is to use the series title plus compilation, collection, collected edition, or omnibus edition (with an optional "The" at the start) e.g. "Lost Solace Collection" or "The Manchester Summer Compilation". If the books are not in a series but are in the same genre then the series name could be replaced with the author and genre e.g. "Karl Drinkwater's Horror Collection". If it is a complete series you could also use the series name, then add "The Complete Series" as a subtitle, or (if appropriate) something like "The Lost Solace Trilogy", or the series name followed by "The Complete Trilogy". Some authors break a series up into multiple collected sets, as mentioned above under pricing. Then you just add a number after each set's name to differentiate them e.g. "The Harvest Festival Collection 1", "The Killswitch Series: Omnibus 2", "Books One Through Four of the Searise Series", or "Lost Solace: Books 1-3". The point is to always be clear and unambiguous about what is offered. Customers who find they have bought the same book a second time may get annoyed.

Book covers. Obviously if the compilation will only be released as an ebook this is much simpler, as you don't need to bother with a spine and back cover.

If it is an ebook compilation then don't use one of those 3D mock-ups of a box set of books as the cover image, because it is misleading, looking like a physical product. Some vendors (such as Apple) won't even allow those.

So, what are the cover options?

- A brand new image for the compilation, which captures the mood of the books that make up the contents. This can give it a fresh appearance.

- Using the existing covers of the individual titles that

have been compiled. They could be overlapped, aligned in a grid, or grouped in any other way. This style makes it clear at a glance that we are dealing with a compilation of titles.

- A combination of the above. A new image, but with the covers of books included in the illustration somewhere. Be inventive: I remember a space opera compilation where the new image was a character sat at a control panel, and the screen displays showed the book covers of the included titles. Another compilation showed the protagonist in a subway station, and the included book covers portraying her adventures were posters behind her.

Alternatives. Instead of putting the books into a single volume, another option open to independent authors is to bundle the separate titles together and sell them via their own platform (such as Gumroad, Shopify, or the author's website) as a discounted bundle. This option doesn't have the reach of distributing the compilation on vendor sites such as Kobo and Amazon, but it sidesteps problems with Amazon pricing penalties, has a higher profit margin, and doesn't require new covers, ISBNs or formatting. Note that if any of the books that make up the compilation receive additions or corrections, ideally you will also update the version within the compilation edition. Also, you can't do a compilation edition incorporating material that is exclusive to Amazon's KDP Select/Kindle Unlimited.

Ethics And Professionalism

One of the differences between an amateur or hobbyist, and a professional, is in the approach we take. A professional mindset is something we adopt at all stages of book creation. It's also something we are mindful of in all our interactions, regardless of whether it is our distributor, a fan – or even someone who doesn't like our work and says so in a review. It's always worth reiterating the etiquette for new authors. In fact, it's a good guide for general life.

Not everyone will like your work. We all have different tastes. It's not personal. Occasionally the negative review may flag up something that you need to think about. Or they may be providing a useful purpose in helping to deter people who would dislike your book – it's better not to sell a copy, than sell it to someone who will hate it.

We all feel an instantaneous reaction to negative comments, but we're civilised beings and don't have to give in to our instincts. So if you feel like posting a reply and saying the reviewer is an idiot: don't. You'll look like a petulant child, and it could lead to all sorts of additional criticism. Remember: be professional. Don't get overly upset. These reviews are part of the inevitable experience of making an element of yourself public. Move on and focus on something else, like writing more words, or reading the positive reviews.

The goal is never to just sell more books, but to *sell more books to people who will enjoy your work*. That's a key difference, often overlooked. Every book its reader, as Ranganathan said. Sometimes a negative review can be doing you a favour in helping you find your audience.

Likewise, if you provided a copy of your book to someone who said they'd review it, but no review appears, just move on. Sure, it's fine to send a single polite follow up, but no more. Nagging doesn't benefit you or anyone else. It would just annoy the would-be reviewer, and that might well affect the final review. Perhaps they didn't review it because they didn't like the book, but hesitated to leave a bad review or upset you, or even to tell you the true reason because it would feel confrontational. If so, they were doing you a favour. Or they might not have reviewed it because they have health issues, or major financial or family worries, something more important than a book review. Again, just be thankful you're not going through those issues. Wish them well. Life is hard at times. In no case is the non-appearance of a review something to worry or get stressed about.

Life's too short. Put your energy into creativity. You want people to think of you as professional and kind, not amateur and psychotic.

In a similar way, a good mindset to have as an author is to see it as an enterprise where we cooperate with each other, rather than compete. Other authors' success does not diminish your own. As they say in the 20BooksTo50K movement: a rising tide lifts all boats. Authors support each other. We share information. We all have the same goal of producing excellent books.

Our competition isn't each other, or libraries (who do an amazing job of fostering literacy and also promoting our work to avid readers), but *people not reading books*. I've heard it said that the average young person spends at least three hours a day on video content (YouTube, Netflix, TikTok) and only a quarter of an hour on written words. Our threat is endless video and social media, which makes people forget about the joys of books. A culture where book-reading is replaced with just TV and games would be a poorer one. So we should all be working together to make reading the imaginative, fulfilling activity it can be, to create a larger audience for all of us. Libraries, bookshops, other authors: we are all allies in that noble quest.

Whatever you do, don't be tempted to manipulate review scores, boosting your own and giving low scores to other writers using fake accounts (known as "sockpuppet" accounts). Not only is that unprofessional behaviour, but it can backfire spectacularly and destroy your career, like this.[247] Sadly, this kind of thing has been going on for years, as this 2016 article shows.[248] As an author I have written critical (in the sense of analytical, not in the sense of negative) reviews of books, but I always prefer to praise the positive. If I was just a reader I could be more honest, but authors must be circumspect in how we relate to other authors. Allies, not enemies.

The Alliance of Independent Authors has an Ethical Author Campaign.[249] It is a set of statements about author ethics. Anyone can sign up to it, whether you're an independent author or a traditionally published one. You can even display a badge, if you like. It's a good illustration of the mindset to adopt as a professional author, whatever route to publication your books take. Here are the statements:

The Ethical Author Code

Guiding principle: Putting the reader first

When I market my books, I put my readers first. This means that I don't engage in any practices that have the effect of misleading the readers and buyers of my books.

Courtesy

I behave with courtesy and respect toward readers, other authors, reviewers and industry professionals such as agents and publishers. I behave professionally online and offline. If I find myself in disagreement, I focus on issues rather than airing grievances or complaints in the press or online, or engaging in personal attacks of any kind.

Aliases

I do not hide behind an alias to boost my own sales or damage the sales or reputation of another person. If I adopt a pen name for legitimate reasons, I use it consistently and carefully.

Reviewing and rating books

I do not review or rate my own or another author's books in any way that misleads or deceives the reader. I am transparent about my relationships with other authors when reviewing their books.

I am transparent about any reciprocal reviewing arrangements, and avoid any practices that result in the reader being deceived.

Reacting to reviews

I do not react to any book review by harassing the reviewer, getting a third party to harass the reviewer, or making any form of intrusive contact with the reviewer. If I've been the subject of a personal attack in a review, I respond in a way that is consistent with professional behaviour.

Book promotions

I do not promote my books by making false statements about, for example, their position on bestseller lists, or consent to anyone else promoting them for me in a misleading manner.

Plagiarism

I know that plagiarism is a serious matter, and I don't intentionally try to pass off another writer's words as my own.

Financial ethics

In my business dealings as an author, I make every effort to be accurate and prompt with payments and financial calculations. If I make a financial error, I remedy it as soon as it's brought to my notice.

Use of Tools and AI

I edit and curate the output of any tool I use to ensure the text is not discriminatory, libellous, an infringement of copyright or otherwise illegal or illicit. I recognise that it is my job to ensure I am legally compliant, not the AI tool or service I use. I declare use of AI and other tools, where appropriate.

Responsibility

I take responsibility for how my books are sold and marketed. If I realize anyone is acting against the spirit or letter of this Code on my behalf, I will refer them to this Code and ask them to modify their behaviour.

Drinky's Digressions: Ghostwriting

While I'm on the subject of ethics, I'd like to mention another thing. Ghostwriting. I have author friends who do this as part or all of their writing career. It's nothing to do with calling on the spirits to do your work for you because you have writers' block today. **Ghostwriting** is where someone is paid to write a book for someone else. For example, they take a celebrity's notes and turn them into a memoir. In exchange, they get a lump sum payment. I'm glad some of my friends can make a living from it whilst providing a useful service.

The element I have an issue with is publishers purposefully misleading customers by not acknowledging when a book has been ghost-written. They often add awful gagging clauses (**NDAs: Non-Disclosure Agreements**) to the contract so my friends can't ever reveal that they worked on the book or that it wasn't actually written by the person listed as the author. And so the official record incorrectly erases them, and names someone else as sole author when they may have not written the book at all, or just done partial work on it, while another author did the hard graft and gets no credit.

I'm not against ghostwriting. I just think that the interests of honesty require the ghostwriter to have the option of including their name on the copyright page as ghostwriter. (It needs to be an *option*, since some of my friends might not want their name to be associated with the end product – they have told me about some awful books publishers paid them to write!) Whether or not the ghostwriter's name is included, the copyright page should still indicate that a ghostwriter worked on it. And no gagging clauses should ever be used in the contract.

If these conditions were always adhered to then people would get credit for their work (if they wanted it), the bibliographic record would be more accurate, and the publisher would be honest with their readers. The current situation where they use ghostwriters, but then erase their existence, is dishonest. Likewise, the way some publishers lie to readers, presenting someone who wasn't the author as if they were the sole creator, is unethical. Always be honest with your readers.

Drinky's Digressions: Sell The Book's Originality, Not Gimmicks

I'm going to end this final long chapter with two digressions in a row. Hey, it's my book! But this is relevant to marketing.

As we've seen, marketing crosses over many areas. The choices to make a book appeal to its target audience are not just what is done after it is published, but also affect decisions on cover design, and metadata such as blurbs and taglines. As such, the points made here apply to all aspects of promoting a book's qualities. And these all come down to "don't copy bad examples, and don't use gimmicky hyperbole to try and sell books".

Don't make twists a selling point. A phrase such as "With a shocking twist you won't see coming!" on a cover or description always makes me cringe. I am well-read and probably *will* see the twist, especially after the spoiler on the front cover that alerted me to one and ruined the surprise. And if I don't spot it after all that neon flashing, it will be because the twist is either badly telegraphed, or not consistent with the rest of the book. Either way, it implies a lack of quality. *All good books have reversals.* It's not a feature to advertise, any more than "Has words spelt correctly".

Describe the book, but don't make claims about an unknown reader. The example above already shows that assumptions about a reader's abilities and preferences can backfire. Don't tell me a book is a "must-read" or I'll avoid reading it just to prove you wrong, and join the billions of other people who aren't reading it. Ditto with sensationalist stuff like "an unputdownable page turner!" (Isn't "unputdownable" a clunky word?) Again, don't tell people they won't be able to put the book down: *show* them. Write a blurb (and a book) that makes them desperate to know more.

Resist the urge to hammer home a point. Do not make some words bold in blurbs, subtitles, and marketing, as I've seen with a few trade-published books. "A **brave**, **breathtaking**, novel that is **powerful** and **heart-breaking**." It's patronising as it implies the readers need to have big fingers pointing at certain words.

Don't make vague claims. Another one we see all too often on books and TV is "Inspired by a true story". Like "bestseller", the phrase is so vague that it just raises questions about how tenuous the relationship is. It rarely seems to be based on verifiable reality. To some degree, *every* novel is based partly on things that happened or were experienced.

All these kinds of gimmicks suggest (to me) that the story and writing aren't strong enough to stand alone, so something more is needed. Treat the reader as an adult, present the work honestly, and you won't need to fall back on bland and overused phrases like these.

While I am on the topic of the ethics of how things are marketed, I've seen a trend of many trade publishers abusing metadata. As we have seen, the title and subtitle of a book appear on the cover and title page, and get recorded as metadata for book sellers. Amazon has unambiguous rules on this:[250]

> "The title field should contain only the actual title of your book as it appears on your book cover. [...] The subtitle must adhere to the same guidelines as your title."

Avoid the misleading practice of creating a fake title or subtitle stuffed with keywords. I've seen things like this: "The Crappy Gun: An award-winning terrifying psychological thriller paranormal horror that will keep you glued to the edge of your seat until the last page where you'll encounter a shocking twist!"

The bit after the colon doesn't appear on the book cover or title page, yet has been added to the title metadata field on Amazon so it shows up in bold large text at the top of the web page. An abuse of the rules, and attempt to mislead customers, but they keep doing it because it is obviously profitable.

Can you make more money by being unethical? Yes, in every area of life. But it's a tacky, sticky, unpleasant road to walk, and anyone with taste and discernment (such as your lovely self) will avoid going that way.

The Secret Sauce

Chapter 10

You've been patient as I meandered around so many topics. Hopefully you've learned something, or at least picked up a couple of tips.

Maybe when you started out reading this book you hoped to learn some secret that will make you successful.

Well, it exists, and it's in two parts.

Here's the first.

Don't stop writing if you enjoy doing it.

The enjoyment of telling stories well, of sharing our words and ideas, is the spark that doesn't go out. Everything else – sales, fame, money, respect – that's lovely, and some of them are necessary to make a living from this game, but they shouldn't be the primary reason you write because they're nebulous, and often fleeting.

But the pleasure of crafting stories and seeing them through to a form that can be shared: that's forever. That can be done even if there's no money to be made. That can be done even if you can only fit it into dinner times and breaks and bus journeys.

Our imaginations are wonderful things, but like a muscle, they need to be exercised if they're to be strengthened. Ignore them and they wither away.

While writing this book I contacted a number of author friends and asked them what advice they'd give. Some of them are independent authors, some are traditionally published, and some are hybrid. Some are even big names in their genre. I was originally going to include all their advice here, but in the end decided against it because it all boils down to the same thing: the first part of the secret sauce, above. So the common sentiments were that new authors should "keep plugging at it and not give up; it frequently takes a lot of luck to have the right work at the right time"; "just keep writing, they'll get there; I wrote many novels before I sold one"; and "they're in this for the long haul so need to write consistently". As one author I respect greatly said: "Luck is fickle. Opportunities are scarce. You cannot predict what's going to catch the public's imagination and soar. The one thing you can predict is that if you give up, it'll never happen. Writers write because they love books, and love writing them, and everything else in the world is crap by comparison."

And that's why not giving up is so important. Like doing any job well, writing takes years of practice, and hard work, and research. It comes down to determination, and persisting despite rejections and disheartening times.

Sticking at it doesn't guarantee success, but giving up guarantees failure. In philosophy terms, continuing to write is a *necessary* but not *sufficient* cause of success. But unless you do it, you'll never get anywhere, and your chances of reaching bestseller lists or selling millions of copies are exactly zero. If you give up you'll never reach the right readers with the right idea at the right time and end up with a hit.

Sure, the authors said more than that. They talked about things like getting short stories published in magazines first, to get a bit of money and recognition. They pointed out that it helps to have some kind of success or existing author platform when you publish your first book: a major podcast, having produced a screenplay, or anything else where you have a (good) reputation can lead to success in publishing. They reiterated the role of luck, and how it may seem random but the more you do, the more chances there are for good luck to kick in. That impromptu contact, that perfect opportunity, that vital connection with the zeitgeist. If luck comes around, you need to be in the right place to take advantage of it, and that requires still being in the game.

In a similar vein, write what you *love*. Not what you think you should write, not what is popular or trendy. If you write what you love – scenes that excite you, characters you want to spend time with – then that joy and passion comes through in the writing. And it helps you to keep going. Writing as a career is a long-term thing.

And I guess the second part of the secret sauce is:

Keep improving.

Even though you can't create luck, there are many factors you *can* control, which increase your chances of success. And this – continued writing and growth – is one of them.

If you never pay attention to craft, if you never try new things, if you don't bother correcting your mistakes, then you'll be stuck in a rut. You don't gain fans with average.

A good writer always seeks to improve. Maybe they focus on characterisation. Then in another book they try more complex plots and subplots. Perhaps they're working on their style, or dialogue, or description. Maybe it's more advanced stuff like embedding theme throughout all elements of a work. But if you're not going to improve, and just want to keep doing the same thing in the same way, what's the point of ever writing more than one book? What's the point of readers following you on your journey if every destination is the same as the last, every town just full of identikit chain stores and concrete? Make the destinations each have something exciting and fresh, local, independent, original. And by improving, you'll also make the journeys between destinations smoother until they become a pleasure in themselves.

Listen to feedback, keep writing, and *read a lot*. Other people's work, not just your own! And read it with a critical eye, analysing what works, what doesn't, how effects are achieved. Do all that and see the quality of your writing soar.

Writing a book is a massive accomplishment that few people ever achieve. You're already a winner. Even if your first book isn't a hit, if you keep improving then your next one might be. Persevere. You've walked this path with me for a while and I think you have what it takes. I'll be cheering you on. I have faith in you. Let's make beautiful words and share them with the world, my friend.

Drinky's FINAL Digression: Plan Your Publishing Route

In March 2024 I ran a workshop as part of a local community arts venue's *Off The Margin Micro Festival*. My session's title was *Publishing: A Super-brief Introduction*. I ended it by asking attendees to think about everything I had discussed, and use some of the elements to plan their publishing route. When we visualise things, it helps to make them real.

You can do this, now.

We will set a goal of seeing your first (or next!) book released, and break it down into some stages needed to achieve it.

Do as many of these as you feel like. All the topics have been covered at some point within this text.

1. Choose the book to be published. (A real one you are working on, or something you'd like to write.) Write down its working title.

2. Write a short summary or elevator pitch, or describe the hook. Try to do it in one sentence.

_____

_____

_____

3. What publishing route will it take? Big publisher and agent? Small publisher? Independent author?

_____

_____

4. Write some of the steps needed to make this happen, and how you will tackle them.

_____

_____

_____

_____

5. Think about the finished product, and note a few details. What would the book cover be? The blurb? How will the book be laid out? Where will it be distributed? What marketing and promotion will be done? What keywords and categories will be chosen? Any publicity stunts? Add anything else you want to record!

_____

_____

_____

_____

_____

6. Where would you like to be a year from now in terms of being an author? What three things would help you get there?

_____

_____

_____

_____

_____

Good luck!

About The Author

Karl Drinkwater is an author with a silly name and a thousand-mile stare. He writes dystopian space opera, dark suspense and diverse social fiction. If you want compelling stories and characters worth caring about, then you're in the right place. Welcome!

Karl lives in Scotland and owns two kilts. He has degrees in librarianship, literature and classics, but also studied astronomy and philosophy. Dolly the cat helps him finish books by sleeping on his lap so he can't leave the desk. When he isn't writing he loves music, nature, games and vegan cake.

Go to karldrinkwater.uk to view all his books grouped by genre.

As well as crafting his own fictional worlds, Karl has supported other writers for years with his creative writing workshops, editorial services, articles on writing and publishing, and mentoring of new authors. He's also judged writing competitions such as the international Bram Stoker Awards, which act as a snapshot of quality contemporary fiction.

Don't Miss Out!

Enter your email at karldrinkwater.substack.com to be notified about his new books. Fans mean a lot to him, and replies to the newsletter go straight to his inbox, where every email is read. There is also an option for paid subscribers to support his work: in exchange you receive additional posts and complimentary books.

Other Titles By Karl Drinkwater

Lost Solace

Lost Solace

Chasing Solace

Hidden Solace

Raising Solace

Finding Solace

Lost Tales Of Solace

Helene

Grubane

Clarissa

Ruabon

Afua

UESI

STANDALONE SUSPENSE
Turner
They Move Below
Harvest Festival

MANCHESTER SUMMER
Cold Fusion 2000
2000 Tunes

CONTEMPORARY SHORT STORIES
It Will Be Quick

NON-FICTION
From Idea To Item

COLLECTED EDITIONS
Karl Drinkwater's Horror Collection
Lost Solace Five Book Edition

Author's Notes

Whenever I discussed this book, and how comprehensive I wanted it to be, authors would suggest I split the book into a series. "You'll make more money with ten books at £2.99 than one book with it all in at £8.99!"

Luckily for you, I would rather always give more to my readers than less. I'd rather give value for money than make more profit. And I always treat people the way I like to be treated. Further, splitting a work like this up means a need to repeat things in each volume for context, so we end up with repetition and padding. As an editor, both are personal bugbears of mine.

I also don't think this book is too big. It's probably smaller than something like *Story* by Bob McKee, which I have read multiple times, and recommend to all authors. If Story had been split into ten books I'd never have picked it up or recommended it! So stick to your values when publishing, whatever route you take.

Thanks

My partner Alyson, for putting up with me, and also reading the whole first draft (before I made extensive cuts!).

My Kickstarter backers.

Barry Hutchison for use of his quote in Chapter 2.

The Alliance of Independent Authors (ALLi) and others who did research or provided statistics.

My proofreader Helen Pryke, who always spots my mistakes; even when I think that *this time* there are none.

My many author friends who provided quotes, support, or feedback on particular chapters. I won't name them all (too many) but the supportive book designer Michelle M. White[251] looked at chapters 5 and 6 and gave useful feedback. She also heartened me by saying:

> "Very thorough and concise. Every time I thought of a point or topic that wasn't mentioned, a few pages later I found it was covered after all. It is well-written and full of information. The pacing is good and it keeps the interest, with a bit of humor here and there to keep it from being text-bookish. The organization is spot on with logical subheadings to help readers navigate to the sections they want to read. I have to say that if the rest of the

book is as thorough as these two chapters, it's going to be a fabulous resource for authors."

All images used with permission. Thanks to Belinda Bauer for sending me the cover of her book *The Beautiful Dead*, and letting me know she created the tagline herself.

Endnotes

1. https://thestove.org/market-of-possibility/

2. https://en.wikipedia.org/wiki/Proofreading

3. https://nypost.com/2022/11/21/penguin-random-house-scraps-2-2b-deal-with-simon-schuster/

4. https://www.writersandartists.co.uk/advice

5. https://blog.reedsy.com/literary-agents/

6. https://www.scottishbooktrust.com/writing-and-authors/getting-published/literary-agents-in-scotland

7. https://www.saltpublishing.com

8. https://www.honno.co.uk

9. https://www.serenbooks.com

10. https://www.lunapresspublishing.com

11. https://arkbound.com

12. https://queryshark.blogspot.com

13. https://barryjhutchison.com

14. https://davidgaughran.com/how-the-author-solutions-scam-works/

15. https://allianceindependentauthors.org/?affid=3558

16. https://www.allianceindependentauthors.org/facts/

17. https://selfpublishingadvice.org/best-self-publishing-services/

18. https://www.allianceindependentauthors.org/members/services-search

19. https://www.allianceindependentauthors.org/members/discounts-deals

20. https://www.ethicalconsumer.org

21. https://selfpublishingadvice.org/author-awards-contests-rated-reviewed/

22. https://www.gladstoneslibrary.org/events/writers-in-residence/submission-guidelines

23. https://www.allianceindependentauthors.org/facts/

24. https://faq.brandonsanderson.com/knowledge-base/should-i-self-publish-ebooks-or-try-for-a-new-york-publisher/

25. https://www.theguardian.com/books/2021/apr/28/disneymust-pay-authors-form-task-force-missing-payments-star-wars-alien-buffy

26. https://www.draft2digital.com/blog/2024-ai-training-survey-results/

27. https://en.wikipedia.org/wiki/Digital_Millennium_Copyright_Act

28. https://www.theguardian.com/books/2010/may/01/blake-morrison-lyrics-copyright

29. https://en.wikipedia.org/wiki/Copyright_Term_Extension_Act

30. https://www.eff.org

31. https://www.caitlinjohnst.one/p/reminder-all-my-work-may-be-freely

32. https://janefriedman.com/key-book-publishing-path/

33. https://faq.brandonsanderson.com/knowledge-base/can-i-make-a-living-as-a-writer/

34. https://www.theguardian.com/books/2014/oct/22/uk-publishes-more-books-per-capita-million-report

35. https://www.worldometers.info/books/

36. https://en.wikipedia.org/wiki/Five_laws_of_library_science

37. https://en.wikipedia.org/wiki/S._R._Ranganathan

38. https://www.theguardian.com/books/article/2024/sep/03/more-than-180-uk-public-libraries-closed-or-handed-to-volunteers-since-2016

39. https://karldrinkwater.substack.com/p/weekly-writers-copyright-licensing

40. https://www.gov.uk/register-for-self-assessment

41. https://www.gov.uk/government/publications/selling-online-and-paying-taxes/selling-online-and-paying-taxes-information-sheet

42. https://www.create.ac.uk/wp-content/uploads/2022/12/Authors-earnings-report-DEF.pdf

43. https://authorsguild.org/news/key-takeaways-from-2023-author-income-survey/

44. https://www.allianceindependentauthors.org/facts/

45. https://www.youtube.com/watch?v=oP3c1h8v2ZQ

46. https://writers.com/freytags-pyramid

47. https://www.dailywritingtips.com/how-to-structure-a-story-the-eight-point-arc/

48. https://www.advancedfictionwriting.com/articles/snowflake-method/

49. http://www.hemingwayapp.com

50. http://www.proz.com/PerfectIt/Consistency_Checker

51. https://prowritingaid.com/

52. https://www.critiquecircle.com

53. https://www.scribophile.com

54. https://www.cabn.info

55. https://selfpublishingadvice.org/prove-your-publishing-rights/

56. https://www.bbc.co.uk/news/technology-47810367

57. https://www.libreoffice.org

58. https://www.bookdesigntemplates.com

59. https://en.wikipedia.org/wiki/List_of_Unicode_characters#Latin_script

60. https://www.atticus.io

61. https://www.draft2digital.com

62. https://www.jutoh.com

63. https://reedsy.com/write-a-book

64. https://www.literatureandlatte.com/scrivener/

65. https://vellum.pub

66. https://en.wikipedia.org/wiki/RGB_color_model

67. https://en.wikipedia.org/wiki/CMYK_color_model.

68. https://getcovers.com

69. https://bookcovers.com

70. https://bookcoverzone.com

71. https://darngoodcovers.com/premadecovers/

72. https://ebooklaunch.com/premade-book-covers-for-sale/

73. https://getpremades.com

74. https://goonwrite.com

75. https://www.paperandsage.com/premades/

76. https://www.gimp.org/

77. https://www.canva.com

78. https://fonts.google.com

79. https://www.dafont.com

80. https://www.fontspace.com

81. https://www.fontsquirrel.com

82. https://www.fontsquirrel.com/matcherator

83. https://fontbundles.net

84. https://pixabay.com

85. https://gratisography.com

86. https://unsplash.com

87. https://www.pexels.com

88. https://nos.twnsnd.co

89. https://depositphotos.com

90. https://www.dreamstime.com

91. http://www.shutterstock.com

92. https://openclipart.org

93. https://creativemarket.com

94. https://designbundles.net

95. https://thehungryjpeg.com

96. https://www.creativefabrica.com

97. https://search.creativecommons.org

98. https://creativecommons.org

99. https://www.shutterstock.com/license

100. http://www.indiebooklauncher.com/resources-diy/gallery-of-clones.php

101. https://blackplume.wordpress.com/tag/similar-book-cover/

102. https://www.bisg.org/complete-bisac-subject-headings-list

103. https://www.bisg.org/fiction

104. https://ns.editeur.org/thema/en

105. https://www.bisg.org/fiction

106. https://nielsenisbnstore.com

107. https://kdp.amazon.com

108. https://authors.apple.com

109. https://press.barnesandnoble.com

110. https://play.google.com/books/publish

111. https://www.kobo.com/writinglife

112. https://www.ethicalconsumer.org

113. https://www.draft2digital.com/newuser

114. https://www.ingramspark.com

115. https://publishdrive.com

116. https://www.streetlib.com

117. https://www.blurb.com

118. https://bookvault.app

119. https://allianceindependentauthors.org/?affid=3558

120. https://www.draft2digital.com/newuser

121. https://www.ingramspark.com

122. https://kdp.amazon.com

123. https://www.lulu.com

124. https://publishdrive.com

125. https://www.blurb.com/pricing

126. https://quote.bookvault.app

127. https://draft2digital.com/podcalc/

128. https://myaccount.ingramspark.com/Portal/Tools/PubComp-Calculator

129. https://kdp.amazon.com/en_US/royalty-calculator

130. https://www.lulu.com/pricing

131. https://www.thegreatbritishbookshop.co.uk

132. https://www.lulu.com/shop/

133. https://deepzen.io

134. https://lovo.ai/text-to-speech

135. https://murf.ai/text-to-speech

136. https://play.ht

137. https://elevenlabs.io

138. https://www.revoicer.com

139. https://synthesys.io

140. https://www.acx.com

141. https://www.audiblegate.com

142. https://distribution.audiobooksunleashed.com

143. https://authorsrepublic.com

144. https://findawayvoices.com

145. https://lanternaudio.com/about-lantern-independent-publishing/

146. https://www.streetlib.com

147. https://en.wikipedia.org/wiki/The_Platform_(film)

148. https://qntm.gumroad.com/

149. https://spiraldance.bandcamp.com/album/the-quickening

150. https://shop.redcandlegames.com/app/devotion

151. https://gumroad.com

152. https://payhip.com

153. https://www.shopify.com

154. https://www.gofundme.com

155. https://www.kickstarter.com

156. https://www.indiegogo.com

157. https://www.buymeacoffee.com

158. https://gumroad.com

159. https://ko-fi.com

160. https://www.patreon.com

161. https://payhip.com

162. https://www.shopify.com

163. https://steadyhq.com

164. https://substack.com

165. https://wordsrated.com/impact-of-book-publishing-on-environment/

166. https://www.isonomia.co.uk/balancing-the-books-the-environmental-impacts-of-digital-reading/

167. https://www2.societyofauthors.org/2023/04/18/tree-to-me/

168. https://www.tonerbuzz.com/blog/how-many-books-are-published-each-year/

169. https://selfpublishingadvice.org/started-as-indie-authors/

170. https://wordsrated.com/impact-of-book-publishing-on-environment/

171. https://www.popsci.com/environment/books-ereader-sustainability/

172. https://www.ethicalconsumer.org/technology/conflict-minerals-tech-goods-home-appliances

173. https://www.ethicalconsumer.org/technology/environmental-issues-tech-industry

174. https://kdgreenparty.substack.com/p/inbuilt-obsolescence

175. https://www.ethicalconsumer.org/technology/e-waste-toxic-techno-trash

176. https://www.iea.org/energy-system/buildings/data-centres-and-data-transmission-networks

177. https://wordsrated.com/impact-of-book-publishing-on-environment/

178. https://www.popsci.com/environment/books-ereader-sustainability/

179. https://www.betterworldbooks.com

180. https://biblio.co.uk

181. https://www.wob.com

182. https://try.carrd.co/testsite

183. https://www.ucraft.com

184. https://www.strikingly.com

185. https://www.imcreator.com

186. https://8b.com

187. https://wordpress.com

188. https://www.squarespace.com

189. https://pub-site.com

190. https://authorwebsites.bookbub.com

191. https://www.shopify.com

192. https://en.wikipedia.org/wiki/Weebly#Censorship

193. https://substack.com

194. https://gumroad.com

195. https://kdp.amazon.com/en_US/help/topic/G200952510#links

196. https://selfpublishingadvice.org/amazon-rules-for-authors/

197. https://www.whois.com/whois

198. https://en.wikipedia.org/wiki/List_of_social_platforms_with_at_least_100_million_active_users

199. https://www.goodreads.com

200. https://www.bookbub.com

201. https://www.thestorygraph.com

202. https://www.librarything.com

203. https://karldrinkwater.substack.com/p/rest-day-ruminations-karl-is-antisocial

204. https://karldrinkwater.substack.com/p/rest-day-ruminations-karl-is-antisocial-ed5

205. https://bsky.social/about

206. https://webkay.robinlinus.com

207. https://blog.reedsy.com/book-review-blogs/

208. https://booksirens.com

209. https://booksprout.co

210. https://storyoriginapp.com

211. https://www.hiddengemsbooks.com/author-services/

212. https://kdp.amazon.com/en_US/help/topic/G201097560

213. https://www.bewitchingbooktours.com/tour-information-and-pricing.html

214. https://www.rachelsrandomresources.com/for-authors

215. https://randomthingsthroughmyletterbox.blogspot.com/p/services-to-publishers-authors-blog.html

216. https://rrbooktours.com/services-rates/

217. https://xpressobooktours.com/services/

218. http://zooloosbooktours.co.uk

219. https://www.amazon.com/gp/help/customer/display.html?nodeId=GLHXEX85MENUE4XF

220. https://books2read.com

221. https://booklinker.com/

222. https://1link.st

223. https://linktr.ee

224. https://geniuslink.com

225. https://ublockorigin.com

226. https://privacybadger.org

227. https://diybookcovers.com/3Dmockups/

228. https://www.gimp.org

229. https://www.photopea.com

230. https://www.canva.com

231. https://bookbrush.com

232. https://placeit.net/c/mockups/?f_devices=Book

233. https://photofunia.com

234. https://partners.bookbub.com

235. https://www.bookbub.com/partners/pricing

236. https://www.bookbub.com

237. https://www.bargainbooksy.com

238. https://bookbarbarian.com

239. http://redrosesromance.com

240. http://bookadrenaline.com

241. http://booksends.com

242. https://www.ereadernewstoday.com

243. https://uk.ereaderiq.com

244. https://robinreads.com

245. https://www.youtube.com/watch?v=K4EdtA4Aeyo

246. https://www.youtube.com/watch?v=ivGHyBTqkjQ&t=5826s

247. https://www.theguardian.com/books/2023/dec/13/cait-corrain-publisher-drops-author-fake-accounts-review-bomb

248. https://www.theguardian.com/books/2016/jan/12/stephen-leather-cyberbullying-steve-mosby-jeremy-duns

249. https://selfpublishingadvice.org/alli-campaigns/ethical-author/

250. https://kdp.amazon.com/en_US/help/topic/G201097560

251. https://mmwbooks.com

www.ingramcontent.com/pod-product-compliance
Lightning Source LLC
Chambersburg PA
CBHW060310230426
43663CB00009B/1655